The Body Code

The Body Code

A Personalized Wellness and
Weight Loss Plan Developed at the
World Famous Green Valley Spa

JAY COOPER, M.S.,
with Kathryn Lance

POCKET BOOKS
New York London Toronto Sydney Tokyo Singapore

The author of this book is not a physician, and the ideas, procedures, and suggestions in this book are not intended as a substitute for the medical advice of a trained
health professional. All matters regarding your health require medical supervision.
Consult your physician before adopting the suggestions in this book, as well as about
any condition that may require diagnosis or medical attention. The author and pub-
lisher disclaim any liability arising directly or indirectly from the use of this book.

 POCKET BOOKS, a division of Simon & Schuster Inc.
1230 Avenue of the Americas, New York, NY 10020

Copyright © 1999 by Jay Cooper

ISBN: 0-671-02619-4

First Pocket Books hardcover printing March 1999

10 9 8 7 6 5 4 3 2

POCKET and colophon are registered trademarks of
Simon & Schuster Inc.

Text design by Helene Wald Berinsky

Printed in the U.S.A.

To my girls,
Barbie, McCall, and Katlin

ACKNOWLEDGMENTS

Thank you for giving me this opportunity to present my work for your consideration.

I'm thankful for the many freedoms that we Americans enjoy. I am grateful to God. To know that he lives and loves us all.

Contemplating my life to date, it appears that the appropriate learning circumstances have been strategically positioned in my pathway. Thanks to all the teachers whose books line my shelves and ideas have stirred my thoughts.

I am thankful for all of you who have influenced my life by allowing me to serve you professionally during the last twenty years. Without you, none of my work would be.

I have many friends, mentors, and role models to be thankful for. First of all for Barbie (my heaven-sent soul mate and friend), what can I say? You are a genuine jewel and the joy of my life. With you these last twenty-three years have been a delight.

For McCall, our older daughter, you are a marvelous young woman, valiant beyond description. For Katlin, our younger daughter, you are fantastic, the quintessential young woman. With you girls, parenting has been a breeze. I love you both with all my heart. I'm lucky to get to be your dad. Thank you for showing me the way.

I'm grateful for goodly parents. For Kenneth, my dad, and Marilyn, my mom, your hard work and dedication paved the way for me. Thank you for all that you have done, been, and are for me. Your unwavering love and support mean more than words can express. I love you both very much and am honored to be your son.

I am thankful for a great family: brothers Herb and Jack, grandmother Blanch, Uncle Tex and Aunt Ila, Uncle Larry and Aunt Pat, and for Gordon Bone, my brotherlike friend.

From my childhood years, I'm thankful for the influence and friendships of Don McCandless, Joe Twitchell, Jesse Torres, Junior Valesquez, Duane Wimmer, John J. Knope, and Bill Foote.

From the young-man era of my life special thanks to Ken Roberts, Bill Stowe, Robert Goodspeed, Mike Haddenham, Billy Hance, John Mabrey, Wendel Bowthorpe, Del Ford, Fred Gay, Rodney Quinn, Dan Dilsaver, Ed Elder, Brett Hardcastle, Ron Stubbs, Mark Clark, Raymond Baker, Ray Zoll, Bob Moore, Harold Hiskey, Jim Cotts, Arnold Pleasant, Marvin and Brenda Hyer, Len Waltershied, Van Mays, and Marie Thomson.

As an adult I've been fortunate to know Garth Barnum, Mike and Carol McCarroll, Darrel and Karen Humphries, George Williams, Dean and LaRae Duke, Jay Ence, Tracy McCoy, Ron Reber, Ross Hurst, Debbie and Tony Zockell, Russ Gallian, John Rogers, Mark Marine, Mark Nilsson, Marc Sorenson, Roy Fitzell, Garth Fisher, Steven Covey, Karl Wegkamp, Kevyn VanLehn, Bonnie Luke, Earl Nightengale, Lora Hinchcliff, Art Ructi, LaDeane Cobabe, Ralph Ofcarcik, Marium Kroff, Karen Westfall, Craig Booth, Denley Fowlke, Neil Roberts, Larry Weber, Judy Anderson, Elizabeth King, Perry and Suzanne Bradford, Steve Allred, Paula Domingues, Dorothy Orton, Gary Colf, Doug Sorenson, Hank Childers, David Clove, Don Cannon, Karl Malone, Rand and Judy Torgerson, Roland Lee, Lyman Hafen, Sue Upwall, Lloyd Carter, Philip McMahill, Greg Kemp, Richard and Sharlene Williams, Ken Iverson, Ben Ford, Richard Whitehead, Conn Wood, Harold and Rose Webb, Eric-Kendall and Charles Allsop, Devon Jones, Kyle Pace, Rich Kelly, Carol and Alan Coombs, Linda Davis, Michelle and Richard Hill, Kim Marshall, Judy Hilsinger, and Kathryn Lance.

For helping transform my book dream into a reality, thanks to Carol Coombs, Kim Marshall, Sandi Mendelson, Gina Centrello, Emily Bestler, Pam Duval, and Laura Ross. And finally, without Ken Cooper, Alan Coombs, Judy Hilsinger, and Kathryn Lance this book simply wouldn't be. Thank you all so much.

I'm humbled by, and grateful for, this opportunity!

Yours for wellness,
Jay Cooper

CONTENTS

PART FOUR

Helpful Hints from the Real World

INTRODUCTION
BY JAY COOPER

The purpose of this book is to share with you the wellness solutions and successes that my clients and I have found over the last twenty-five years. Solutions that will give you vibrant health. I believe that this message for you is part of why I am still alive today.

In the summer of 1990, Dr. Phil McMahill, the oncologist at Dixie Regional Medical Center, looked me directly in the eyes and said, "Jay, get your affairs in order. You may have only months left to live." He explained that I had a life-threatening cancer—a highly metastatic form of testicular cancer.

That shocking prognosis, scary as it was, was actually a disguised blessing for me and my girls. It was one of those wake-up calls that you hear about, I believe sent straight from the heavens to me. That crisis has blessed our little family in many ways. One of the results is this book, which had been one of those weekend-only projects. Now, suddenly, it was a priority. I realized that all of my life's work might be lost if I failed to get it into print. So I got busy!

The essence of my message for you is that you are one of four possible Human Types, and each type has an ideal diet and exercise regimen. I'll show you which type you are and how to access vibrant wellness, a process we call unlocking the code.

This book is for those who have not yet found their way into the wellness movement. I'll show you a proven way to get hooked on exercise and ease into a diet of balancing foods.

This book is also for those who struggle to eat right and exercise regularly. I'll show you time-tested solutions that will make you efforts pay off.

Join me now as we explore the process of unlocking your Body Code.

A NOTE FROM THE COAUTHOR

Back in the seventies, I was one of the pioneers of the fitness movement, having written two of the first exercise books for women. I continued to exercise and watch what I ate, which was a basically vegetarian diet of whole grains, pasta, and veggies. I considered myself quite fit when I met Jay Cooper two years ago, so imagine my surprise when he told me my exercise program was pretty good, but I was eating all wrong!

I was a Communicator, he explained, the genetic type worst suited to a grain-based, vegetarian diet. I was skeptical but decided to put Jay's program to the test. I didn't return to eating meat but did start eating free-range eggs and soy protein and switched my snacks from whole-wheat pretzels to peanuts and almonds.

Now, nearly two years later, I have to say the new way of eating works! I have more energy than before and, most important, have almost completely stopped suffering the midafternoon low-blood-sugar crashes that began when I was a teen and dramatically worsened with menopause.

Though I occasionally "cheat," I would no more go back to my old way of eating than I would stop seeking the "flow" through exercise. My body knows what it needs, and the Body Code principles provide it.

Jay Cooper's message is honest and true. I urge you to read what he has to say, find out your own genetic type, and give the Body Code program a try!

Kathryn Lance, October 1998

PART ONE

All Humans Are
Not the Same

1

THE JAY WAY

Hi, I'm Jay Cooper, Wellness Director of the Green Valley Spa in St. George, Utah. For more than twenty years I've helped thousands of clients unlock the secrets of their Body Code. This unique genetic programming, which is different for each individual, determines our general body build and dictates the best food and exercise plans for each of us.

Now, I'd like to help you discover your own Body Code. Whether you want to lose weight, find more energy, or simply become more healthy, I invite you to join the thousands who have improved their lives through understanding the Body Code.

At Green Valley Spa, clients arrive from all over the world. They're stressed out, overweight, underexercised, and overfed. Some are recovering from their umpteenth diet, or worn-out from doing too much of the wrong kind of "no pain, no gain" exercise. Many have low energy and wonder if they'll even be able to make it through the week.

After a few days on our program, most have turned completely around, feeling relaxed, energetic, and losing weight. Some feel better than they've felt in decades.

They're not counting calories or fat grams. For the first time in their entire lives these clients are eating the foods that are right for their metabolism. They're performing the type and amount of exercise that keeps their body-fat thermostat low and their energy level high.

Our clients are working *with* their bodies instead of following a one-size-fits-all diet and exercise plan that is *supposed* to work for every human being, but simply does not. The bottom line is that some approaches work for some people and not for others. I know you've observed this yourself. Some people, no matter how they eat, stay slim. Others, no matter which diet and exercise regimen they follow, always battle to keep their weight down.

I understand this reality very well, because I am one of the latter types. Although I've been medium-sized since 1979, I was born and raised fat. In my family, my mom served good old American food. You know, the stuff that sticks to your ribs: meat, potatoes, gravy, heavy sauces. My father and brothers all thrived on this diet, but my mom and I kept battling weight and getting fatter. I remember looking at my bony younger brother and wondering how it could be that we'd eat the same things, day after day, and yet I kept gaining while he remained so thin. By the time I was a sophomore in college, I was up to 242 pounds—and I'm only five feet nine inches tall.

By then I was also an accomplished couch potato. From time to time, I'd try to diet or just cut down on eating, but it never worked. I made feeble attempts to exercise. I even tried out for the wrestling team, until the other boys laughed at me and dubbed me "fat boy." Luckily for my self-esteem and sanity, I was interested in music and theater and was able to get roles that fit my physique, such as Snoopy in *Charlie Brown*, and Tevye, the portly milkman, in *Fiddler on the Roof.*

Later in my sophomore year, I had the good fortune to badly twist my ankle. I say good fortune because that mishap may have saved—and certainly changed—my life. It sent me to a doctor, who discovered that my blood pressure and resting heart rate were very high for my age. After the exam, he skillfully used shock therapy by sternly asking me, "Jay, how are you going to spend these last ten years of your life?"

It worked. I was petrified. What did he mean, the last ten years? I was still a kid. But deep inside I knew he was right. I knew it was time I grew up and faced that my eating and exercise habits were literally killing me. He said, "Some people wear themselves out. You, on the other hand, are luxuriating yourself to death."

I immediately moved off campus so I'd be forced to walk to school. I didn't change my eating habits, not then, but I did notice that just walking was having a noticeable effect, both on how I felt and how I looked. Encouraged by this interplay of exercise and well-being, I was determined to return to a more natural lifestyle. I continued to study, in school and on my own time, to better understand biology and physiology.

By the time I graduated from college, I was only moderately over-weight, but far more fit. I was also a newlywed! My new bride and I moved to St. George, Utah, in the heart of canyon country, where I began to test the principles I had been studying. Most of my diets would work a little, for a while, but I was still overweight.

As I continued my walking program, I gradually progressed from a mosey to a walk to a fast walk to a walk/jog to finally running. One day it dawned on me that quite by accident I had evolved into a runner. I had even melted down to a trim person and have been medium-sized ever since. These changes in my body convinced me that exercise really works. I began to study human typology (the study of human characteristics) to find more specific information about weight loss and metabolic functions. I read the works of Dr. William Sheldon, who wrote about constitution-al types. According to Sheldon's team of medical researchers, most of us are one of three basic somatotypes, or body builds. I scored as a meso-morph—the compact, muscular type. The other two anatomical types are the ectomorphs, the thinner, lanky-type folks, and the endomorphs, who tend to be more rounded or pear-shaped. Sheldon established that body type and personality type are roughly correlated, with the mesomorphs tending to be hard-driving type A's; endomorphs the calmer, more delib-erate type B's; and ectomorphs either the high-strung or the reclusive types.

Around this time I also reread a book by Dr. Henry Bieler that I had originally read in 1968, which steered me to the works of a group of physicians, including Dr. Herman Rubin. These scientists had followed up on the earlier work of Dr. Lewellys Barker of Johns Hopkins, and Francis Pottinger, who had medically confirmed an association between our body shape, personality, and our Endocrine System. This was what I needed! The association made sense, and I soon became a disciple of the meta-bolic-types movement.

In a nutshell, what these physicians had found through studying tens of thousands of people was that each of us is genetically programmed to be influenced by one dominant endocrine system gland or glands: the adrenal, thyroid, pituitary, or gonads. The dominant gland or glands gov-ern metabolism—food intake and energy output. Bieler and the others showed that all the major glands are designed to work synergistically like members of a chorus. The dominant gland is like a chorus section that has the strongest voice. If that section overwhelms the others, the balance is lost.

This information changed my life. I identified myself as an adrenal type and began to eat the foods that were recommended for that type. The results were miraculous. Keeping my weight down and eating right were no longer a battle. I simply felt fantastic and wasn't hungry.

During this period of my life I became a certified personal trainer. and began training clients to run marathons. I knew for sure that I wanted to make my career as a fitness/wellness educator. Within a few months I made a business proposal to Dr. Mark Sorenson, an exercise physiologist. Together we built the National Institute of Fitness (NIF) into one of the top-destination wellness retreats in the world. Although my job title was "general manager," my real function was client counseling and tweaking the diet and exercise programs. I coached literally thousands of clients. I weighed them, measured them, and tracked their progress. My task was to keep all clients losing weight systematically and feeling great. By taking body-site measurements and skin-fold calibrations weekly, I began to document that humans are not only built differently, but also store body fat in different parts of their bodies. Furthermore, we lose weight at very different rates.

Some of my clients, for example, would store excess weight in their stomachs, while others would gain in the hips. Still others tended to gain weight all over, even in their fingers and toes. Some of my clients thrived on a basically vegetarian diet, while others felt well only when consuming more protein and fat.

Some would lose four to seven pounds in a week, while others would actually gain weight on their new regimen, even though all were started on the exact same program of diet and exercise.

The more clients I worked with, including various ethnic types from all over the world, the more crystal clear it became to me that there are four different basic metabolic types, and each type responds quite predictably to specific diet and exercise principles.

At this time NIF was continually growing, and moving in the direction of keeping all clients on the popular and less expensive low-fat, high-carbohydrate, near-vegetarian diet. I knew that that diet was healthy and had helped most people. But I also had stacks of evidence showing that it wasn't working for everyone. Some people not only didn't respond favorably, they even gained weight and felt bad.

Since I had this "built-in laboratory" of clients arriving weekly from all regions of the world, I began to record and study the data in an attempt to get my clients the results they were so willing to work for. I was the troubleshooter. I began putting thyroid-dominant clients on a thyroid-type diet, and adrenal-dominant clients on an adrenal-type diet. My clients began to lose weight more predictably through this individualized approach.

Over the next six years, I became thoroughly convinced that putting everyone on the same diet was often counterproductive. So it was time to put my beliefs into practice. I resigned from NIF and started my own fitness center. My client base grew steadily as I succeeded with people who had failed on the one-size-fits-all program.

And then, in 1990, I received another life-changing wake-up call.

I was diagnosed with a highly metastatic type of testicular cancer. I had been so passionate about my work that I had been putting in seventy to ninety hours a week. I'd been running marathons and triathlons. I had overstressed my body and mind—and now I had to pay the price. But this experience, frightening as it was, taught me one more piece to the wellness puzzle that I had not really understood.

That missing piece was the energy component. I realized my mistake as I restudied the ancient Indian system of Ayurveda. Ayurveda, which is actually a complete science of life, sees all humans as made up of vibrating waves of energy. This body of thought dovetails quite nicely with what we know today about quantum physics. The literal essence of what we are is not tangible mass, but the vibrating fields of energy between particles of matter. According to Ayurveda, each person is a combination of three energy types or *doshas,* but one dosha is always a stronger influence than the others. The dosha types correspond categorically with the anatomical and glandular types I mentioned earlier. Your dosha type actually determines which anatomical and glandular type you are. This is the fundamental system behind all the others. Your dosha type shapes your energy patterns, temperament, and personality. Thousands of years ago, the Eastern World cultures had stumbled on what is only now being studied in modern medicine as psychoneuroimmunology, the science of how our thoughts, feelings, and behaviors affect physical health.

I experienced the reality that allowing one's doshas to become unbalanced can lead to illness. For my dominant dosha, the pitta type, one of the most serious dangers is too much intensity, which can certainly come from overworking. The pitta dosha types are the prototypical type A's, hard-driving, task-oriented, and intense. For us pitta types, as for all the dosha types, balance is the key. I had lost that balance, weakened my immune system, and needed to regain the balance.

After the surgery that followed my diagnosis of cancer, I took some time off to ponder and pray. I decided that for me a cure lay not in taking the poisonous chemical treatments that had been prescribed, but rather in slowing down, regaining balance, and continuing to work. I systematically decreased my workload, sold my fitness center, and came to Green Valley Spa, where without the long hours I could still help others pursue wellness. I modified my diet even more, bringing it more in line with the principles of my Ayurveda energy type.

As I lived this less intense lifestyle, my cancer regressed, and I've now been cancer-free for nine years. I continue to integrate the principles of Ayurveda with the anatomical and metabolic systems to fine-tune the most balanced diet and exercise regimens for the four mind-body types.

From this book you will get these time-tested principles. I will show you the four basic human genetic types, identify which type you are, and most importantly give you the specific diet and exercise approach that is best for *you*.

My ultimate goal is to help you evolve toward a healthier, happier lifestyle, where you will feel and look your best.

2

THE FOUR HUMAN
GENETIC TYPES

In the late 1970s, the age-old argument over nature versus nurture shifted dramatically toward validating the nature side of the debate. Molecular biologists studying sets of twins from around the globe concluded that, while environment does influence who we are, the dominant influence is certainly heredity. We are like a computer's motherboard, hardwired with inherited characteristics woven into the fabric of our DNA.

Long before the theory of genetic inheritance, Ayurvedic physicians from India recognized that specific inherited traits come in groups. Oriental skin and hair come with brown eyes, not blue eyes; solid musculature comes with heavier bones and supportive connective tissues, not delicate ones. The Ayurvedists concluded that we are each packaged in complementary ways to help promote natural balance and homeostasis.

Today, as we observe different peoples from around the world, it is obvious that all humans are not the same, in size, shape, or way of life.

For example, the Inuit groups of arctic Canada and Greenland have thrived for generations eating several pounds of whale blubber every day, without any measurable adverse effects, such as high blood cholesterol. Yet by the FDA's measure, these people consume enough saturated fat to clog the arteries of an army.

Most native Chinese live from cradle to grave without consuming any calcium-rich dairy food at all. They don't get near the FDA-recommended

1,000 mg of calcium per day, yet they still have among the world's lowest rates of osteoporosis.

Vegetarians in East India thrive on a diet that provides them with less protein than the FDA says is needed to avoid negative nitrogen balance.

The point is, no one diet or exercise plan or lifestyle is ideal, or even reasonable, for all human types. Over countless generations, our physiologies have adjusted to our environments through natural adaptation and mutation. Governed by a survival mechanism, our gene pool has evolved to enable the perpetuation of our species by incorporating the many different threads of human history that have contributed to it.

Each of the 100 trillion cells in each of our bodies is carrying this history. It is our history, the history of the human race, perpetuated through all generations of time into this living conglomeration that is today . . . you and me.

Since America is one big ethnic melting pot, and since most of us don't know our genealogy very well, we may not know exactly which threads from the strand of human history are predominant in our physiological makeup. That's why we must use the tools that we have to discover the lifestyle choices that are most harmonious for our own genetic type.

How We Can Understand Our Own Differences

For centuries, physicians, philosophers, and researchers have tried to place humans into categories that would give meaning to the differences between people. Some earlier classifications categorized people according to race, religion, class, or the time of year they were born. Other early methods focused on gender, anatomical build, blood type, oxidation rate, or personality type. Most of these methods have at least some validity, but modern researchers have established that, for purposes of determining diet and exercise needs, the anatomical, glandular, and energy methods are the most useful.

Anatomical Types

The modern Western pioneer in this field was Dr. William Sheldon of Harvard, who, working with a team of research physicians in the 1940s and 1950s, grouped humans into anatomical types according to body shape or general build. This classification system was based on which of the three embryonic tissue layers were most prominent in an individual.

The embryonic layers are the three types of body tissue that develop from a growing fertilized egg. In each individual, one of the tissue types—ectoderm, mesoderm, or endoderm—predominates, giving rise to structures that are *relatively* more dominant in that individual's anatomy.

The anatomical classification system works by measuring and comparing a number of anatomical parameters, including height, weight, and thickness and relative length of the limbs. This "somatotyping," or body typing, then places all humans in one of three general categories:

The **ectomorph** is the usually taller, bony, thin, small-framed, sharp-featured person who generally has difficulty gaining weight; the ectomorph tends to have a preponderance of body tissue from the embryonic ectoderm layer (skin and nervous system).

The **mesomorph** is the compactly built, muscular type with a broad chest and small buttocks and hips; she has a tendency toward more muscle and connective tissue from the embryonic mesoderm.

The **endomorph** is the rounded type with relatively short limbs and a larger abdominal component. His digestive system, which comes from the embryonic endoderm layer, is relatively larger than his musculoskeletal and nervous system, resulting in a tendency to gain weight.

Although Sheldon recognized that not everyone fits exactly into one of these categories, his classification method proved applicable to a wide range of subjects, predicting not just body type but also some basic personality tendencies.

At Green Valley, we have also found that your anatomical type determines your biological need for body motion (how much and which types). Anatomical body typing also helps to explain why exercise is easier for some people and a struggle for others. Through the years, we've found that exercise is much more enjoyable and more likely to become a continuing part of your life if you do the exercises that are right for your anatomical type (body build).

I'll never forget Judy, a spirited, red-haired client in her thirties. When she came to me, she was already exercising a lot—in fact, she exercised nearly every day. She was strong and curvy in her lower body, with plenty of lean body mass. Yet Judy was dissatisfied with her body shape.

"No matter what I do, I'm just too big in my hips and thighs," she said.

I told Judy about the basic body types and explained that the weight training was actually working against her desired results. "Your body is programmed to have curvier legs," I said. "All the weight training you're doing is just making them more muscular."

"But my trainer said I had to lift weights to burn more fat," she objected.

I told Judy that was true for certain anatomical types, but not for hers. In fact, a strength-building program would cause her to bulk up and actually hinder weight loss. After we talked a little more, Judy agreed to try my suggestions. She gave up her intensive strength-training regimen while continuing to pace walk and swim, and within a few months she'd returned to her optimum size.

Glandular (Metabolic) Types

I told you earlier how I identified that I was an "adrenal" type. In the glandular (metabolic) approach, people are classified according to the characteristics determined by the dominant gland in the endocrine (glandular) system. This classification system, invented by Dr. Lewellys Barker of Johns Hopkins and later refined and popularized by several physicians, posits that we are each born with a dominant gland that influences our body's biochemical functioning. Your dominant gland determines differences in body-chemistry balance, metabolic function, and energy usage. Your glandular type, like your anatomical type, is programmed by your genes.

Your glandular type affects your body's usage of basic macronutrients—air, water, protein, fat, and carbohydrates, along with micronutrients such as vitamins and minerals—that create the energy and building materials necessary for cellular regeneration. This process of converting raw materials into the building blocks of life is known as metabolism. Each person has slightly different ways of using these raw materials and needs different relative amounts of them: some require more protein, others need more fat or carbohydrates.

The four major endocrine glands are the adrenals, which regulate appetite and reactions to stress and danger; the gonads, which control growth, sexuality, and reproduction; the thyroid, which governs metabolic rate and energy usage; and the pituitary, the "master gland" that regulates all of the other glands.

Each of the body's four major glands is nourished and stimulated by specific foods. You often crave those foods that most stimulate your dominant gland. The secretions from this gland affect your brain and body chemistry balances, causing specific feelings. When the gland becomes repeatedly overstimulated, however, the excess hormonal flood can throw your body chemistry out of balance. The gland can become overstimulated to the point of exhaustion and stop functioning properly.

To restore a healthy balance among your glandular secretions, you must cut back on foods that stimulate your dominant gland and eat more of the foods that stimulate the subordinate glands.

In this process, the key to health is balance—although one gland is always dominant, it should not be *too* dominant, or it will overpower the contributions of the other glands. You can think of the glandular system as a barbershop quartet, where your dominant gland sings the melody but for good harmony mustn't drown out the others.

Your glandular type is determined by analyzing related characteristics, such as physical shape, the size of your skeleton, the location of body-fat pads, your energy patterns, and how your body responds to proteins, fats, carbohydrates, and exercise.

The glandular approach divides humans into four body-chemistry types:

> **Thyroidal**—long, lanky, and restless; corresponds in many ways with Sheldon's ectomorph.
>
> **Adrenal**—solid, driven, and warm; corresponds categorically with the mesomorph.
>
> **Pituitary**—detached, dreamy, and rounded; corresponds basically with the ectomorph, though some pituitary types have an endomorphic base.
>
> **Gonadal**—applies only to women. This type is generally quite slender above the waist but tends to be larger, with more body fat, below the waist. Although her body has an endomorphic or mesomorphic foundation, she may actually be a combination of anatomical types. Her personality is usually warm, outgoing, and people-oriented. At Green Valley, we refer to this type as the **ovarian** type.

Your glandular-metabolic type determines how your body processes nutrients, and the best fuel ratio of protein, fat, and carbohydrate for optimum functioning. It also explains why you crave certain foods, and how best to neutralize those cravings.

Eating incorrectly for your metabolic type can have serious health consequences. It took me many years to understand that the high-protein, high-fat, all-American meals my brothers thrived on were overstimulating my dominant adrenal glands and contributing to my growing obesity.

Energy Types

There is yet another classification system we use at Green Valley, the oldest of them all. Based on the ancient Indian study of Ayurveda, it classifies people according to their underlying energy patterns, or doshas. Named vata, pitta, and kapha, all three doshas work together to achieve balance in all aspects of our biology. Vata regulates movement, pitta controls metabolism, and kapha oversees structure. Together, the doshas provide the architecture of our being, and as any architect will tell you, there is more than one way to design a building.

The ancient Ayurvedic physicians anticipated modern physics in realizing that all matter, including the physical matter that makes up human beings, is largely vibrating waves of energy between particles (quantum units). Most of what we truly are is not a tangible mass, but the energy fields between the tangible, physical components.

Ayurveda deals with how the energy fields and the physical mass interact to influence how we feel. In a sense, modern science is beginning to catch up. The new science of psychoneuroimmunology studies the interactions among the nervous system, endocrine (glandular) system, and immune system. It is the key to how body chemistry works in practice. Even though scientists cannot always be sure how these communications take place, more and more evidence shows that our bodies produce a complex network of chemicals (neurotransmitters, neuropeptides, and related molecules) that our brain uses to communicate with the rest of the body.

Although all three doshas influence every human, one is generally dominant in each of us. The practice of Ayurveda applies herbs, foods, movement, and other principles to the doshas, bringing balance to the entire system. You can think of the doshas as the meeting point between mind and body. Good health is a result of balance between these elements. If you are spiritually minded, you will recognize this as the realm of the spirit or soul, the essence of what you are.

Although the doshas do not correspond exactly with the anatomical and glandular typing systems, there is a basic common ground:

Vata dosha corresponds to the ectomorphic, thyroidal type, and to the sleeker version of the pituitary type.

Pitta dosha corresponds to the mesomorphic, adrenal type.

Kapha dosha corresponds to the endomorphic ovarian type, and also to the less common cherub, or puffy, endomorphic version of the pituitary type.

Your Ayurvedic energy type determines how you respond to sensory stimulation and gives you the understanding of how to apply such holistic practices as massage and meditation to balance your body and mind.

At Green Valley Spa, we use all of these classification systems—anatomical, glandular, and Ayurvedic—to help us understand the four genetic types, which determine which diet and exercise plan will work best for you.

When you know which anatomical body build you are—ectomorphic, mesomorphic, or endomorphic—you will know which kinds and amounts of body motion are most effective for you. You'll discover what your type needs from exercise in order to make it an enjoyable, regular part of your life.

When you know which glandular-metabolic type you are—the pituitary, thyroidal, adrenal, or ovarian—you'll discover the nutritional principles that are essential for your good health. You'll learn why you crave certain foods, and how to neutralize those cravings, so that you will feel satisfied on a balanced diet.

When you know which Ayurvedic energy type you are—vata, pitta, or kapha—you'll begin to understand the principles for balancing your mind and body. You'll see what types and amount of sensory stimulation are right for you. You'll discover what parts of the day are best for you, and what sort of environment you require for optimum well-being.

The Challenge

Throughout this chapter, I've talked about how our individual genetic programming—the Body Code—determines our body build, our need for exercise, our appetite, how effectively we're satiated by different foods, our metabolic rate, and even to a certain extent what happens to our excess energy if we overeat. Genetic programming determines what different body types will do with those excess calories, whether the calories will go to expand fat pads or build lean body tissue.

The essence of my program—and what we do in the Body Code wellness plan—is to adjust those elements over which we have control *within our genetically programmed range*. Each of us possesses a group of protective measures that will help us to stay within that range—as long as we provide the basic types of stimulation that our body needs to work toward that state of balance or homeostasis.

No matter what you eat, no matter how much or little you exercise, you cannot change your basic Body Code. If you are programmed to be an ectomorph, you cannot turn yourself into a natural mesomorph, no matter how hard you try. You will always tend toward long and bony; you cannot realistically make yourself into a compact, muscular mesomorph.

The Pima Indians of southern Arizona and northern Mexico stand out as casualties of the attempt to be something other than what they are genetically programmed to be. Until the mid–twentieth century, these people had been very healthy, living on a natural diet of mostly desert plant foods, and getting an enormous amount of physical exercise by farming, gathering food, hunting, and walking. All that changed when the twentieth century invaded their lives and they had to give up their traditional ways. Now, the Pimas eat the way many Americans eat, relying on processed, greasy convenience foods. They exercise the way most Americans exercise—very little. But the effects of those unhealthful habits on the Pimas have been dramatic and far more obviously harmful than for most Americans.

Today the Pima Indians (and some other related tribes) are among the most obese people in the world and have the highest rate of diabetes in the world. Various experts and scientists have been trying to reprogram the Pimas' attitudes and ideas, to get them to change their behaviors and eat less, to follow the sort of low-fat diet often recommended for overweight people. The Pimas are encouraged to work exercise into their lives in small ways—to walk more, for example. But all these attempts aren't working—and I don't think they will work until the Pimas begin to more closely approximate the living conditions they evolved from. Until they again begin to eat the native foods that kept their blood sugar levels stable, and most important, to perform the higher levels of body motion their bodies evolved to need, they won't get better.

Because of their unique genetic coding, the Pimas offer dramatic proof of the negative influence of the typical American diet. But they are not alone. The relatively recent changes in lifestyle and food choices have taken a toll—though somewhat less dramatic—on most of us Americans. Until a short time ago we didn't have so many refined foods available. We didn't have remote controls, and most work didn't require hours of sitting in front of a computer terminal. Inactivity and rich foods have combined to make us, as a people, out of shape, overweight, and unhealthy.

And now, it's time to invite you to participate in the Green Valley Body Code Plan. I invite you to discover which genetic type you are, and to use the specific foods, herbs, and physical stimulation that will give you what your type needs for balance of mind and body. Simply follow the plan for a few weeks and watch what happens. You will be at least delighted—and maybe even amazed.

3

WHICH TYPE ARE YOU?

The Green Valley genetic types are a synthesis of anatomical, metabolic, and Ayurvedic energy types. Learning your genetic type will give you the keys to meeting the specific needs of your mind and body. In other words, you will be able to take control of your health.

There are two basic human genetic types—strong and sleek. Each of these two categories contains two subdivision types that are similar, but not exactly the same. The strong types are generally more solid and have more muscular builds. They need more body motion and a relatively low-protein, plant-based diet. The sleek types are generally leaner and more delicate than the strong types. They need somewhat less body motion and more protein in their diets.

For convenience, we have given each genetic type a totemic name based on ancient archetypes that symbolize important features including temperament. The two strong genetic types are the **Warrior** and the **Nurturer.** The two sleek genetic types are the **Communicator** and the **Visionary.**

The Genetic Type Shapes

To determine more exactly which is your unique human genetic type, answer one of the following questionnaires. For each question, choose the answer that is most like you. If a question doesn't seem to apply to you, then leave it blank.

18

Questionnaire for Women

Below are drawings of the four genetic types. Look them over carefully. You may find immediately that you match, say, Figure 1. Or you may see features of your own body in two of the genetic types. Choose the one that most closely matches your dominant body-shape characteristics.

THE NURTURER TYPE
Ovarian Driven—Women Only

Body-shape characteristics
More substantial lower body—thinner neck—heart-shaped head—curvy-looking lower body—smaller and/or leaner upper body.

Excess body-fat locations
Buttocks—outer thighs—hamstrings—inner thighs—triceps.

Mind-personality type
Warm—caring—compassionate—service-oriented—extroverted.

Favorite foods
When balanced: fruits—most veggies—lean dairy—spices. When out of balance: creamy fats—greasy foods—flour—and spices.

THE WARRIOR TYPE
Adrenal Driven

Body-shape characteristics
More substantial upper body—shorter neck—solid-chesty-looking physique—sturdy-square features—flatter buttocks.

Excess body-fat locations
Stomach—rib cage—chest—back—triceps—upper body mostly.

Mind-personality type
Assertive—orderly—decisive—task-oriented—extroverted.

Favorite foods
When balanced: starchy veggies—grains—lean dairy and meats. When out of balance: fats—meats—salts—flour—and alcohol.

THE COMMUNICATOR TYPE
Thyroid Driven

Body-shape characteristics
Thinner—oval-shaped head—lanky—sleek—longer-looking physique—bony hands, feet, clavicles.

Excess body-fat locations
Spare-tire area—top front of legs—triceps.

Mind-personality type
Creative—lively—verbal—quick—moody—spirited—extroverted—perfectionist.

Favorite foods
When balanced: proteins—all veggies—grains. When out of balance: sugars—flour—caffeine.

THE VISIONARY TYPE
Pituitary Driven

Body-shape characteristics
Medium- to large-sized head—less developed physique—youthful appearance.

Excess body-fat locations
Pouch below navel—between the knees—face—hands—feet—all over body evenly.

Mind-personality type
Either reserved—calm—introverted—intellectual—idealistic—or childlike—curious—witty—and extroverted.

Favorite foods
When balanced: cooked veggies—spices—proteins. When out of balance: sweets—grains—flour.

1. Which best describes your body build or body shape?
   a) Naturally smaller, less curvy, teenage-looking
   b) Sleek, rangy, lanky, bony-looking body
   c) Strong, solid, sturdy, chesty-looking body
   d) Very curvy, pear-shaped, smaller upper body

2. My natural waistline is:
   a) slightly defined, long-waisted
   b) well-defined, high-waisted
   c) moderately defined and long-waisted with a wider rib cage
   d) well-defined with a very bony rib cage

3. Use a mirror, or have someone look at you from the back, to describe your basic body build:
   a) not particularly curvy
   b) balanced hourglass
   c) more substantial upper body
   d) curvy with a smaller upper body

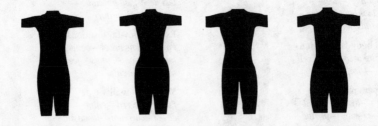

4. The amount of sway or curve in my back, and the shape of my buttocks, most resembles:
   a) slight sway in back with a smaller, rounded buttocks shape
   b) moderately swayed back with a moderately rounded buttocks shape
   c) straighter back with a flatter buttocks shape
   d) very swayed back with a very rounded buttocks shape

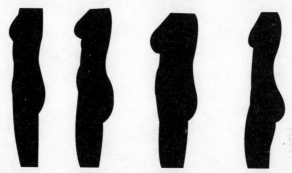

5. As a relatively younger woman (age 22–25), which weight-gain tendency best describes you:
   a) basically did not gain weight, tended to be trim, waif-looking; not bony
   b) basically did not gain weight, tended to be trim, even lanky, and bony-looking
   c) could gain weight if sedentary, but easily controlled it with exercise or diet
   d) gained weight easily, had to diet and stay active to stay trim

6. The absolute first place on my body that I notice excess body fat is:
   a) just below the belly button
   b) upper legs or abdomen
   c) stomach, rib cage, or back
   d) buttocks, outer thighs, or legs

7. In my waistline and buttocks areas, I tend to gain:
   a) all through the waist and buttocks evenly
   b) in a spare tire around the waist and more through the top area of the buttocks
   c) all through the stomach area but little through the buttocks
   d) little through the waist but all through the buttocks

8. Generally speaking, my weight gain tends to be:
   a) all over evenly, even the head, hands, and feet
   b) middle of my body only
   c) upper half of my body mostly
   d) lower half of my body mostly

9. Read the following snack choices as though calories and other nutritional values do not matter. If you could eat anything you wanted and continue to feel and look great, what would you usually choose?
   a) fruit, yogurt, cheese
   b) candies, cookies, muffins
   c) crackers, pretzels, popcorn
   d) chips and salsa, potato chips, cheesecake

10. Which description is generally most true regarding your appetite?
    a) mild appetite; can skip meals if mentally busy
    b) unpredictable appetite; generally stronger from 1–5 P.M.
    c) strong appetite, sharp pangs; cannot skip meals; often hungry
    d) moderate appetite; strongest from 5–10 P.M.

11. Which statement best describes your general relationship with food?
    a) I eat only to live. I am not oriented toward food or food-related activities.
    b) I feel best if I eat smaller amounts more often. I enjoy food, but it is not a prime focus for me.
    c) I live to eat. I think about food often during the day. Food and food-oriented festivities are important to me.
    d) I love food and the "togetherness" of meals.

12. For these questions, choose the response that is generally representative of the way you were at about age eighteen.

    Physical Look/Body Build:
    a) not very curvy
    b) lanky, bony, sleek
    c) athletic, strong, chesty
    d) very curvy, athletic build with smaller or leaner upper body

    Fat-Gaining Tendency:
    a) none; very trim, even with no exercise
    b) little gain, easily controlled with just a little exercise
    c) moderate tendency to gain, controlled with steady exercise
    d) moderate to strong tendency to gain, had to exercise diligently

    Regional Location of Fat Gain (If Any):
    a) just below belly button
    b) upper legs or spare-tire area
    c) stomach, rib cage, or back
    d) buttocks, saddlebags, and/or legs

Temperament or Personality Type:
a) intellectual, introverted
b) creative, moody
c) assertive, confident
d) social, extroverted

Favorite Foods:
a) anything, really; food wasn't important
b) sweets and starches
c) salty or fatty starches
d) spicy starches or creamy foods

Which column did you choose the most often? a b c d

13. Generally speaking, I think of myself as:
    a) an intellectual, detailed thinker who enjoys solitude
    b) a quick, creative type who enjoys change
    c) a decisive, intense type who enjoys orderliness
    d) a compassionate, social type who enjoys interaction

14. My true personality type is actually:
    a) reserved, calm
    b) creative, moody
    c) purposeful, intense
    d) nurturing, tolerant

15. My energy type would best be described as:
    a) calm, best in the morning, needing solitude and quiet
    b) high-strung, best after meals, less comfortable in cold weather
    c) strong and consistent, less comfortable in hot weather
    d) lowest in the early morning, best from 5–11 P.M.

16. Which group of conditions do you tend toward? (If none apply to you, choose the group that affects the parent you are most like.)
    a) colds, allergies, asthma
    b) blood sugar problems, moodiness, constipation
    c) high blood pressure, high cholesterol, anxiety
    d) depression, cramps, codependence

17. The overall description that generally reflects the "essence of me" is:
    a) I love to stay in my head. I am intellectual and tend to overthink things. Expressing emotion is not easy for me. I can seem detached to others.
    b) I love variety. I often have many projects going at once. I can seem too changeable to others.
    c) I love orderliness. I am bold and pragmatic. I tend to exude intensity. I can seem critical or too demanding of others.
    d) I love belonging. I tend to look for ways to serve others. I can seem too gregarious or social-oriented.

Questionnaire for Men

Below are drawings of the three genetic types for men. Look them over carefully. You may find immediately that you closely resemble one. Or you may see features of your own body in two of the genetic types. Choose the one that *most closely* matches your general build.

Illus. 5–7

THE VISIONARY TYPE
Pituitary Driven

Body-shape characteristics
Medium- to large-sized head— less developed physique— youthful appearance.

Excess body-fat locations
Pouch below navel—between the knees—face—hands—feet—all over body evenly.

Mind-personality type
Either reserved—calm—introverted intellectual—idealistic—or child- like—curious—witty—and extroverted.

Favorite foods
When balanced: cooked veggies— spices—proteins.. When out of balance: sweets—dairy—flour.

THE COMMUNICATOR TYPE
Thyroid Driven

Body-shape characteristics
Thinner—oval-shaped head—lanky—sleek— longer-looking physique— bony hands, feet, clavicles.

Excess body-fat locations
Spare-tire area—top front of legs—triceps.

Mind-personality type
Creative—lively—quick— moody—spirited— extroverted—perfectionist.

Favorite foods
When balanced: proteins— all veggies—grains. When out of balance: sugars— flour—caffine.

THE WARRIOR TYPE
Adrenal Driven

Body-shape characteristics
More substantial upper body— shorter neck, square jaw—solid- chesty-looking physique— sturdy-square features— rounded buttocks.

Excess body-fat locations
Stomach—rib cage—chest— back—triceps—upper body mostly.

Mind-personality type
Assertive—orderly—decisive— task-oriented—extrovert.

Favorite foods
When balanced: starchy veggies—grains—lean dairy and meats. When out of balance: fats—meats—salts—flour— and alcohol.

1. Which best describes your basic body shape?
   a) naturally smaller, less defined, teenager-looking
   b) sleek, rangy, lanky, bony-looking
   c) strong, solid, chesty-looking

2. At about age 18–22, which choice best reflects your tendency to gain body fat?
   a) started to gain a little
   b) did not gain
   c) tended to gain

3. My favorite foods at age 18–22 were:
   a) anything, really; food was not important
   b) pasta, cookies, cakes, cereals
   c) burgers and fries, sandwiches, pizza

4. As an adult, how much cardiovascular exercise is required to keep you trim?
   a) little; I stay trim without a structured plan
   b) moderate amounts; 20–40 minute sessions, 3–4 times a week
   c) lots; 40–60 minute sessions, 4–7 times a week

5. The first area that I notice excess body fat is:
   a) just below my belly button or in my face
   b) in my spare tire, all the way around my waist
   c) in the upper front of my body

6. As/if I continue to gain excess body fat, most of the excess is located:
   a) all over me evenly, even in my face, hands, and feet
   b) only in my spare tire, chin, and upper legs, while my hands and feet remain bony
   c) mostly in the upper front of my body (chest and abdomen)

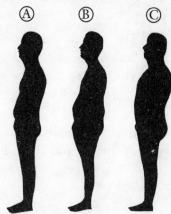

7. Nutritional value aside, my taste buds prefer the following snacks:
   a) none at all or ice cream, sherbet, or cheese
   b) cookies, muffins, sodas, coffee
   c) chips, crackers, pretzels, nuts

8. Generally speaking, I think of myself as:
   a) an intellectual, detailed thinker who enjoys solitude
   b) a quick, creative type who enjoys change
   c) a decisive, confident type who enjoys orderliness

9. My true personality type is actually:
   a) reserved, calm
   b) creative, moody
   c) purposeful, intense

10. My energy type would best be described as:
    a) calm, best in the morning, needing solitude and quiet
    b) high-strung, best after meals, uncomfortable in cold weather
    c) strong and consistent, uncomfortable in hot weather

11. Which group of conditions do you tend toward? (If none apply, choose the group that affects the parent that you are most like.)
    a) colds, allergies, asthma
    b) blood sugar problems, moodiness, constipation
    c) high blood pressure, high cholesterol, anxiety

12. The overall description that generally reflects the natural "essence of me" is:
    a) I love to stay in my head. I am intellectual and tend to mentally dwell on things. Expressing emotion is less comfortable for me.
    b) I love variety. I often have many projects going on at once.
    c) I love orderliness. I am bold and intense.

Scoring

Each question is worth one point. Add up your answers for each letter. Whichever letter has the highest number of answers indicates your genetic type.

If you had the most answers for letter **A**, you are a **Visionary.**

If you had the most answers for letter **B**, you are a **Communicator.**

If you had the most answers for letter **C**, you are a **Warrior.**

If you had the most answers for letter **D**, you are a **Nurturer.**

Tiebreaker: If you have the same total number of answers in two or more columns, count the answers to the first ten questions only (for women) or the first six questions only (for men) to determine your genetic type.

Note: If three or more columns still have approximately the same number of answers, you are a Visionary.

The Four Genetic Types

The Two Strong Types

WARRIOR.

If you are a Warrior, your anatomical type (body build) is generally mesomorphic, from the embryonic layer that gives rise to bone, connective tissue, and muscle. Your dominant glands are the adrenals, and your energy type is pitta—the fiery dosha. As a Warrior, you have a generally strong, steady constitution. You are probably rather rectangular in build and tend to be muscular. You tend to have broad shoulders and chest— if you are a woman, you probably have a large bust. You usually have square hands with sturdy fingers. You may have had a problem with weight gain from your childhood days. When you put on weight, it tends to concentrate in your upper body, resulting, in men, in the traditional "beer belly."

Your exercise regimen should emphasize cardiovascular training for a healthy heart and flexibility to prevent injury and stay supple. Because you are naturally muscular you should minimize heavy strength training. Though you often crave meat and fatty foods, which stimulate your dominant glands, you are healthiest on a plant-based diet including whole grains, fruits, and vegetables. Warriors generally have strong, steady energy throughout the day.

The Warriors are the leaders of the world—adventurous, task-oriented, and opinionated. They are often found in positions of authority, as entrepreneurs, administrators, and managers. Famous people who appear to be Warriors include Demi Moore, Kirstie Alley, Cindy Crawford, Lynda Carter, Madonna, Oprah Winfrey, Bette Midler, Roseanne Barr, Garth Brooks, Robin Williams, Arnold Schwarzenegger, Evander Holyfield, and Mark McGwire.

For complete details on a nutrition and body-motion program for Warriors, see chapter ten.

NURTURER.

If you are a Nurturer, your dominant glands are your ovaries, which govern growth, sexuality, and reproduction, and your energy type is usually a combination of kapha, the slow dosha, and vata, the more changeable dosha. Anatomically, you are very curvy, fuller-figured below the waist with a slender build above. Your head is oval or heart-shaped, your shoulders are narrower than your hips, and you have a small, low waistline and medium- to small-sized breasts. Your hands are usually small to medium-sized, with tapering fingers. When you gain weight, it tends to go to your hips, thighs, and legs. An overweight Nurturer can still be quite slim above the waist.

You need more exercise than the sleek genetic types and thrive on exercise programs that include social interaction. You should emphasize cardiovascular training, with strength training for the upper body only. You often crave creamy and/or spicy foods, but you do much better on high-water-content foods, including lots of fruits and vegetables. Your energy level can be variable throughout the day, though you usually get a burst of energy in the evening.

Nurturers are sensitive, caregiving, service-oriented people and can often be found in the healing professions and teaching. Famous people who appear to be Nurturers include Jodi Foster, Whoopi Goldberg, Julia Louis-Dreyfus, Jennifer Aniston, Sandra Bullock, Meg Ryan, and Goldie Hawn.

For complete details on a nutrition and body-motion program for Nurturers, see chapter eleven.

The Two Sleek Types

COMMUNICATOR.

If you are a Communicator, your anatomical type is ectomorphic, from the embryonic layer that gives rise to skin and nerves. Your dominant gland is the thyroid, which governs energy levels, and your energy type is vata, the more changeable dosha. Your shape is generally symmetrical. Your shoulders and hips are about the same width. You tend to be slim and lanky, even bony looking, with long arms and legs and long, thin, bony hands and feet. When you put on weight, it's in the middle of your body, around the waist, abdomen, and upper hips. An overweight Communicator will still have relatively thin arms and legs.

Communicators enjoy variety in exercise and should be sure to include cardiovascular training, strength training, and flexibility exercises. Your dominant thyroid gland keeps your metabolism revved up. Though you love sweets and carbos, you thrive on "high-octane" fuel, including steady amounts of high-quality, animal-based protein. Your energy level is the most variable of all the genetic types. If you don't regularly eat small meals that include protein, you can experience severe energy crashes in the afternoon.

In temperament, Communicators are creative and easily bored. You are change-oriented and are often found in communications professions, such as writing, entertainment, and teaching. Famous people who appear to be Communicators include Julia Roberts, Candice Bergen, Barbra Streisand, Alan Alda, Ted Danson, Whitney Houston, Carol Burnett, Joan Collins, Uma Thurman, Michael Jordan, Patrick Ewing, Reba McEntire, Jane Pauley, George Bush, and Randy Travis.

For complete details on a nutrition and body-motion program for Communicators, see chapter twelve.

VISIONARY.

If you are a Visionary, your anatomical type is either ectomorphic, from the embryonic layer that produces skin and nerves, or endomorphic, from the layer that produces the digestive organs. Your dominant gland is the pituitary, which governs all other glands, and your energy type is either vata (changeable) or kapha (slow and steady). You probably are not very curvy; instead, your body is like a teenager's. You generally have a somewhat large head, a slightly defined, low-set waistline, and small hands and feet. When you become overweight, you tend to puffiness, even in your fingers and toes.

Exercise does not come naturally to you, but you'll feel best on a strength and flexibility program with a smaller cardiovascular component for overall health. As for fuel, you thrive on the foods now known as "healthy": light proteins and vegetables with few or no dairy products. Your day should start off with a substantial breakfast. Your energy level is strongest in the morning and tends to wane as the day goes along.

Visionaries are cerebral, idea-oriented, and generally introverted. They are often found in intellectual jobs that allow them to work on their own, such as researchers, inventors, artists, and musicians. Famous people who appear to be Visionaries include Nancy Reagan, John Travolta, Michael J. Fox, Tom Hanks, Paul McCartney, Bob Dylan, Kate Moss, Gwyneth Paltrow, Kate Winslet, Calista Flockhart, Michael Jackson, Albert Einstein, Elvis Presley, and Sammy Davis Jr.

For complete details on a nutrition and body motion program for Visionaries, see chapter thirteen.

4

CONTROLLING BIOCHEMISTRY

You may be wondering how people can be so different. Do we really have such different needs? To understand the reasons for the very real differences among humans, we need to take a look at how the different genetic types developed.

The Ancestry Connection

The biochemical differences between humans begin with the reality that each of us has a unique set of ancestors, going back tens of thousands of years. We did not all come from the same geographic location, nor did we develop under the same sets of climatic conditions or with the same available foods.

Many of our ancestors' physical characteristics, such as hair and skin color and texture, varied according to where they lived. Skin and hair pigment lightened in those who moved to cooler climates, and hair loss increased, to take advantage of the limited sunlight available.

Some of our forebears lived in warm climates with abundant plant foods. Their digestive systems and body chemistry slowly evolved to process these plant foods for optimum health. Other groups of humans evolved in harsher climates, with short growing seasons. Their bodies adapted to richer foods, such as meat, eggs, nuts, and fish. Still other early humans developed in fertile agricultural areas, where it was easy to grow food, and where grains were the staple foods of the diet.

Over time, the functional characteristics of each of these types—their digestion, absorption, assimilation, and elimination processes—adapted to use the basic types of nutrients most easily available to them. Those who developed in harsh climates, for example, developed relatively shorter intestines, to better utilize the energy and more quickly eliminate the wastes provided by animal-based foods. These people ate fewer carbohydrates, so their systems never developed to efficiently process them.

Those who subsisted on plant-based foods developed longer digestive systems, better suited to breaking down grains and other slower-to-digest, fiber-based nutrients, but not as well suited to a heavily protein-based diet.

Well, so what? you might think. That was then, and this is now. Yet if you think about it, "now" isn't so far removed from our ancestors in evolutionary terms. It took nature tens of thousands of years to develop genetic variants to take advantage of the local conditions. These built-in variations in body build, type of metabolism, and energy patterns/usage could not be changed in a few—or even several—generations.

When the hunter-gatherer humans began migrating, they found themselves in changing conditions that did not match those they had evolved from. Thus, certain problems, such as allergies and food intolerances, sprang up. If you find that milk products make you feel gassy and uncomfortable, some of your ancestors probably originated in a place where the only milk available was human milk, so their bodies never evolved to process cow's or goat's milk effectively.

Our ancestors' bodies also evolved in a time when much physical activity was necessary just to survive. They needed the stamina to spend long hours hunting for food, running from predators, and defending their territory. We no longer have to worry about those sorts of physical survival strategies—although our bodies are still genetically coded to need the body motion.

Our metabolisms are still geared to the lifestyles of our primitive forebears. They are still coded to require the same basic mix of fuel and activity that our ancestors experienced. They don't adjust overnight to having transportation, computerized conveniences, and a never-ending supply of concentrated foods.

Just as a Volkswagen and a Mercedes require different fuel mixtures and maintenance schedules, so do two humans of fundamentally different metabolic types. Thus, the sleek types—the Communicator and Visionary—who have faster metabolisms, require meals containing high-octane fuel (protein and fat), while the strong types—the Warrior and Nurturer—with slower metabolisms, do better with lower-octane fuel, meaning a more plant-based diet. And all types—sleek and strong— require a specific amount of body motion nearly every day.

Venus and Mars

I'd like to offer a word now about the deepest human difference of all— the difference between the sexes. Many recent books that delve into explaining our "humanness" have done extremely well because they answer age-old questions about behaviors and relationships. Recently Dr. John Gray's *Men Are from Mars, Women Are from Venus* has resonated as true to millions of us. His work focuses on some aspects of the biochemical differences between the male-aggressive and the female-nurturer.

This work has some relevance to the Body Code genetic types because, despite one's primary genetic type, all males are categorically more adrenal/pitta/mesomorphic, while all females are categorically more ovarian/kapha/endomorphic. Because the pitta/mesomorphic men generally have more lean body mass, they can more effectively burn off excess calories. This basic biological fact helps explain why it is generally easier for a man to lose weight than for a woman.

Confronting Conventional Thinking

If you've ever tried a diet and failed, you've absorbed a lot of conflicting dietary and exercise information. You've heard that it's essential to control calories if you want to lose weight. On the other hand, you may also have heard that calories don't count—that it's more important to be aware of fat grams, or the amount of protein or carbohydrate you consume. Some books and articles tout a low-fat diet with lots of carbos as the best route not only to losing weight but also to optimum health. Other recently popular books stress a higher-protein diet with higher amounts of fat and limited carbohydrate consumption.

Likewise, exercise recommendations are widely varied. Some books tell you that all you need is a little activity—say, gardening—a few times a week. Other experts promote an intensive regimen of running, weight lifting, and stretching for maximum fitness.

All this advice comes on top of the "wisdom" we've been taught, through repetition, down through the years. For example, the old saying that if there's no pain (in exercise), there's no gain. Or the idea that if food tastes good, it has to be bad for you, or that breakfast is the most important meal of the day. Or that as we age, we're destined to put on weight.

I'm here to tell you that a lot of these ideas are downright false. In the medical world, we've recently unlearned some ideas that were thought for a long time to be true. For example, it was long held that ulcers were primarily due to stress; then it was discovered that most ulcers are caused by a bacterium.

Many of the old truths about diet and exercise have likewise been proven untrue. For example, the notion of "no pain, no gain" is definitely wrong. You should not feel actual pain when you exercise, although, when you are first getting started, a slight amount of tightness or soreness may result. Likewise, the foods that taste good to us are primarily the foods we are used to. Skim milk, for instance, often tastes bland and "chalky" until it becomes the milk flavor we are accustomed to. Once that happens, for most of us, whole milk comes to taste over-rich and cloying. Breakfast is the most important meal of the day only for the sleek genetic types (Communicator and Visionary); it is the least important meal for the strong types. And it is *not* natural to put on weight as we age; it happens primarily because the metabolism slows with age and most of us don't do enough body motion to make up for that slowing.

The truth is that we learn as we go. No one has all the answers. In your own area of interest, whatever it happens to be—computers, teaching, business—you've undoubtedly noticed enormous changes in recent years. The same thing has happened in the nutrition/exercise/wellness industry. Yet most of us are still dragging around outdated information about diet, exercise, and disease prevention that may in fact be false.

Part of my goal in writing this book is to help you rethink some of these things, to see them in a different light. To stop believing the fallacies that you've stored as truth. And the biggest fallacy of all—the one that is the crux of my work—is that all human beings are biochemically the same.

It has long been believed that all of humanity can be served by one basic recommendation. That we all need a diet with the same ratio of proteins, fats, and carbohydrates. That we should all exercise a certain set amount of time every week. The Dietary Council has specific sets of recommendations for the nutrients that we need—basically the same for everyone; and most exercise physiologists likewise have programs detailing how we should all exercise.

My twenty years in the wellness industry have proven to me, beyond any possible doubt, that there is not a more fundamental truth than this: *Human beings are quite different in their needs for exercise and food choice, and in how we respond to mental and sensory stimulation.*

So why, you may ask, have past popular diets and exercise plans actually worked for some people? The answer is simple—those plans worked because they approximated the specific diet and exercise needs of *some* of the people who tried them. But every one of those plans failed for some people too.

The bottom line is that one wellness plan cannot possibly work for all metabolic types because the food and exercise needs for each genetic type are so totally different.

Just as an example, proponents of the low-carbo, high-protein diets claim that when deprived of carbos, your body will burn fat, producing a state known as ketosis, in which your body eliminates metabolic waste products known as ketones. Unfortunately, ketosis is a toxic state that can be dangerous for some types. However, another aim of the high-protein, low-carbo diets is to keep the insulin levels low, thus avoiding energy swings, which is a reasonable goal for both Communicators and Visionaries, who may have problems with fluctuating energy. But this sort of diet—which also tends to be high in fat—will not work in the long run for a Warrior or Nurturer. In fact, it will ultimately raise their body-fat thermostat and could lead to heart disease for some Warriors.

Likewise, the currently popular low-fat, low-protein, high-carbohydrate diets are probably the most healthful of the diets recommended for everyone. These diets have been useful in helping to prevent or even cure certain ailments, such as heart disease. The trouble with these diets is that the sleek genetic types, especially the Communicator, are constantly hungry when on them. Such a diet might actually make a Communicator more prone to severe energy fluctuations.

An incident in the early years of my career helped me see this reality clearly. Back when I worked for the National Institute of Fitness, two oriental sisters in their early twenties came to us to lose weight. Jean and Monica were both attractive Visionary types, but both were puffy and unhealthy looking, and about twenty pounds overweight. Monica told me that she and her sister had tried several diet plans but that nothing had seemed to work for them.

At the time, we were putting everybody on a low-fat, high-carbo diet, so I tried it with the sisters too. Between the boot-camp exercise levels and the presumably healthy diet, I expected Monica and Jean to lose about two to four pounds of body fat per week, as most of my other clients did. But to my surprise and their dismay, at the end of a week they had each lost barely a pound.

I decided to experiment, and over the next few weeks I eventually adjusted them toward a higher-protein, low-carbohydrate diet, which began to work immediately. Both women began to lose weight—the pounds just melted off. "I have more energy now than I've had in years," Jean told me.

This experience was one of the most memorable of my early career because it demonstrated for me that what I'd been taught in school was not always true. Since then, I've met thousands of other "tough cases," and in nearly every instance it has turned out that the person was simply following a plan that was wrong for his or her genetic type.

It's the same thing with exercise plans. If you notice, most of the exercise writers in the early seventies advocated jogging or brisk walking for half an hour a day, three to five times a week, which is the ideal amount of aerobic exercise for Communicators. By a not-so-strange coincidence, most of these experts, such as Jane Fonda, Ken Cooper, and Covert Bailey, are themselves Communicators.

The naturally thinner vata types—the Communicators and Visionaries—do need less aerobic (fat-burning) activity, and more activity that stimulates lean body mass (builds muscle). The opposite is true for the sturdier pitta and kapha types, the Nurturer and Warrior. These types need more fat-burning and less muscle-toning activity. The right body motion for you isn't determined by what some expert says—it's determined by your body build.

We recognized these differences years ago at the National Institute of Fitness and Green Valley Spa. Our Body Code approach takes them into account. In devising our Body Code programs, we take advantage of your body's built-in genetic needs for fuel and activity, working with your natural propensities.

Generating Feelings

We all have a way we like to feel that's comfortable or familiar to us. We say things like "I feel great today." On the other hand, sometimes we're out of sorts. We'll say, "Oh, I just don't feel like myself." Yet there's nothing we can actually measure that's wrong with us. Something is just not right.

Whether we realize it or not, the feelings we look for—those that make us "feel like ourselves"—can be stimulated by outside stimuli—things we do or eat or wear or interact with. Thus, each of us prefers certain foods, certain clothing, a certain type of job or industry, particular exercises, relationships, and activities. Our reasons for choosing these things are to create these specific feelings we are seeking, which are genetically coded. A Warrior, for example, who needs physical activity and thrives in a cool climate, may seek a physically demanding job or gravitate to an industry located in the snow belt. A vata-dosha Communicator or pituitary may seek the literal warmth of a tropical climate.

In seeking our preferred feeling, some of us are a little more power-oriented, some of us are a little more relationships-oriented, some of us are a little more cerebral or creative. We tend to fill our lives with the types of external stimuli that will give us those comfortable feelings of power or security or creativity.

The Body Code wellness system uses this inborn desire to feel a specific way to improve our health and well-being. Its various components are designed to use external stimuli to change the way we feel. You can think of it as a program of *feelings generation*. Its purpose is to help us stop doing the things that are counterproductive and start doing the things that are balancing.

What this program is really about, then, is learning to choose certain foods, herbal remedies, and physical stimulation that will create the specific kinds of feelings that our genetic types are coded for—and will also optimize our physical and mental well-being.

Unfortunately, we often make the wrong choices when seeking our desired feelings. We may choose something because someone else does, or because the media tell us to choose it, ignoring that it may not be right for our unique genetic type. Or we may find ourselves craving certain foods or experiences because they cause us to have a certain feeling. These cravings may give us what we're looking for in the short term, but in the long term they are actually counterproductive, especially if we overdo them.

For the Communicator, for example, with her uneven energy levels, the desired feeling is one of being able to process information, hence she seeks nutrients and activities that will keep the mind quick and alert. Too often, she tries to get, keep, and intensify that feeling by taking in a concentrated source of quick energy—sugar or caffeine—which will ultimately backfire on her, since her body may react to these substances with an overload of insulin, causing a rebound blood-sugar crash (hypoglycemia) and even greater feelings of low energy.

The Warrior, who has plenty of steady energy, needs to feel strong, steady, and in control, so she seeks the stimuli that will cause an increase of hormones from her adrenal glands to affect her brain chemistry balance.

The Visionary needs to ponder and create, so she seeks sustained mental focus—which she can get from dairy foods and carbohydrates that tend to throw her into the dreamy state.

The Nurturer likes the warm-fuzzy feeling of belonging or having purpose, so she too seeks stimulation sources, including pungent, spicy foods. These tastes initiate increased secretions of estrogen and progesterone, which increase the nurturing component of human beings.

The primary control site for this information exchange between the mind and body is the hypothalamus, which is located at the junction between the spinal cord and the brain. The main function of the hypothalamus ("the brain's brain") is to maintain homeostasis—or a steady state within the body. It does this through its control of body temperature, respiration, heartbeat, and the secretions of the pituitary gland, sometimes called the "master gland" of the body.

The hypothalamus is linked to the brain by a network of nerves; together the nerves and the hypothalamus are part of the limbic system. The limbic system is like a switchboard, mediating messages between your brain and your body. It is also responsible for many of our most primal, deep-seated drives and emotions, including the strong feelings of pain, anger, sex, hunger, thirst, and desire for pleasure.

We still don't fully understand the communications process in the limbic system, but we do know some of the key players. Serotonin, for example, is a brain chemical connected with feelings of well-being that responds directly to the types of nutrients we consume. We also know that these complex biochemical interactions affect a wide variety of body functions. For example, the body-fat thermostat—or setpoint—is governed by the hypothalamus.

Your body-fat setpoint is a genetically encoded ideal percentage of body fat that is programmed into the hypothalamus. A series of control mechanisms—checks and balances—defends this range tenaciously. Thus, if you overeat occasionally, you don't immediately become fat, because your hypothalamus can direct the body to burn up the excess calories. Likewise, if you're too busy to eat much for a few days, your setpoint adjusts your metabolism and keeps you from wasting away.

Setpoint theory explains why some people—those with low setpoints—can seem to generally overeat and never gain weight, while some of us—with a higher setpoint—put on pounds by just "looking at" chocolate cake. Your setpoint will stay within its genetically encoded range if you eat the foods and get the amount of body motion that you are genetically encoded to need. The problem comes when, over a long period of time, you eat the wrong foods and/or get insufficient or inappropriate body motion. Eventually, the body-fat thermostat becomes reset to a higher level. And the body will work just as hard to maintain this new setpoint as it did the original one, which explains why it's so difficult to lose weight once you have gained it.

Your success in returning to your previous weight range—in resetting the body-fat thermostat—depends on using the right combination of fuel and body motion. The Body Code program gives you the nutrients and body motion that your genetic type is programmed for to help you more quickly reset your body-fat thermostat to your ideal.

The Green Valley/Jay Cooper Laboratory

I've been fortunate in my work at the National Institute of Fitness, my local fitness centers, and the Green Valley Spa. In over twenty years I've been privileged to work with all kinds, shapes, and sizes of clients from literally all regions of the world. I've had the opportunity to observe them as they tried different food and activity regimens. Most of our programs have been weight-loss oriented, but we have also helped world-class athletes, runners, cyclists, body builders, tennis players, and triathletes to maximize their performance.

This "natural laboratory" has enabled me to refine these principles, to create the best possible eating and exercise plans for the four genetic types. In formulating my thinking, I've relied on the industry pioneers who came before me. I've discovered that a lot of what they said has proven to be true—but also found a lot of it false, saw that it didn't work in the laboratory of real conditions. I'm sure that future experts will improve on the work I'm doing here at Green Valley.

In the meantime, what I'm offering you represents the culmination of my experience with thousands of clients. In the following pages you'll find proven principles on nutrition and body movement for your genetic type. These principles will show you how to lower your body-fat thermostat, achieve a healthier, trimmer body, and increase those centered "feelings."

PART TWO

Unlocking Your Body Code

5

THE EXERCISE CONNECTION

I often use an anatomical chart, a picture of a human body showing all the muscles beneath the skin, to visually remind myself and my clients of what we are. When you *see* all of the muscles, bones, ligaments, and tendons, it becomes undeniably apparent that our bodies are designed for motion. That may seem obvious, but in today's information age, most of us spend much of the day working at semi-sedentary jobs. Yet our bodies are composed mostly of lean body mass, which consists of muscles, bones, ligaments, organs, and other connective tissues designed to *move*. To be fit, these parts of our body must be allowed to do what they were designed for.

If you confine a fish to a small enough fishbowl, he will be unable to move sufficiently to force a flow of water through his gills; unable to extract enough oxygen, he sickens and dies. If you confine a human to a sedentary lifestyle, he also begins to degenerate.

Back in the days when our ancestors were evolving, movement came naturally in the course of the day. Our ancestors spent most of their time hunting or gathering or farming or ranching. Even as recently as one hundred years ago, our predecessors spent up to ten or fifteen hours a day, six to seven days a week, rigorously using their bodies.

Today, few of us *have* to engage in much body motion to earn a living. In fact, approximately 75 percent of all Americans are basically sedentary, with no regular exercise program. The lifestyle of most of us involves moving each day only as much as is necessary to climb into the car and then push a button to roll down the windows. We don't plow fields. We don't even hang our laundry out to dry. We don't physically do the things we used to do that kept our fat thermostats where they should be, maintaining a low percentage of body fat. Today our bodies have no physical reason to be lean.

I'm not saying we should go back to the old days before modern conveniences, but rather that if we don't make up for that body motion we used to get, we will pay the price in how we feel, function, and look.

I can't emphasize enough that this is more than a lifestyle choice. Our bodies must have movement in order to efficiently process the fuel they take in. We need movement to keep our body parts functioning efficiently and to prevent them from rusting out too soon. And we need movement to keep our brain chemicals in balance and stay in a good mood.

Research scientists have established that a specific amount of body motion is necessary for those brain chemicals to be produced in the right amounts to affect our entire biochemistry. Certain types of body motion release endorphins and enkephalins, which contribute to a sense of well-being. Body motion helps promote the release of serotonin, which produces a happy flow and optimism. Body motion even affects the release of insulin to keep blood sugar in balance and to help lower the body-fat thermostat, or setpoint.

Body Motion vs. Exercise

The word *exercise* has come to have a negative connotation, perhaps because the way many of us have been introduced to it has generated less than warm, fuzzy feelings. For many people, exercise means an uncomfortable, regimented routine of difficult activities that make us sweat and grunt. Yet the truth is, exercise is nothing more than intentional body motion. Daniel, a middle-aged man I know, is typical of those who have negative feelings about exercise. "I don't want anyone telling me what to do," he says. "I never do exercise for its own sake. If I'm going to exercise, I have to be accomplishing something."

I suggested to Daniel, who was quite overweight, that he begin by walking to many destinations instead of using his car. As he advanced to pace-walk speed, he lost weight and regained a sense of well-being. Once he noticed how much better this activity made him feel, he eventually chose to schedule body motion into his life—and he doesn't ever need to call it "exercise."

If I accomplish little else in this book, I'd like to help those of you who have negative feelings about exercise to unlearn those attitudes. It really does feel great when you do the right kind of motion at the correct intensity. I'd like you to recognize that the biomechanical essence of what we all are is movement-oriented. We're not only comfortable when we're moving, movement is something that our bodies actually seek out and crave. Kids are into body motion all the time. Our pets do it. It's only we adult humans who don't do it, because we're not paying attention to what our bodies are telling us.

I call exercise *body motion* to convey the idea that it doesn't have to be a lot of joyless huffing and puffing and running like a hamster on a wheel. There's no specific type of body motion that anyone has to do. *Any type* of body motion performed at the effective level of intensity will cause the release of those good brain chemicals and give you that feeling you're seeking.

Once you learn to fill your need for body motion, you'll also find the type of body motion that you most enjoy. Some people will say, "Oh, you have to be a runner, or you have to do weight training, or you have to do jazz dance." The reality is that most types of body motion can be effective if done correctly, so the choice is yours.

Three Basic Types of Body Motion

Although some people have always known the value of body motion, it wasn't until the 1970s that getting regular exercise became what could be known as a (pardon the pun) *movement.* The exercise classes and books that evolved from those early days, as well as the program I am offering, simply provide a modernized way of condensing the hours of body motion that our forefathers routinely performed down to an equivalent amount of higher-intensity activity.

No matter what your body type, you need twenty-five to sixty minutes of rhythmic exercise, three to six times a week, to keep your body chemistry balanced.

The exact amount and combination of exercise you need depends on your specific body type.

The three basic types of exercise that everyone needs are:

Aerobic (cardiovascular conditioning)

Strength training

Flexibility

Aerobic (Cardiovascular Conditioning) Exercise: Finding the Flow

Aerobic body motion, which I prefer to call *zone-time* body motion, is the most effective type of exercise for conditioning your heart, lungs, and circulatory system. The name *aerobic* means "in the presence of oxygen." Aerobic exercise efficiently moves oxygen through your body, nourishing all of your tissues. It strengthens the most important muscle in your body—the heart. In addition to improving your general health, aerobic exercise also helps to balance your body chemistry, including the mood-governing chemicals in your brain, and turns down your body's fat thermostat, enabling you to stay at your ideal weight.

Exercise-induced release of the brain chemicals beta endorphin and enkephalin imparts the feeling of "the flow," sometimes known as runner's high. This feeling is so pleasurable that once you've experienced it regularly, you won't be willing to be without it.

In fact, the primary reason why most people don't engage in regular body motion is that they fail to reach that state that I call the flow. But I want to assure you right now that everyone can find the type of activity and intensity level that will produce the flow and cause those physiological changes. You—yes, even *you*—have the potential to become both physiologically and psychologically addicted to body motion. Just follow the guidelines for your genetic type in the next chapters, experimenting with the suggested activities as necessary until you find the activities that put you into the flow.

All four genetic types need some cardiovascular conditioning.

Many people still think aerobic exercise is the dancelike steps performed in "aerobics" classes. While it is true that those classes are aerobic, they are far from the only aerobic activities. Aerobic exercises are any activities that cause your heart, lungs, and circulatory system to work together at an elevated rate for a sustained period. Generally, twenty minutes is considered the minimum time necessary for fitness training.

In an aerobic exercise, you can feel your heart beating (but not pounding), notice your breathing has become faster (but not so fast that you are gasping), and you may break out in a sweat. The most effective ways to train aerobically involve using the biggest muscle groups in your body at a steady rate. Some of the most popular aerobic exercises are "aerobics," including aerobic dance; running/jogging; walking, power walking, walk-jogging, race or pace walking; rope jumping; cycling; spinning; power yoga; elliptical cross-training machines; stair climbing; rowing; step bench; NordicTrack; cross-country skiing; in-line skating; backpacking; mountain biking; circuit-style weight training; swim exercise classes; and swimming.

Among the most practical and effective activities for most of us, particularly if you are just starting a body motion program, is rhythmic walking, or pace walking.

Although a number of sports increase your heart rate, their elevated activity is not sustained long enough to get the aerobic benefits. These sports are enjoyable and good for you, so by all means enjoy golf, bowling, racquet sports, and team sports, but don't rely on them for the aerobic exercise you need.

To be aerobic, an activity must take place in the "aerobic training zone," or target zone, which is determined by your pulse rate. For information on determining your own training zone, see pages 56–58 in chapter six.

If you work out at a heart rate higher than your target zone, you are straining, not training. At this *anaerobic* level of intensity, your oxygen delivery system can't deliver oxygen fast enough to keep up. Anaerobic exercises include weight training and sprinting, or any activity in which the effort comes in relatively short, high-intensity bursts. These activities can be good for you too—they strengthen your muscles and improve your speed—but they are too intensive to confer an aerobic benefit. When you're first beginning to work body motion into your life, the temptation may be to go full steam ahead, running or walking or bicycling as fast as you can, but this will ultimately defeat many of the purposes of exercise. When it comes to cardiovascular conditioning, rhythmic and steady is your aim.

On the other hand, if you train at too *low* a heart rate, one that does not cause you to breathe faster, you are getting some benefit but not a truly aerobic one. A friend of mine named Robert, a career diplomat in his late fifties, made this common mistake. When Robert came to town to visit not long ago, I was surprised at how much weight he had put on in the four years since I'd last seen him.

I invited Robert to join me on a hike in a nearby canyon. As we began, my friend told me that he worked out every day for almost an hour. Yet as we began the walk at a moderate pace, Robert began to struggle. By the time we'd gone only a couple of miles, he was huffing and puffing and his face had become quite red. He told me that he just couldn't seem to breathe. I quizzed him more closely about the amount and type of exer-

cise he was doing and found that while he did walk for forty minutes nearly every day, he walked so slowly that his heart rate didn't get into the aerobic zone. In other words, though he was engaging in an aerobic exercise, Robert was not performing it *aerobically.*

When I explained to Robert how he could gradually increase his fitness level, he thanked me. "This has been a great wake-up call," Robert
told me at the end of our walk. "Next time I'm here, you'll see—I'll beat
you to the top of the canyon."

I hope he does. And I hope he does increase his activity level, for his
own health.

Strength Training

Strength training, another important component of fitness, is exercise
that conditions and strengthens the muscles, bones, and connective tissues. Research has shown that strength training is especially important for
women, who may be more prone to osteoporosis, the weakening of bone
that can lead to skeletal degeneration.

Strength-training exercises are those in which a muscle contracts
against applied resistance. That resistance can be a free weight, such as a
dumbbell, the weights found in weight-training machines, stretch bands,
or the weight of your own body, as in calisthenics, isometrics, and some
forms of yoga. Most weight training is done according to the principle of
progressive resistance, in which you challenge the muscles with resistance,
and when the muscles grow stronger in response, you increase the resistance.

Weight-training exercises are important for all four genetic types, but
especially so for Communicators and Visionaries, who tend to have weak-
er muscles. Warriors should limit their training, as they are naturally
strong, and Nurturers should limit weight training to the upper half of
the body.

Flexibility

The third component of fitness is flexibility, which primarily has to do
with the range of muscle motion and mobility of your joints. Flexibility
exercises help your muscles maintain elasticity and tone. They also help
to prevent injuries, such as dislocations or torn cartilage, tendons, or ligaments. Stretching exercises, such as slow stretch and yoga, help pro-

mote flexibility, which is especially important for Warriors, who tend to be stiff.

Are You Sleek or Strong?

As I explained in chapter three, human physiques fall into one of two basic classifications, the strong and the sleek. The sleek types, the Communicators and Visionaries, are naturally more linear, with thinner skeletons and longer muscles. The strong types—the Warriors and Nurturers—are naturally more muscled and/or curvy, with medium to thick skeletons and thicker muscles.

The Body Code plan takes a rather different approach to body motion depending on whether you are sleek or strong. The sleek types need less physical stimulation to stay in balance, while the strong types are biomechanically designed to need more physical stimulation to stay in balance. We simply need longer periods of physical stimulation to give us the physical and emotional benefits of body motion.

Within the two basic anatomical types, the exercise regimens are then fine-tuned for each of the four genetic types, taking account of the strengths and weaknesses of each type. Thus, the Warrior, who is naturally muscular and can be subject to heart disease, needs more aerobic exercise for cardiovascular fitness, and less emphasis on strength training; while the Visionary, who tends to flabbiness, needs to combine strength-building exercises with a more moderate aerobic regimen.

"Do I Really Have to Do As Much Exercise As You Recommend?"

Most of the people who come to see me at the Green Valley Spa are moderately active people anyway. To go from a moderate exercise program to a more rigorous one is not a dramatic step for them.

But if you're now basically sedentary, if you've rarely exercised in your life, or if you exercise less than one or two hours a week, hearing that you need to get five to ten hours of body motion a week can be discouraging. If you have health complications, or you live in a city, you may feel that you're already doing everything possible just to keep up. But don't panic—there is a gradual and proven process for you to follow.

First, remember that we're working toward an ultimate goal. Eventually, you'll be able to incorporate more body motion into your life.

For each of us, it is a process of starting right where we are, taking one day at a time, and complying with the "flow zone" principles. Your natural progression will take over from there. It has happened to literally millions of us formerly sedentary types. As you will see in the section on your own genetic-type exercise prescription, I offer gentle and realistic guidelines for easing into your body motion plans.

If five or six times a week isn't possible for now, then aim for one or two sessions per week, of ten to twenty minutes. If you start doing some activity after having a lifestyle without body motion, you'll get results right away. You'll immediately start to feel better. The exercise will start to lean you out, pulling your body-fat thermostat down toward the body shape you're genetically coded to have.

In the meantime, try to modify your lifestyle and career to enable you to gradually fit more body motion into the week. Just take small steps in that direction. Soon you will be choosing to do more than you ever imagined, and somehow everything will still get done. Remember that this is *your* lifestyle modification program, and it's yours to adjust.

I encourage my clients to memorize and apply this old principle: "What your mind can conceive and believe, you can achieve."

What you can conceive and believe, you can achieve! We must be able to conceive (see—visualize—imagine) our desired outcome, then believe (have hope or positive expectations) that we can accomplish our goal, to give us the stimulus to achieve (do) it.

If I tell you that you can run (every step of) a full marathon (26.2 miles) one year from today, you might assume that I am a bit wacko. Your response is based upon your *beliefs* about running for 26.2 miles. But you have never run that far and don't really know what it takes. My beliefs are based upon having trained literally thousands of clients to run marathons, many just like you, who thought that they couldn't when they began training. You believe that you can't; in fact, you can't even picture yourself running five miles or even two miles.

Over twenty years ago I went through this very process. I had already evolved into a runner by that time. I was routinely running three to five miles almost every day when I heard a local runner state that almost anyone could run a marathon. I thought, "Yeah, right—he doesn't know how my legs feel after only five miles." But his statement stayed with me and I began to wonder, "How far can I run?" So I took off one Saturday morning to find out. At that time, I believed that I could run six—maybe eight—miles max. I just knew that I could not run for ten miles. To my surprise, I ran eleven and a half miles that day. "Hmm," I thought. "Maybe I can run in the upcoming half-marathon," a 13.1-mile distance. I did, and from there to the twenty-five-kilometer (15.5 miles) distance, and so forth on to the marathon distance.

Here I was, running for four hours nonstop, when only a couple of years earlier I literally could not walk nonstop for even one mile. I've since worked with many athletes who run, cycle, and swim for two to six hours a day, every day, year after year. You probably don't want to even consider such a prodigious workout schedule. But I guarantee you can gradually work your way to whatever amount of body motion you desire by following these guidelines.

First, you need to *conceive* that you're capable of doing a specific amount of body motion. So start with an amount that you can actually picture yourself doing. Let's say you choose ten minutes of body motion once a week. Once you can actually see (conceive) that goal as possible, the next step is to *believe* it—construct your lifestyle in a way that will give you the opportunity to put in that amount of body motion.

Once you can conceive and believe your one body-motion session a week, then you can realistically *achieve* it. Spend as much time as you need on achieving this first goal, then begin to picture yourself doing slightly more, adding, say, another ten-minute session per week, or adding five more minutes to your one session. Once you can picture the new goal, find a believable way to fit it into your life, then work on achieving it.

The law of perpetual motion says that a body in motion tends to stay in motion until acted upon by an outside force. This law applies to body motion as well. Whatever you are doing today is laying the groundwork for your future. As your body chemistry changes, as your oxygen delivery improves and your body gets stronger, you'll feel better—lighter and leaner. You'll gather momentum as you go. The law of perpetual motion really does kick in, making it easier to keep going.

In the sections for each genetic type, I offer specific programs for systematically incorporating body motion into your life. You can take as long as you need to work up to the ultimate goals. This is your life. You are taking the reins in hand and taking responsibility for how you feel.

General Body Motion Guidelines

You will find detailed, specific instructions for the amount, duration, and type of body motion that's best for your type in the following chapters.

But in the meantime, here are some general guidelines for getting started.

• Get a doctor's okay. This is especially important if you are over fifty, have been inactive for a long time, or have been diagnosed with any chronic disease, such as heart disease, high blood pressure, obesity, or diabetes.

• Start slowly. Don't try to do too much too soon. When you begin your new activities, intentionally do less than your capacity. Don't try to go several miles on your first pace walk. Don't try to bench-press a Volkswagen during your first strength-training session, and don't try to put both your legs behind your head the first time you do yoga.

• Exercise within your exercise training zone. See the guidelines on pages 56–58.

• Don't skimp on equipment. You needn't go out and buy a set of color-coordinated spandex workout clothes. But it's essential for aerobic activities such as pace walking, running, or aerobics to have a good pair of well-fitting shoes designed for that specific activity. You'll also need good socks—synthetics are excellent, as they wick perspiration away from your skin. Invest in quality by choosing one of the industry leaders in footwear. Now is not the time to try to be thrifty. Choose a running specialty store and get fitted by an adult, runner salesperson.

• Don't use exercise equipment before receiving proper instructions.

• Consider joining a health club. While you can certainly do all the exercise you need elsewhere, there are definite advantages to a health club membership. For one, you'll have access to a wide variety of newer exercise equipment, both for cardiovascular and strength training. You'll also receive instruction on how to properly use the equipment. Inclement weather will no longer hinder your progress. Most health clubs also offer a wide curriculum of classes for variety, including yoga for the flexibility component of your fitness program.

Another advantage (especially for the gregarious Nurturer types) is that health clubs offer a social aspect to working out, without forcing those who prefer more solitary activity (such as Visionaries) to be social.

6

BODY MOTION GUIDELINES

Aerobic Training Zone (Flow Zone, Target Zone)

I explained in the last chapter that to get all the euphoric and other benefits of flow-type body motion, including improved cardiovascular health and a lowering of your fat thermostat, you must perform such activities in the aerobic training zone. This zone has been technically defined as a range between 65 and 85 percent of your heart's maximum pumping capacity. Studies show that some people enter the aerobic state at about 60 percent, and some stay aerobic up to about 85 percent of maximum.

I've already told you about how I came to run marathons. I've trained hundreds of other people to run them too, and I've found that the key to success in marathon running as well as in adherence to any body motion program is in finding the flow. The flow, you recall, is the level of intensity—the speed—at which you release brain chemicals that produce the euphoric high that enables you to run . . . or cycle . . . or swim for literally hours. I can't overemphasize that *anyone* and *everyone* can get to that level, if you just know how. This discovery has helped me to help thousands who felt they couldn't get into any type of exercise and stay with it. I first discovered this principle for myself, and later on I found it for my many running clients.

Approximately 22 percent of Americans exercise systematically. Why, you may wonder, do we do this to ourselves? The answer is that this 22 percent of the population has found the flow. In other words, we have found the type of activity that sustains our heart rates at the flow-zone level for long enough to get the payoff—the exercise high. For some of us it is running, for others it may be cycling or tennis or yoga or any of a myriad of other activities. What produces the flow is somewhat different for everyone, and anyone can get it if he or she complies with the basic principles.

When I started training clients back in the late seventies, I was determined to understand why some people got into the flow and some didn't. I found the answer when I began to work with Mark, a local "George Plimpton"–type writer for the local newspaper. Like George Plimpton, Mark's job was to enter into unusual events and write about the experience. They had him ride a bull in the local rodeo, parachute from a plane, box in the county fair, and run in the St. George Marathon. That's where I came into the story.

Training Mark was a riot. At 211 pounds, he began reluctantly, having never run more than five miles before. To make matters worse, we only had sixteen weeks to get ready, so we were on the "hurry up" approach. As I strategically increased the mileage and experimented with the pace, I recognized that Mark could run all day at 65–75 percent of his maximum capacity, but move him to 75–85 percent and he fizzled fast. This was an *aha* experience for me, leading me to realize that the optimum training zone was very different for different clients.

Since that experience, I've refined my understanding and application of that principle on thousands of clients, with outstanding results. And by the way, Mark weighed 175 on race day and ran every step of the marathon, in four hours and five minutes.

I firmly believe that the key to getting "hooked" on exercise is based almost *entirely* on your proper application of what I call the zone-flow principle.

So, bear all this in mind as you begin your own zone-type exercise. Experiment within your training zone to see which range works best for you.

Finding Your Own Training Zone

The aerobic training zone is indicated by your exercising pulse rate. To calculate your own training zone, follow these instructions:

1. First, *subtract your age from 220,* which will give you your estimated maximum heart rate.

2. *Multiply the figure you obtained by .60 and again by .85.*

3. The two resulting numbers will give you your aerobic training zone, a top and bottom pulse rate within which you should maintain your heart rate when exercising.

For example, if you are forty, your maximum rate (220−40) would be 180.

Then, $180 \times .60 = 108$; $180 \times .85 = 153$. This would be your aerobic training zone. To receive aerobic benefits, you would need to exercise at a pulse rate of no faster than 153 beats per minute and no slower than 108 beats per minute.

In the real world, we need to make adjustments in the training zone. Specific genetic types find "the flow" at different ranges within the target zone. For Warriors and Communicators, that range is 70–85 percent of the maximum heart rate; for Nurturers and Visionaries, it's 60–75 percent. However, if you are beginning a training program, it's best to begin working out much closer to the 60 percent end of the zone, while a highly trained athlete may comfortably train at the upper end of the zone.

To measure your level of intensity, simply do the Quick Test: take your pulse rate by placing the tips of two fingers to the left side of your Adam's apple and adjust finger positions till you can feel your heartbeat. Count how many times your heart beats in one six-second period and then just add a zero to that number. The result is your current estimated heart rate.

When you are first beginning to exercise, you needn't be so exact; use the following rule of thumb: do your body motion activity at a pace that is fast enough to make you breathe harder and break out in a sweat, but not so fast that you can't carry on a conversation (or sing). If you're gasping and can't talk, you're going too fast; if your breath rate is not elevated, you're going too slow.

Whether you are a beginner or an experienced athlete, I seriously recommend investing in a heart-rate monitor, which measures your pulse rate as you train. Monitors are comfortable and effective. They consist of a thin strap that holds a flat receptor on your skin close to your heart. The receptor picks up the electronic impulses sent as your heart pulsates and sends that message to what looks like a sports watch worn on your wrist.

Some models alert you with a beep if you exceed or drop out of your training zone. These are especially useful if you're trying to lose weight or are training for athletic competition. They also help prevent overexercising, which is the most common mistake made by beginners. The models of heart-rate monitors I recommend most often are made by Polar Electro Inc. For information on ordering a Polar Monitor, see appendix C.

Strength Training

I explained previously that strength training generally follows the principle of *progressive resistance,* which means that you move the target muscle (the one you are training) against a given amount of resistance or weight; when the muscle grows stronger in response to that weight, you increase the amount of resistance, so the muscle is still challenged. This is usually done by increasing the amount of resistance (adding more weight), by increasing the number of repetitions of the exercise, or by increasing the training frequency.

Strength-training exercises are customarily divided into repetitions *(reps)* of each movement, grouped together in *sets.* Thus, you might do ten reps of a given movement for one set; rest, then repeat the same movements ten more times for a second set. (Each set does not need to contain the same number of reps.)

In general, many reps (20–30) with lighter weight are best for toning and firming, while fewer reps (6–15) with heavier weight are best for strength and muscle building. The strong-body types (Warrior and Nurturer) need to adjust their activity to light weights and high reps, while the sleek types (Communicator and Visionary) should focus on using heavier weights with fewer reps.

The primary methods to perform strength training are free weights, training machines, stretch bands, and calisthenics. The methods you choose will depend on your personality, current level of strength, and access to equipment.

Free weights are dumbbells and barbells, mostly. For beginners, any easily graspable objects that can be lifted will do nicely. For many exercises, household objects, such as cans of vegetables, can be used to get started. Advantages of free weights are that they are relatively inexpensive and easy to use.

Weight-training machines are perhaps the easiest way for most to begin a strength-training program. These machines, technically called selectorized variable-resistance machines, are mechanical contraptions in which you sit or kneel, then push, pull, raise, or lower a weight, depending on the given machine. Advantages of weight-training machines are that they are relatively safe, easy to use, and when used correctly, effectively isolate the specific muscle groups. Disadvantages are that they take up a great deal of space and can be quite expensive. Most people choose to go to a health club to use them.

The machines found in most health clubs these days are Nautilus, Universal, Cybex, Keiser, Body Master, and Life Fitness. They work in slightly different ways, but all of them provide a good workout for the body's major muscle groups.

Stretch or resistance bands are thick, strong rubber bands of different sizes that can be used to train various muscle groups. Once you learn how to use them, they can be very effective. Their advantages are that, obviously, they are affordable, take up little space, and are portable, so you can travel with them. Disadvantages are that they may be difficult to learn to use correctly, and the rubber can deteriorate or stretch out of shape, necessitating replacement.

Calisthenics are whole-body exercises that strengthen various muscle groups. The weight you work with in calisthenics is your own body weight; to increase resistance you must increase the number of times you perform the exercise. Examples of calisthenics include push-ups and chin-ups. Advantages of calisthenics are that they can be performed in a group setting, which is advantageous to the socially oriented Nurturer. They require no purchase at all and can easily be performed anywhere. A number of strength and toning classes, including power yoga, make use of calisthenics.

What about Isometrics?

You may have heard of isometric exercises, in which a muscle is strengthened by contracting it and holding it at the maximum contraction for several seconds. Although these exercises can be excellent for toning the body and can even increase strength, I don't recommend them for a general strength-building program for two reasons. In the first place, when you hold a muscle contracted in only one position, as with most isometrics, that muscle is strengthened *only in that position,* rather than throughout its range of motion. In the second place, we now know that only weight-bearing exercises, such as weight training and calisthenics, strengthen the bones, helping to prevent osteoporosis.

Examples of isometrics are a number of yoga postures in which the extreme position is held for several seconds with the muscles tensed.

Body Code Basic Strength-Training Routine

I recommend learning how to do strength training at a health club, gym, or YMCA, if possible. A fitness instructor or trainer can show you exactly how to do each exercise correctly, as well as recommend a good basic strength routine. When you are beginning, it is easy to do strength exercises incorrectly, which will slow your progress and could even cause injury. But if you want to get started in a smaller way, I offer the following routine, designed to challenge each of your major muscle groups.

Refer to Key #2 in the section on your body type to determine which muscle groups you should work on. Remember that these exercises are suggestions only. There are literally dozens of exercises for each of the major muscle groups. When you have mastered one exercise for each group, learn another, which will challenge the muscles in a slightly different way and also help to keep you from getting bored.

Remember also, when lifting weights, to perform slow and steady motions. Begin with a weight that you can lift in a controlled motion; if you need to "jerk" or "throw" the weight, then that weight is too heavy for you at your present level of strength. Remember also to breathe naturally as you work out. *Never hold your breath* while training; your muscles need oxygen to sustain the activity.

Group One: Hips and Thighs (Buttocks, Quadriceps, Hamstrings)

These large muscles, found in your thighs and extreme lower back, are responsible for moving your legs in nearly all body motion. They are naturally stronger in the strong-body types; Communicators and Visionaries need to do extra work to keep these muscles toned and strengthened.

SQUAT

Stand comfortably, your feet hip-width apart and your arms stretched out in front of you for balance. Keeping your back straight, bend your knees and lower yourself toward the floor as if to sit down; when your thighs are parallel to the floor pause, then slowly stand back up. Repeat 10–30 times.

If this exercise is too difficult at first, you can begin by leaning against a wall, your feet twelve to fifteen inches from the wall, and "sit on air," your back supported by the wall.

Warrior: omit

Nurturer: omit

Communicator: include

Visionary: include

Other strength exercises for the quadriceps and buttocks include the lunge and leg press.

Group Two: Chest and Front of Shoulders

These muscles, which include your pectorals and deltoids, are important in nearly all activities in which you use your arms. They are naturally strong in the Warrior, but may need strengthening with the other genetic types.

BENT-ARM LIFTS (FLYS)

This exercise is best performed on an exercise bench, but you can start on the floor with light weights. Lie on your back on the floor or an exercise bench with your knees bent, your arms straight out to the sides (or slightly bent, if lying on a bench), holding a weight in each hand with your palms facing the ceiling.

Slowly raise your slightly bent arms off the floor (or from just below the top of the bench) toward each other, until your hands almost meet in the air above your chest. Maintain a slight curve in your arms, as if you were trying to grasp a barrel. Pause a moment, then slowly lower. Repeat 10–30 times.

Warrior: omit or *use light weights only*

Nurturer: include, but *use light weights* if already strong above the waist

Communicator: include

Visionary: include

Other exercises for this muscle group include push-ups, modified push-ups (push-ups performed with the legs bent behind you), negative

push-ups (in which only the lowering part of the push-up is performed),
and bench press.

Group Three: Upper Back

These muscles, which include the latissimi dorsi (lats) and trapezius
(traps), are responsible for moving your shoulders and protecting your
shoulders and neck from injury.

BENT-OVER ROW WITH BENCH

Stand with your right foot on the floor and left knee resting on a
bench (or hard wooden chair seat). Lean forward, balancing yourself with
your left hand on the seat. Keep your back straight, parallel to the floor,
your right arm hanging down, holding a weight in an overhand grip (your
palm is facing your body).

Slowly raise your right hand, bringing the weight up, until it touches
the outside of your chest. Your elbow should be pointing up in the air,
above your back. Pause, and slowly lower.

Complete 10–30 reps, then repeat on the other side.

Warrior: omit or *use light weights only*

Nurturer: include, but *use light weights* if already strong above the
waist

Communicator: include

Visionary: include

Other exercises for the upper back include the chin-up, pullover, lat
pulldown, and seated row.

Group Four: Lower Back

These muscles are important for stabilizing your trunk and ensuring
good posture. The following yoga pose is good for flexibility of the lower
back as well as strength.

LOCUST

Lie on your stomach with your forehead on the floor, your arms at
your sides, your hands tucked underneath your abdomen and groin,
palms facing up.

Keeping your upper body on the floor, slowly lift your legs straight up
as far as you can, hold for ten seconds, then slowly lower. If this is too dif-

ficult, begin by lifting one leg at a time until you have gained greater strength. Repeat 10–30 times.

Warrior: include

Nurturer: include

Communicator: include

Visionary: include

Other exercises for the lower back include forward bend with weights, stiff-legged dead lift, and lower-back hyperextension.

Group Five: Shoulders

These muscles, the deltoids, are used whenever you raise your arms. Strong deltoids are essential in most sports.

STANDING PRESS

Stand with your feet comfortably apart, your back straight, your knees slightly bent, and a weight in each hand at shoulder level in an overhand grip (your palms are facing forward).

Slowly raise your right arm straight up until it is fully extended above your shoulder. Pause a moment, then slowly lower to the starting position; *at the same time,* raise your left arm until it is fully extended. Continue, alternating arms. Repeat 10–30 times.

Warrior: omit or *use light weights only*

Nurturer: include, but *use light weights* if already strong above the waist

Communicator: include

Visionary: include

Group Six: Front of Upper Arms

The biceps, the muscle that bulges when you "make a muscle," is responsible for bending your elbow and for pulling and lifting.

BICEPS CURL

Stand comfortably with your arms at your sides, a weight in each hand in an underhand grip (your palms are facing the front, your knuckles are facing the floor).

Slowly raise your right forearm, keeping your elbows back and held to your sides. Try not to move your shoulders. When your hand has reached shoulder level, pause momentarily, then begin to lower your arm back to starting position. *At the same time,* start to raise your left arm. Continue alternately raising and lowering; try to concentrate on the lowering part of the exercise, keeping both arms in a steady and controlled motion. Repeat 10–30 times.

Warrior: omit or *use light weights only*

Nurturer: include, but *use light weights* if already strong above the waist

Communicator: include

Visionary: include

Other exercises for the biceps include negative chin-ups and chin-ups.

Group Seven: Backs of Upper Arms

The triceps muscles straighten your arms and are used in pushing movements. They are generally undeveloped in most women, resulting in upper-arm flab.

CHAIR DIP

Sit on the edge of a bench or sturdy wooden chair, placing your hands next to your hips so that you're almost sitting on your thumbs. Walk your feet out until your hips are off the bench or chair. Your knees should be bent at a ninety-degree angle, your thighs parallel to the floor.

Tighten your abdominal muscles, bend your elbows, then lower your body until your upper arms are parallel to the floor; pause a moment, then push your body straight back up. Repeat 10–30 times.

Warrior: do one set only of 10–12 reps

Nurturer: do 2–3 sets

Communicator: 3 sets

Visionary: 3 sets

Other exercises for the triceps include the triceps press, French curl, and triceps extension.

Group Eight: Forearms, Wrists, Hands

This group of several muscles, primarily involved in gripping, is usually underdeveloped in the sleek types.

WRIST CURLS

Sit or stand at a table, bench, desk, or anything that supports your forearms while allowing your hands and wrists to hang off the edge.

Part 1: With your arms and palms facing up, grasp a weight in each hand (underhand grip) and raise them as far as possible, while keeping your forearms on the table. Slowly lower the weights, then repeat.

Part 2: With your arms and palms facing down, grasp a weight in each hand (overhand grip), then proceed as for Part 1. Repeat 10–30 times.

Warrior: omit

Nurturer: omit

Communicator: 1 set

Visionary: 2–3 sets

Another good exercise for the hands and wrists is slowly squeezing a hard rubber ball in each hand.

Group Nine: Abdominals

This important group of muscles, found in the center and sides of your abdominal area, is responsible for bending, turning, twisting, and stabilizing your trunk. These muscles are undeveloped in many people of all genetic types.

MODIFIED CRUNCH

Some form of crunch is the best overall abdominal exercise.

Lie on your back with your knees bent, your hands clasped behind your head. Keeping your chin tucked into your chest, slowly curl up until your head, shoulders, chest, and arms are just off the floor; hold a moment, then curl back down. Repeat 10–30 times. Be sure to keep your lower back flat on the floor.

Note: The position of your hands makes a difference as to the difficulty of the exercise. The easiest position is with your arms folded across your chest; the hardest, with your hands behind your head. If you find the latter too easy, hold a weight just under your chin with both hands.

To strengthen the lateral abdominal muscles, proceed as for the basic crunch, but alternately bring each elbow to the opposite knee; hold a moment, then lower. Repeat 10–30 times.

Warrior: 1 set

Nurturer: 1 set

Communicator: 2 sets

Visionary: 2–3 sets

Other exercises that are good for the abdominals include straight and bent-legged push-ups and abdominal machines.

Stretching

The strong types need to spend more time on stretching than the sleek types, because their muscles and tendons tend to be tight. But all types benefit from a stretching routine. There are many books and articles on stretching; no matter what sort of routine you use, try to involve all of your major muscle groups.

To get the benefit from stretches, perform them slowly, then *hold* at the extended position for fifteen to thirty seconds. Stretches performed violently, or in a herky-jerky motion, can have the opposite effect from that desired and can actually tighten the muscle groups you're hoping to lengthen and relax.

Basic Stretch Routine

1. BACK WARM-UP

Bend over from the waist, keeping your legs straight and letting your arms and head drop, and just *hang*. Don't try to force yourself any closer to the ground, and don't tighten any of your muscles. Just relax and let gravity do its work of unkinking your back and stretching the muscles of your back and legs. Hold for one minute. Repeat two or three times.

2. ARM WARM-UP

Stand with your feet comfortably apart, your hands and arms straight overhead. Reach upward, slowly, as high as possible with one hand, as if you were trying to touch the ceiling. Hold at the extreme position for a few seconds, then reach slowly with the other hand. Repeat several times with each hand.

3. SIDE STRETCH

Stand with your feet comfortably apart, your right hand on your waist, your left arm overhead. Now gently bend to the right side until you feel a stretch on your left side. Hold for fifteen to thirty seconds, then reverse the positions of your hands and bend to the other side. Repeat several times on each side.

4. CALF STRETCH

Stand about two feet from a wall, facing it. Stretch out your arms and lean against the wall, supporting yourself with your hands. Keep your feet flat on the floor as you lean into the wall, hold fifteen seconds, then push yourself away from the wall, as if you were doing a push-up against it. You should feel a stretching in your calf muscles. If you don't, move your feet farther from the wall. Repeat two or three times.

This exercise is especially good for women who wear high heels, or for anyone with tight calf muscles.

5. HALF-FORWARD BEND

Sit on the floor with your legs stretched out in front of you. With your right leg straight and keeping both legs on the floor, bend your left leg and bring your left foot as close to your body as possible (your left knee should be on the floor, and your left heel should rest close to your groin). Now, without bending your right knee, reach forward with both hands and grasp your right leg, ankle, or foot, as far down as you can reach without straining. Try to bend from the waist, keeping your back as straight as possible (some rounding is inevitable).

Hold for thirty seconds, relaxing into the pose. Reverse the position and repeat with your other leg. This is not only a great hamstring stretcher, it also loosens your back.

6. CROSS-LEGGED STRETCHER

Lie on your back with your right leg bent, the foot on the floor. Cross your left ankle over your right thigh, then, holding your hands behind your right thigh, gently pull the right leg toward your chest. Hold for a moment, then release and switch sides. You should feel a deep stretch in your quadriceps and hips.

There are literally thousands of other stretching exercises. Check a video out from your library or rent one. Take a stretch or yoga class and find the stretches you like to create your own routine.

7

NUTRITION ESSENTIALS
FOR ALL TYPES

Thirty years ago, before the information age, we needed a more concentrated fuel mixture to provide the energy for our physically active lifestyles. Today we are far less active and no longer need the big meals and high calories. Still, for too many of us, food is the main event of the day.

However you view mealtimes, food is one of the basics in everyone's life—it's the fuel that keeps your body going, the way gasoline fuels your car. But just as you wouldn't put an inferior brand of gasoline in your car, or a diesel fuel containing extra ingredients that are known to be harmful to your car's engine, so you shouldn't take in fuel that is known to be harmful to your body—yet that is what many of us do every day when we choose processed, unwholesome foods.

Another nutritional mistake many of us make is eating foods that are wrong for our genetic type, which is also like using the wrong type of fuel. If you continue to eat this way, these foods can overstimulate your dominant gland, eventually exhausting it and creating an imbalance in your glandular system. The entire system becomes sluggish, you begin to put on weight, you don't feel right. In the Body Code way of eating, we shift the emphasis from foods that stimulate the dominant gland to foods that stimulate the other glands, bringing the entire system into balance.

In the beginning, the changes may seem dramatic to you, and sometimes they are. But the recommended food-choice plans will bring your body chemistry back into balance quickly enough to give you a notice-able benefit in how you feel and how you look. The idea is to enable your body to heal itself, so your system can once again function as designed.

Once you're hitting on all eight cylinders, so to speak, when your immune functions are stronger and steadier, your digestion is proceeding smoothly, and your energy levels are more steady, then you may begin to add back in those foods that right now you think you can't do without. You'll discover that your cravings are easier to control when you are balanced.

One of my clients, a Communicator, though a dedicated vegetarian, gradually brought her diet into line with my recommendations. Before she began the Body Code diet, she ate what most would consider a healthy breakfast of rice or other grain and vegetables. Unfortunately, that was too much carbohydrate too early in the day for a Communicator, and not enough protein. "It's really hard to get all the protein," she told me. But she started eating egg whites from free-range chickens, and some soy products. "I basically don't eat any carbos now before noon," she said. "And I don't really miss them."

A year and a half after she began the program, she is no longer suffering from the midafternoon blood-sugar "crashes" that had plagued her her entire life. Now in her midfifties, she claims to have as much energy as she did in her thirties. And as she reported with a grin, "I have a plate of pasta now and then, and even an occasional hot-fudge sundae."

That occasional sundae is fine—as long as she doesn't overdo it, and as long as she continues sufficient body motion to keep her insulin levels steady. The point is that the Body Code nutrition plan isn't a diet of deprivation. It's a foundation eating plan designed to avoid overloading your system with input that it can't handle. In the next section of the book, I'll give you specific guidelines for the best foods for your genetic type. Below is a list of the foods that are known to stimulate each of the dominant glands:

Foods that stimulate the adrenal gland (Warriors should limit):
- high-cholesterol foods—egg yolks, cream, organ meats
- flesh foods—red meats, deli meats, all high-fat dairy
- salt, high-sodium foods—cheeses, packaged foods
- alcohol

Foods that stimulate the ovaries (Nurturers should limit):

- Creamy foods—high-fat dairy, chocolate, sauces, dips, gravy
- Spicy foods—hot, zesty, tangy foods and spices: cumin, cayenne, chiles, curries

Foods that stimulate the thyroid (Communicators should limit):

- Refined carbos—cookies, cakes, crackers
- Sweets—sugar, sodas, cookies, honey, jelly, candy
- Caffeine—coffee, teas

Foods that stimulate the pituitary (Visionaries should limit):

- Dairy foods—milk, cheeses, butter
- Sweets—sugar, sodas, cookies, honey, jelly, candy

Macronutrients

You probably know that the fundamental components of food are carbohydrates, proteins, and fats. Each of the four genetic types needs sufficient amounts of foods containing these components. They contain the basic building blocks of life, as well as the micronutrients necessary for all processes of metabolism. The nutrients in our food are used not only to build and repair body cells, but to create hormones, neurotransmitters, and other chemicals used for communication within our body.

Carbohydrates are our basic fuel. Carbohydrates are either used for energy immediately, in the form of simple sugars; stored for later use (as glycogen, a complex sugar); or converted to fat for long-term storage. Carbohydrates include not only flour and sugar, but all plant foods. The different genetic types need different kinds and amounts of carbohydrates. The Communicator, for instance, needs a lot of green and leafy vegetables that grow above the ground, while the Warrior thrives on those as well as starchier veggies, grains, and fruit. All four types, however, should avoid highly refined and processed carbohydrates, such as white flour and refined sugar.

This is true for several reasons. For one, refined flour and sugar have had most of the real "nutrition"—the micronutrients and bran, or fibrous matter—removed. Therefore they supply mostly extra calories, which most of us don't need.

Because they have so little fiber, refined carbos are not useful for helping food to move quickly through the digestive system. This is particularly a problem for Warriors, who have a longer bowel and are prone to colorectal ailments.

Refined flour and sugar are also undesirable because of what usually goes with them—quantities of undesirable additives and fats.

Proteins are the building blocks of life. Amino acids, the constituents of proteins, are used for building the scaffolding of all cells. Sources of protein include all kinds of meats, nuts, seeds, and dairy products. There is also some protein in many plant foods other than nuts and seeds, but most are second-best sources, except for beans (soybeans are especially high in protein).

As with carbohydrates, the different genetic types need different amounts and types of protein. Communicators need the most protein, to help keep their blood sugar levels stable, while Warriors need the least. In fact, Warriors are genetically the best suited to a traditional vegetarian diet.

Fatty sources of protein, such as marbled meats and high-fat dairy foods, including butter, are not ideal for any of the genetic types and should be limited, even by Communicators.

No matter what your genetic type, be aware that most meat available in supermarkets is heavily contaminated with antibiotics, growth hormones, and pesticides. These residues concentrate in the fat deposits of meat, which is the main reason that I don't recommend eating beef, pork, and delicatessen meats. For the sleek genetic types, who do need animal protein, better sources are those found in free-range animals not raised in factory-farm conditions. (See sources list in appendix C.) Also healthier are the increasingly available exotic meats, such as buffalo and ostrich. When seeking meat, remember to look for sources that are lighter, leaner, and cleaner.

Although we generally think of **fats and oils** as "bad," forbidden foods, they are actually every bit as essential to life as carbohydrates and protein. Fatty acids—components of fat—are found in every cell of the body and provide energy, insulate nerves, and cushion and protect cells and organs. They are also essential components of hormones and other chemical messengers. You could not survive on a diet that eliminated all fats. But in terms of health, the key is in knowing which fats to eat.

The best fats—the ones that all of us need to include regularly in our diets, though in small amounts—are those that contain essential fatty acids (EFAs). These fatty acids are called essential because they cannot be made by the body; they must be supplied by the diet. Research has established that some of the essential fatty acids play a role in regulating appetite and maintaining the body-fat thermostat. According to some studies, when the body does not get enough of the essential fatty acids, appetite increases in an attempt to supply them. Among the fats that contain the highest percentage of essential fatty acids are the mono-unsaturated oils, found in olives, avocados, peanuts, cashews, and canola oil.

Less beneficial for everyone are the highly saturated fats found in red meat and whole-fat dairy products, such as egg yolks, cream, cheeses, and butter. Not only do these fats lack the essential fatty acids, they also contain a lot of cholesterol and calories. Also undesirable are hydrogenated fats and transfats. These are fats that have been chemically changed to improve their stability for cooking or storage. Unfortunately, changing them also makes them unhealthful and more likely to end up as deposits in our arteries.

To understand why these chemically changed fats are so bad for you, try thinking of them as keys that fit chemical "locks" in your body. The locks are keyed to be opened by fatty acids, enabling various metabolic processes to take place. Hydrogenated fats have been changed in such a way that their "keys" no longer fit in the locks or will only turn the locks partway. The transfats are even worse; they may fit into the locks, but then they jam, preventing the correct keys—the essential fatty acids—from opening the locks and thus preventing the given metabolic processes from continuing.

The following chart gives a brief summary of the most common sources of carbohydrates, proteins, and fats in the American diet. Each category offers subcategories, which group similar food sources together.

MACRONUTRIENT CHART

Sources of Carbohydrates
Group 1—Fruits, citrus and tropical (all common fruits
   except tomato, avocado, melon, and berries)
Group 2—Melons and berries
Group 3—Leafy and/or green vegetables, squash, cruciferous
   vegetables (cabbage, broccoli, cauliflower, bok choy), sea
   vegetables (kelp, nori, kombu, bladder wrack)
Group 4—Starchy vegetables, including roots, potatoes,
   yams, carrots, onions, turnips, parsnips, rutabagas, beets

Group 5—Legumes, including lentils, chickpeas, lima and butter beans, peas, black-eyed peas, soybeans, tofu, miso, tempeh

Group 6—Other beans, including black, pinto, navy, kidney, white, wax, and pole

Group 7—Whole grains, including oats, corn, rice, wheat, millet, barley, quinoa, and rye

Sources of Protein

Group 8—Nonfat dairy, including skim milk, yogurt, white cheeses

Group 9—Extra-lean proteins, including white and pink fish, skinless poultry, egg whites, Egg Beaters

Group 10—Medium-fat proteins, including exotic meats, such as buffalo, elk, emu, venison, ostrich, free-range-fed beef and pork

Group 11—Medium-fat dairy proteins, including low-fat milk, cheese, yogurt, and kefir

Group 12—Higher-fat protein, including lamb, pork, beef, egg yolks, organ meats, and deli meats

Group 13—Higher-fat dairy proteins, including whole-fat milk, creams, cream cheese, butter, ice cream, sauces, and spreads

Group 14—Shellfish*

Group 15—Vegetable proteins: legumes, nuts, seeds, seitan (wheat gluten)

Sources of Fats

Group 16—Monounsaturated: olives, olive oil, canola oil, avocado, almonds, cashews, macadamias, peanuts

Group 17—Polyunsaturated: vegetable and grain oils— sunflower, safflower, sesame, flax

---

*A note on shellfish: Although shellfish are a good source of protein, I don't recommend them for any of the genetic types. This is because generally speaking shellfish (oysters, clams, shrimp, etc.) are coastal dwellers and bottom feeders, which means that they consume toxic chemicals and other pollutants that are dumped or drained off our coasts. If you love shellfish, eat it only occasionally, don't eat it raw, and avoid consuming the veiniest parts and the digestive systems. Warriors and Nurturers also need beware of the high fat and cholesterol content of some shellfish, especially shrimp and squid.

Group 18—Saturated fats: all animal foods (meat and dairy except for nonfat)

Group 19—Hydrogenated and transfats: all packaged and/or hermetically sealed foods such as crackers, potato chips, etc.; fried foods, fast food

Food Preparation

Food preparation is an individual matter, and I offer few guidelines, except to recommend that you bake, broil, grill, steam, or stir-fry, which do not require adding a lot of extra fat to foods. When you do use oil in cooking, make it a monounsaturated oil. Canola oil is best.

The strong genetic types should try to eat as much plant food as possible, preferably raw. The strong types—Warriors and Nurturers—are designed to be more physical, which includes chewing, so raw vegetables, salads, fruits with their skins on, are ideal foods for these types.

Conversely, the sleek genetic types, especially Communicators, do better with warmer or cooked foods. Excesses of cold and raw foods can hinder metabolic functions in Communicator types. Also, they don't need as much chewing stimulation as the strong types to cue the digestive process.

General Supplements

In addition to the basic macronutrients, I recommend numerous food supplements, ranging from herbs, teas, and condiments to vitamins and minerals. All foods and condiments, through their taste and smell, can influence glandular secretions. These influences affect the different genetic types in different ways, so specific combinations of supplements are suggested for each type.

In general, teas are used to control appetite, though some are valuable for both calming and invigorating effects. Herbs can aid digestion and help balance biochemistry, while vitamins and minerals also balance biochemistry and help to ease cravings.

For more details on herbs, vitamins, and minerals for each genetic type, see chapter fifteen.

Alfalfa or Kelp—These supplements are used as glandular support and bulking agents, to aid digestion and help prevent constipation. The nondigestible fiber creates a feeling of fullness, which hastens satiation. Alfalfa is especially good for Warriors and Nurturers; kelp is preferred for Communicators and Visionaries.

Flaxseed—This is an excellent source of essential fatty acids and an appetite suppressant. I recommend it for all types, sprinkled on your food in the evening. You can also buy flaxseed oil and mix it with juice, or grind the flaxseed in a coffee mill and mix with other foods.

Condiments

Garlic—Garlic can be used by all types. It can increase metabolism, aid digestion, and in sufficient amounts, lower cholesterol. Garlic has long been used in folk medicine as a general health tonic. I suggest using plenty of raw garlic to season your food, or use garlic capsules. (See specific recommendations for each genetic type.)

Ginger—This root, which is a staple in Eastern cooking, has long been used as a general tonic, a digestive aid and calmative, and an anti-inflammatory. Use powdered ginger in cooking, or chew on crystallized gingerroot to calm your stomach and help suppress appetite.

Artificial Sweeteners—As a general rule, I don't recommend artificial additives of any kind because they are not pure, whole foods. Still, the sweetener known as NutraSweet is made of synthetic amino acids, so one to two packets per day is not the worst thing in the world for a sleek type to eat when craving something sweet.

The problem with relying on artificial sweeteners is that, since they are sweet, eating them will help perpetuate your craving for sweets. Also, some studies have suggested that artificial sweeteners can create an insulin response in some hypersensitive individuals, which could be a problem for Communicators.

Avoid artificial sweeteners that contain saccharin, which has been proven to cause cancer in laboratory animals.

Gymnemia, an herbal extract available in health-food stores, can be helpful for those, such as Communicators, who have blood-sugar problems. Sprinkled on sweet foods, it slows the absorption of sugar into the digestive tract.

Stimulants

Ginseng—This folk remedy is a proven adaptogen that has long been used to boost metabolism, increase energy and mental clarity, and improve the sex life. It is particularly good for the sleek genetic types, especially Communicators, who can use an energy boost in the midafternoon. Nurturers should avoid or limit their intake of ginseng, as it may overstimulate their dominant glands. Ginseng can be taken as a tea or in capsules. Choose one that has actual "ginsenosides" in the ingredients.

Ma Huang/Ephedra—These herbal extracts have long been used as central-nervous-system stimulants and bronchial dilators. They are not recommended for Communicators or anyone who has difficulty sleeping. Follow the directions on the package for use.

Teas

Many types of teas can be useful on the Body Code plan. Below are some of the teas I recommend for the different genetic types.

Green Tea—If you really have to drink caffeine, green tea is the best way to do it. Green tea is an unfermented version of the black tea that many Americans are used to drinking. It contains a small amount of caffeine, but is much milder than either black tea or coffee. Green tea also has several health benefits: it contains a mild antibiotic and is believed to contain antioxidants that can help prevent cell aging and cancer. Although Communicators can drink some green tea, they should limit the amount because of their hypersensitivity to caffeine.

Ginger Tea—Ginger tea has long been used as a digestive stimulant, as it enhances the digestion of protein. It can also be used to calm an upset stomach, and there's evidence that it may be an antibiotic and help prevent osteoporosis. You can buy gingerroot tea in tea bags at a health-food store. Or try crystallized gingerroot: rub off the sugar, then cut a slice the size of a quarter and chew it before meals to aid digestion and satiation. (See individual sections for other specific-function tea recommendations.)

8

BALANCING PRINCIPLES

Body motion and diet are two of the most important principles in living a healthy life, but they are not the only principles. Psychology, religion, and philosophy have always recognized the importance of the psyche; now, with recent discoveries in psychoneuroimmunology, it is becoming clear that the mind and spirit need to be nourished too. From modern stress-reduction techniques to ancient yogic breathing practices, activities that calm and center the mind also appear to boost the immune system and help the entire mind/body system function better.

Other ancient practices, such as massage, do not work directly on the mind, but affect the mind/body system in numerous beneficial ways. All of the following techniques will make you feel better overall and make it easier to adapt to the guidelines of the Body Code program.

Some of the following are recommended especially for certain body types, but all of them can be practiced by all the types, though the benefits will be greatest for those for whom they are specifically recommended.

Meditation

Meditation has been practiced for thousands of years. Ranging from the devotional, prayerlike meditation in some religions to the more pragmatic "relaxation response" style taught in some business seminars, meditation has a number of medically proven beneficial effects. Practiced regularly, meditation enables you to move into a deeply relaxed state in which your worries and anxieties melt away. The effect is more than temporary too: studies conclude that meditation can lower blood pressure and heart rate. Cancer patients who are taught to meditate find their toxic treatments much easier to handle.

Although meditation can be beneficial for all four genetic types, I especially recommend it for Communicators, who are more high-strung than the other types and therefore more vulnerable to life's vagaries. The vata-dosha, ectomorphic version of the Visionary type can also benefit greatly from meditation. Meditation works best when it is practiced for approximately twenty minutes every day at the same time, but even two or three times a week will have a noticeable effect.

How to Meditate

There are many different meditation techniques. If you already have one that works for you, by all means continue using it. If you are new to meditation or want to get an idea of what it is like, try the following technique, which was developed by Dr. Herbert Benson, a Harvard cardiologist and author of *The Relaxation Response*.

Sit comfortably, with your body relaxed, your hands in your lap, and your eyes closed.

Breathing through your nose, focus on your breathing. Breathe in and out, paying attention to the movement of the air going in and out through your nostrils. Dr. Benson also recommends silently repeating a word to yourself each time you breathe out. Any word that feels calming to you is just fine.

As you practice, thoughts will pop into your mind. Don't pay attention to them. Simply let them come and let them go, by steering your thoughts back to your breathing. This is difficult at first, but gets easier with practice.

Remember also that there's no such thing as "succeeding" at meditation. The important thing is to do it consistently.

Pineal Gland Stimulation

The pineal gland, located in the middle of the front brain, was believed by the ancients to be the remnant of the "third eye," or sixth sense. It was also long believed that the gland caused clairvoyant abilities in adept individuals. Today, we still don't know all of the functions of this gland, but it is thought by many researchers to be the site of the biological clock: the part of the brain that sets circadian rhythm balances that determine our waking and sleeping cycles. The pineal is known to secrete melatonin, the hormone that governs those cycles and that also has a mellowing and calming influence on us.

The pineal gland is stimulated by sunlight, causing secretion of melatonin. Sunrise and sunset times have the best healthful influence. Those who do not receive enough direct sunlight (people living in the far north) often report SAD (seasonal affective disorder), or feelings of irritability, lethargy, and anxiety. This condition, also called cabin fever, is often related to insufficient stimulation of the pineal gland.

For pineal gland stimulation, I recommend exposure to direct sunlight several times a week for all four genetic types. I also recommend supplements of ginseng, especially for the sleek types. For specific guidelines, see the sections for each genetic type.

Occasional supplements of melatonin itself can also be useful for jet lag.

Lymphatic Massage

The lymph system is an essential part of the body's cleansing mechanism, transporting cellular waste to the lymph glands. The lymphatic system has no pumping mechanism, as does the circulatory system, and relies more on muscular contractions to help move the flow of lymph fluid along.

This process is often inefficient in the kapha-dosha types—some Visionaries and some Nurturers—allowing waste products to accumulate, resulting in sluggishness and/or puffiness. To speed lymph fluid along, I recommend frequent mini-self-massages of the whole body for Visionaries, and of the lower body for Nurturers.

How to Do a Lymphatic Self-Massage

This procedure is best done lying in bed first thing in the morning, before you get up. Begin by lifting your left arm straight up in the air. Then, using your right hand, gently knead your left arm from fingertips all the way to the armpit, squeezing and "milking" the lymph fluid down toward the lymph nodes. Repeat the milking three to six times on each arm.

Next lift your left leg up into the air, knee bent, and using both hands, knead and squeeze from the tips of your toes all the way down to your groin. Repeat three to six times on each leg.

Sit up, and starting at the top of your head, gently massage the skin of your head, face, and scalp, milking the lymph fluid toward the lymph glands in your neck.

Finally, using both hands, stroke/massage the skin of your torso toward the lymph nodes in the groin. Repeat three to six times on the front, back, and sides of your trunk.

Yogic Breathing

The physician and alternative-medicine pioneer Andrew Weil says that the breath is the connection between the conscious and the subconscious. The yogic tradition has focused on the breath for thousands of years, devising a number of techniques that can be used for calming, invigorating, and increasing oxygen flow to all the tissues.

I recommend some form of yogic breathing for all the genetic types. In addition to the benefits listed above, yogic-style breathing can help to take the edge off anxiety-related appetite, calming you so you won't overeat.

For specific guidelines for your genetic type, see the individual sections.

Energy-Boosting, Mind-Refreshing Power Stretch

I've found this technique to be one of the most effective in helping clients maintain their focus and stay with the Body Code plan. It refreshes both the body and mind, unkinking tight muscles and oxygenating the brain.

Whenever you're feeling taxed, try this combined breathing and stretching routine. Stand with your feet about shoulder-width apart, your knees slightly bent for the entire five-minute routine. Place your hands on your hips as you inhale through the nose for three to six counts. Hold your breath for eight to twelve counts, then exhale through your mouth for two to four counts. Close your eyes, let your chin fall comfortably toward your chest, place the palms of your clasped hands on the back of your head, then let your elbows fall comfortably toward your forehead. Now let the weight of your arms *only* press your chin into your chest. *Do not pull down on your head.*

Inhale through your nose for four to eight counts, hold your breath for ten to twenty counts, exhale through your mouth for three to six counts. Clasp your hands behind your back, bend forward gently from the waist, then raise your clasped hands comfortably toward the ceiling. Again, inhale four to eight counts through the nose, hold for ten to twenty counts, and exhale through the mouth for three to six counts.

Straighten up and cross your right arm over the front of your body, reaching out to the left side. Repeat the breath cycle. Drop your right arm to your side and cross your left arm over your body, reaching out to the right side. Again, repeat the breath cycle.

Bend your arms so that your hands are in front of your chest, facing your body, your fingers together. Now grasp the fingers of the left hand (excluding your thumb) in the palm of your right hand and gently flex the fingers of the left hand toward the floor. Hold and repeat the breath cycle. Repeat, flexing the right fingers.

This concludes the power-breath process. As you become more proficient, keep your eyes closed and visualize your muscles lengthening and relaxing. You may also modify the stretches to include your favorites. With only a little practice, you will find the process far more stimulating than a cup of coffee. I do this routine daily at 2 or 3 P.M., and then again at 5 or 6 P.M.

Sesame-oil Gum Massage

This technique, borrowed from Ayurveda, is one of the most useful for the strong types—Warriors and Nurturers—in helping to curb appetite. It works by preparing the mouth for heightened taste sensations. The result is increased enjoyment of your meal and quicker satiation, so you are less likely to overeat.

A number of clients have thanked me for teaching them gum massage. Charlotte, a Warrior in her early fifties who was a self-described food addict, told me that she had never experienced *not* being hungry until she began using this technique. "The most valuable thing I learned at Green Valley was the gum massage," Charlotte told me after she had dropped about twenty pounds. "I couldn't believe something so simple would work, but it completely changed my life. It took me away from compulsive overeating in the evening. For the first time ever, I was able to actually taste and to enjoy the food I was eating."

How to Do Gum Massage

Spoon one tablespoon of sesame oil into your mouth and swish it around thoroughly for thirty seconds. (You may also use olive or canola oil.) Then tilt your head slightly back, open your mouth, and use your index finger to thoroughly massage the entire inside of the mouth, including gums and tongue. Continue the massage for one to two minutes, then expel the oil and rinse your mouth. Combine this practice with chewing thoroughly and dining in a serene environment. Brush your teeth immediately after dinner to help quiet evening cravings.

Stay in Touch with Nature

Most of us are creatures of nature, though living in cities, in high-rises and modern houses, it's easy to lose touch with that dimension. I recommend that all types consciously and frequently retain a connection with nature.

For Communicators, it's balancing to keep fresh foliage—houseplants or fresh-cut flowers—in their surroundings. For Visionaries, keeping aromatic plants around helps to maintain that connection.

Warriors and Nurturers can also benefit from keeping plants in the house, but even more important for these types is to maintain a strong sensory connection with nature. Get outside often, walk barefoot in the grass, watch a sunrise or sunset three or four times a week, listen to a babbling brook, watch and listen to the air moving through the trees.

PART THREE

Taking Control of Your Metabolism: The Body Code Genetic Type Plans

9

FINDING THE KEYS
TO YOUR SUCCESS

A Note on Balance

Taking control of your metabolism is vital to long-term wellness. Research shows that those who take responsibility for their own health are generally healthiest. Not one of us experts can do as good a job as you can at getting and keeping yourself well.

The following pages show you the keys that unlock the code for each genetic type, to keep your metabolism in balance. Most of us come into life balanced and basically stay balanced until our systems can no longer compensate for our poor lifestyle choices. The overload of rich foods, stress, and a sedentary lifestyle eventually overwhelm our systems.

The ultimate key to the Body Code program is bringing your body back into balance and leading your anatomical, glandular, and energy aspects types into the homeostatic range. You may be starting this program because you want to look and feel better, improve your health, stabilize your energy levels, or lose weight. Following the guidelines for your genetic type will help you do all of these things, but it will not happen overnight. After all, you didn't get out of balance overnight; your system is designed to change slowly, responding to your built-in checks and balances.

Neither will bringing your body into balance change your basic genetic type. If you are a Warrior, this program will never make you into a lanky Communicator or model-slim Visionary. And you are in for a lifelong battle as long as you deny your genetic design.

Another obstacle for many people is clearly defining balance. For example, what is fat? I believe we need to redefine this term, especially for women. A lot of us in Western society seem to be obsessed with the magazine version of what the female is supposed to look like, which the media often present as tinted, touched up, tucked, and liposuctioned. This is not really a realistic look or lifestyle for 90 percent of us, and most of us say we know that. But we still beat ourselves up because we don't seem to be able to reach those unrealistic goals.

Unless you have that exact body type, those goals are unsustainable and generally unreachable. The answer is to forget about this hyped-up image and learn what look is best for your own body type. Then celebrate the reality that some types of women are supposed to be curvier, and certain types are supposed to be a little more sleek or delicate in their body build. Likewise, some men are supposed to be more muscular and stronger, while others are naturally smaller. There is no such thing as an unappealing-looking body of any type, as long as that body is balanced, trim, and radiating wellness.

A number of years ago an airline flight attendant named Stephanie came to see me because she had been deemed too fat for her job. Stephanie, then in her late twenties, stood five feet eight inches and weighed 145 pounds. As a Nurturer, she carried a lot of that weight below her waist; overall she had a curvy, womanly looking body with a small, twenty-five-inch waist. Her body fat measured only 19 percent—a healthy amount even by today's obsessive standards.

"As soon as I hit puberty, I started to get more muscular in my legs," Stephanie told me. "No matter what I do, I can't seem to take that weight off."

I reassured Stephanie that she was at an ideal weight for her body type and named some famous and attractive women with her body shape. Then I set about writing a letter to the officials at her airline. I told them about our research findings on the different body types and documented that for her body type Stephanie was in a range that was not just acceptable, but actually very good. I challenged my correspondents to compare their percentage of body fat to Stephanie's to help them gain some perspective.

It took a couple of years, but eventually the airline people adjusted their position and revised their guidelines, making it possible for Stephanie and other curvier types to maintain their jobs.

The key for Stephanie and for anyone interested in a healthy body image is to understand that your basic appearance is coded right into your DNA helix, and that if you'll do the things necessary to be balanced, you'll look attractive and feel terrific—for your type.

Mixed Types

When you took the genetic-type quiz back in chapter three, you may have scored higher on two of the body types, and you may thus wonder if you are, say, part Warrior and part Communicator.

Each of us is actually a blend of all of the glandular types and energy doshas, but one is dominant in everyone. If we observed your hair under a microscope, we would see a myriad of colors, but looking at your hair from a distance shows a definite dominant color. Your glandular, energy, and anatomical types are a similar blend, but one is always dominant. Remember the analogy of the barbershop quartet, where one voice is slightly stronger and usually sings the melody. Under some circumstances, a different voice may take over and sing the melody for a while, but it doesn't change the basic structure of the quartet. If one of your lesser "voices" seems to have temporarily taken over the melody, it simply means that you are out of balance.

To get the whole quartet back in harmony, you first need to start with the melody or lead "voice." So follow the Body Code diet and exercise plan for your dominant genetic type. Once the dominant gland is rejuvenated, you will find that you don't need much in the way of fine-tuning.

The relative balance of the influence of your glandular system and doshas may shift a little throughout your life for various reasons, but you remain basically one type. Don't be tempted to try the program for another type; it simply will not work for you in the long run. Remember that you want to balance your dominant gland and dosha, because that's the foundation or essence of who you are. The other components will follow the lead influence.

The Six Keys

The next four chapters present the individualized programs for each genetic type. Each section starts off with an overview of your genetic tendencies and vulnerabilities, then offers you the six keys to balance your body and mind.

The six keys are:

1. Body motion: cardiovascular zone-time conditioning (finding the flow)
2. Strength training: keeping the engine well tuned
3. Flexibility: maintaining the range of motion
4. Nutrition: basic principles, including sample menus
5. Staying focused: motivation and the mind-set
6. Energy-balancing principles (fine-tuning)

10

THE WARRIOR'S WAY

Overview

The Warrior is one of the two **strong** genetic types. If you're a Warrior, you're generally a higher-energy person with lots of drive—sometimes too much. The two sides of your personality are the Warrior and the Controller. You tend to take charge and are often found in positions of power, as a business owner or entrepreneur. You are responsible and enjoy a challenge, but you can also be stubborn, overbearing, combative, sometimes losing your temper. You have a tendency to excess in all things— exercise, work, and eating. You can be a workaholic, forgetting to take care of your health.

Your anatomical type is usually mesomorph, meaning that you have a preponderance of muscle, bone, and connective tissue, which developed from the mesodermal embryonic layer. Because of this, you generally are strong, and when you do strength training, you quickly bulk up. All your energy and drive is most effective when focused. You benefit greatly by doing a lot of cardiovascular-type body movement to maintain balance (see Key #1).

When in balance, you have a solid, muscular body, with prominent shoulders and chest, and relatively slim hips. Your head is usually rectangular or oval-shaped, your hands and feet are solid and square. When out of balance, you can easily gain weight. Usually the fat goes straight to your trunk—your stomach, rib cage, chest, and back, resulting in more upper-body fat gain at first. My research shows that about 50% of all American men are warrior types.

Your glandular type is adrenal, which gives you your drive. You often crave adrenal-stimulating foods such as saturated fats (meats), salty foods, and/or alcohol. These foods generally exacerbate your tendencies toward excessive intensity and compromise your health by raising your blood pressure and clogging your arteries. You will be healthiest and most in balance on a more vegetarian-type diet (see Key #4).

Your Ayurvedic energy type is pitta dosha, which lends "fire" or intensity to everything you do and can cause you to be irritable and short-tempered. You are uncomfortable in warm rooms or hot weather and tend to perspire easily. To help maintain your balance, seek a cool environment with calming influences, and schedule leisure into your lifestyle (see Key #6).

Genetically, you have vulnerabilities to cross-linkages (stiffness in all your tissues), cardiovascular disease, and high blood pressure. You are also vulnerable to cancers of the digestive tract, including colorectal cancers. Your longer digestive tract allows carcinogenic agents to remain in contact with the cell walls of the large bowel for too long. Cardiovascular exercise and a vegetarian diet can help speed intestinal transit time, improving the health of your digestive system.

WARRIOR KEY #1:
Cardiovascular Conditioning (Finding the Flow)

As an intense, purposeful Warrior type, the most important thing you can do is to include some serious body motion in your lifestyle. Warriors need more cardiovascular conditioning (zone-time exercise) than any other genetic type.

Why do Warriors need the most body motion? The short answer is that it speaks to the physical essence of who you are. Your biomechanical build is stronger than the other genetic types—you generally have thicker bones; greater bone density; stronger muscles, ligaments, and tendons, with a more balanced combination of slow- and fast-twitch muscle fibers. Anatomically, you have a worker body. Your constitutional essence is that you are very physical. A thousand years ago, the Warrior's ancestors were performing physically challenging work in middle, eastern, and northern Europe.

As a physical person, you need an outlet for all that stored-up energy. You're like a Jeep, which is designed to be driven. You need to sweat often and systematically move.

Biochemically, what's going on is that as an adrenal-driven Warrior, epinephrine, an adrenal-gland secretion, keeps you prepared for fight or flight. You need an outlet for that. You need adventure or competition, or at least to be very physical for extended periods.

In this high-pressure modern world there are not many built-in outlets for your pent-up Warrior spirit. You don't have saber-toothed tigers to fight, or a village to defend. Yet your body continues to produce that flow of epinephrine. What you really need, and what you are really looking for, though most Warriors don't realize it, is a more calmed-down feeling. This sense of being centered can come from having worked your body rigorously. You need the calming, centering, relaxing feelings that you get from the brain chemicals that are produced by higher levels of exertion. Thus, you need to stay in the target heart zone for a longer time, and more often, than the sleek genetic types in order to maintain a centered consciousness. You need to find the flow consistently.

Remember that the flow is the level of intensity in the target zone that generates the release of beta endorphin and enkephalins, creating that euphoric, morphinelike high that makes zone-time feel so great. This elevated state stays with you for hours afterward. Exercising in the aerobic zone, but out of the flow zone, will not promote the euphoria necessary for long-term addiction. To become physically and psychologically addicted to exercise, you *must* find the flow.

Warriors generally find the flow at an intensity level of 70–85 percent of aerobic capacity.

In addition to keeping you balanced physically and emotionally, these higher levels of exertion will also improve the overall health of your heart and cardiovascular system, which tends to be problematic for Warriors.

The best kinds of body-motion exercises for you are any that you can enjoy for extended periods, such as pace walking, walking/jogging, lap swimming, brisk walking/jogging, step bench/aerobics, NordicTrack, treadmill, cycling, and in-line skating. Among the best exercises are those that involve the arms and legs swinging rhythmically. I don't have controlled studies to prove it, but I've noticed over the years that both Warriors and Nurturers do extremely well with rhythmic, bipedal body motion.

I also recommend that Warriors do body motion in the water as often as possible—at least two or three times a week. Working out in a pool keeps your body temperature down while the resistance of the water tones and firms your muscles without bulking you up. Warriors tend to be physically rigid and inflexible, easily losing range of motion. Most pool exercises take all of your larger muscle groups through a full range of motion, helping to improve flexibility.

Try water aerobics, swim laps, or join a cardio swim class. You can also power walk/run using Aqua-Jogger flotation devices (for information on purchasing Aqua-Jogger, see appendix C). Just be sure that your water activities are performed in the target heart range.

I realize that making regular body motion a part of your life is not always easy. From personal experience I know that our type must *make* time for it in our busy lives. As a Warrior myself, I'm usually trying to fit thirty hours' worth of activities into a twenty-four-hour day. But I've learned the hard way that body motion is so essential to my well-being that I make it a priority in my life. I've learned to stop fighting the reality and just get up a few minutes earlier in the morning. Later on I'll offer a number of practical suggestions for ways you can fit body motion into your life.

When to Do Body Motion

The best time for Warriors to do body motion is when it's cool—either before or after the heat of midday. Warriors tend to get hot, red-faced, and to sweat profusely when training. If you're working out on a machine indoors, use a fan. Don't let yourself get dehydrated: drink about eight ounces of water every fifteen to thirty minutes while you're exercising in your target heart zone.

WARM-UPS AND COOLDOWNS.

Before your body motion sessions, always warm up by doing your scheduled activity at a slower pace for five to ten minutes, then cool down after every workout by moving more slowly for eight to ten minutes.

Weight-Loss Tips

If you're trying to lose weight, or you want to reach the peak of leanness possible for you, you'll need to do a little bit more than the basic recommended program.

The best, most efficient way to achieve your ideal of leanness is to add short bursts of activity to your basic body motion workout one or two times a week, as detailed in the guidelines below. Pushing your heart rate through the anaerobic threshold for short times stimulates the release of

ACTH by the pituitary gland. This adrenal-stimulating growth hormone lowers the fat thermostat.

Longer workouts are another way to lean out. Twice a week extend your usual amount of zone-time by up to 25 percent. Twice-a-day workouts once or twice a week also speed the process. Space the workouts at least six to eight hours apart.

Another way to speed weight loss is to fool your body into thinking it weighs more than it does. Do this by carrying nine pounds of weight while you pace walk. Your limbic system feels the weight and thinks, "Hey, we're heavier than I thought. That doesn't feel like us." It responds by lowering the fat thermostat, and you lose more quickly.

It can be dangerous to wear ankle weights—you can injure your legs that way. Far better is to put a five-pound bag of grain in your backpack and carry two-pound dumbbells in each hand. Then do your pace walking as usual.

Still another strategy for the strong genetic types is to include at least three sessions per week of striding (pace walking, jogging, power walking). If your basic zone-time exercise is one of these bipedal activities, you will quicken the balance of circadian rhythms in your brain, again lowering the fat thermostat.

Following is a stepped-level program that will allow you to gradually work toward the amount of zone-time body motion that your body needs.

Start at a level that is appropriate for you, and stay at each level as long as you need. For some, that might mean staying at level one for several weeks or even months. If you have previously been sedentary and/or are recovering from any illness, this is a good start and will get your body on the road to balance. It will also give you time to make the needed lifestyle changes that will allow you to gradually ease more body motion into your life.

Level One

Amount of Body Motion

One or two sessions per week of cardiovascular exercises, of ten to twenty minutes each, in your target heart zone.

I suggest walking/pace walking to start with, because it is effective, easy, and requires no equipment other than a good pair of shoes. The important thing is to do something you like, something that you'll be able to do regularly for the recommended amount of time.

When you have worked up to and can comfortably do two sessions per week of twenty minutes each at your target heart rate, you are ready to move on to level two.

Level Two

Amount of Body Motion

Two to three sessions of cardiovascular exercise, of fifteen to twenty-five minutes each, at your target heart rate.

Again, I recommend pace walking, unless you prefer another rhythmic exercise.

Speed Bursts

After you have been at this level for a week or two, it's time to add speed bursts to hasten weight loss and increase your fitness level. During one of your regular body-motion sessions, throw in one thirty-second burst of maximum-intensity effort. These "speed burst" sessions will get you lean sooner than any other training principle.

When you can do the maximum amount of body motion suggested for this level—three sessions of twenty-five minutes each, with one burst of maximum-intensity effort during one of the sessions—move on to level three.

Level Three

Amount of Body Motion

Twenty-five to thirty-three minutes of aerobic activities, three to four times a week, at your target heart rate.

If you've reached level three, congratulations! You're doing well and are much closer to your ultimate goal.

Speed Bursts

Add two more thirty-second bursts of maximum-intensity effort to one of your workouts, for a total of three. Space the bursts five minutes apart, allowing your heart rate to decrease back down to your target heart zone before beginning the next burst.

Endurance Training

After you have been at this level for two or three weeks, it's time to extend one of your basic body-motion sessions for endurance and stamina. Gradually extend the time you spend on one of the three to four total sessions per week to forty-three minutes of zone-time.

When you can do the maximum amount of body motion suggested for this level—four sessions of thirty-three minutes each at your target heart rate, including three bursts of thirty seconds each, and one longer session of forty-three minutes—it is time to move on to level four.

Level Four

Amount of Body Motion

Thirty-three to forty-three minutes of aerobic exercise, four or five times a week.

Speed Bursts

Add one more thirty-second burst of maximum-intensity effort to one of your workouts, for a total of four. Space the bursts five minutes apart, allowing your heart rate to decrease back down to your target heart zone before beginning the next burst.

Endurance Training

Extend one of your basic body-motion sessions to fifty-three minutes.

When you can do the maximum amount of body motion suggested for this level—five sessions of forty-three minutes each at your target heart rate, including four bursts of thirty seconds each, and one longer session of fifty-three minutes—it is time to move on to level five.

Level Five

Amount of Body Motion

Forty-three to forty-eight minutes of zone-time training, five to six times per week.

This is almost the top level. By now you're leaning out and feeling great about yourself. You are to be commended for your efforts!

Speed Bursts

Add one more thirty-second burst of maximum-intensity effort to one of your workouts, for a total of five. Space the bursts five minutes apart, allowing your heart rate to decrease back down to your target heart zone before beginning the next burst.

Endurance Training

Extend one of your basic body-motion sessions to sixty-three minutes.

When you can do the maximum amount of body motion suggested for this level—six sessions of forty-eight minutes each at your target heart rate, one of the sessions including five bursts of thirty seconds each, and one of the sessions lasting sixty-three minutes—it is time to move on to level six.

Level Six

Amount of Body Motion

Cardiovascular training six times per week, at your target heart rate, for forty-eight to sixty-three minutes.

Speed Bursts

Add one more thirty-second burst of maximum-intensity effort to one of your six total workouts, for a total of six bursts. Space the bursts five minutes apart, allowing your heart rate to decrease back down to your target heart zone before beginning the next burst.

Endurance Training

Extend one of your basic body-motion sessions to seventy-eight minutes, which is 25 percent longer than the average workout.

*　*　*

Great work! This is the top level—the one you will thrive on and basically be following for the rest of your healthy life. By now you feel and look much better, you have more energy, yet you feel calmer and more centered.

I realize that this basic program may seem like a lot of exercise, and it is—but I also know that this amount will balance your body and keep you feeling and looking your best! Right now you may be thinking that you can never do so much exercise, but you not only can, your genes are programmed to be exhilarated by it.

Following is a progression chart that shows your cardiovascular progress at a glance.

WARRIOR-TYPE CARDIOVASCULAR CONDITIONING

Level Number	Total Number of Zone-Time Sessions per Week (Including Endurance Session)	Total Number of Zone-Time Minutes per Session	Total Number of Speed-Burst Sessions per Week and Number of Bursts per Session	Length of Endurance Session
One	1 or 2	10–20	None	None
Two	2 or 3	15–25	1 session 1 burst	None
Three	3 or 4	25–33	1 session 3 bursts	1 session 43 minutes
Four	4 or 5	33–43	1 session 4 bursts	1 session 53 minutes
Five	5 or 6	43–48	1 session 5 bursts	1 session 63 minutes
Six	6	48–63	1 session 6 bursts	1 session 78 minutes

WARRIOR KEY #2:
Strength Training

Because you are naturally stronger, you need less emphasis on strength training than the other types, but you do need to work on muscle tone, and to maintain full range of motion.

See the guidelines in chapter six on how best to perform strength exercises.

Two times per week, perform *one set only* on free weights, selectorized machines, or with stretch bands, for each major muscle group (see pages 60–66). Use light enough resistance to perform twenty to twenty-five repetitions without feeling muscle pain or burning.

All varieties of toning, firming, sculpting, and calisthenics-type activities are fine, but do not use heavy enough weights or high enough repetitions to reach muscle failure (the burning or shaking feeling). When doing toning activities, emphasize the full range of motion to increase your flexibility.

You may want to perform abdominal crunches and back hyperextensions daily.

WARRIOR KEY #3:
Flexibility

Warriors need to emphasize flexibility exercises, to avoid becoming rigid and to help prevent strained muscles, tendons, and ligaments.

Stretch four to six times a week.

See the general guidelines on stretching in chapter six. The best way to limber up is to do static stretches—meaning that you hold the stretch, without bouncing—for twenty to thirty seconds for each major muscle group. For the lumbars (lower back) and hamstrings (upper backs of legs), both of which tend to be tight in Warriors, hold the stretches for forty-five to sixty seconds.

It's my experience that the best—and sometimes the only—way to get Warriors to stretch regularly is to make it an "autopilot" activity, to have it memorized so you can do other things while you stretch. To do this, follow the stretch routine I present here, or find an equivalent routine you like better. See appendix C for information on ordering exercise videos. Memorize the routine by doing it a dozen times until it becomes as easy and automatic as brushing your teeth.

Once the routine has become automatic, you can go on autopilot while your consciousness is involved in some other activity, such as watching TV, listening to a taped book, or reading. I often bump into people I helped years and years ago, and they tell me, "You were right. It did become automatic, even though I didn't believe you when you told me about it."

As you continue to practice the body-motion routines recommended in this section, remember that, just as the other genetic types can never hope to achieve the athletic appearance you have naturally when balanced, you will never resemble a willowy model. You will, however, radiate health and well-being from your well-toned physique.

EXAMPLE OF AN IDEAL EXERCISE WEEK FOR THE WARRIOR

Monday: A.M.—pace walk or jog 60 minutes. P.M.—stretch.

Tuesday: A.M.—Lifecycle and cardio-style weights, 50 minutes total.

Wednesday: A.M.—pace walk with weights 55 minutes. P.M.—stretch.

Thursday: A.M.—in-line skating 60–75 minutes. P.M.—stretch.

Friday: stair-climber or elliptical, cardio-style weights, 50 minutes total.

Saturday: endurance pace walk/jog 90 minutes.

Sunday: rest, relax. P.M.—stretch.

WARRIOR KEY #4:
Nutrition

Your basic theme as a Warrior focuses on plant-based foods, because animal foods overstimulate your dominant adrenal glands, pulling you out of balance. Every day you should emphasize lots of vegetables, fruits, roots, and grains, which stimulate your nondominant glands and balance you. Higher-calorie plant foods, such as nuts and seeds, should be restricted if you are trying to lose weight.

To remember the foods you need to avoid or minimize, use the acronym FAST: F = Fats, especially saturated and hydrogenated, A = Alcohol, S = Salts, and T = Transformed foods (refined grains and flour). Each time you get ready to eat, pause and ask yourself, "Is this a FAST food?" If it is, it will trigger your cravings and appetite.

Your main dietary challenge is your cravings for those FAST foods, all of which pull you metabolically out of balance. Unfortunately, the more unbalanced you become, the worse your cravings will be. This process is a negative downward spiral; once you get into it, the harder it is to break free. Your appetite is strongest between 5 and 10 P.M., so you need a satisfying evening meal. Warriors do best by resisting the temptation to skip meals and to snack. Fasting for a day once a month is good for the body and great for the spirit.

The table below shows you three groups of foods. These are your **plenty foods,** those you can basically eat as many of as you like, within reason (unless otherwise noted); your **moderation foods,** those that you may have sparingly, in small amounts; and your **seldom foods,** those foods that you should eat very rarely. Most of the foods in the seldom list are those that stimulate your dominant adrenal glands and cause you to become physically and, eventually, emotionally unbalanced.

Included under the plenty foods are "extras"—herbs, condiments, and teas that are beneficial to Warriors and should be added to your daily regimen. These foods will help control your appetite and balance your biochemistry.

See also the list of supplements at the end of the foods list. These are micronutrients that are necessary for your body's basic processes. Including them as recommended will help ease cravings.

WARRIOR FOOD CHOICES

Plenty Foods
—all fruits, especially melon and berries
—all vegetables
—all whole grains
—all white and pink fish, white poultry (skinless), egg whites and Egg Beaters
—all nonfat dairy products
—extras
  ginger tea—3 times a day (dandelion and parsley-leaf teas also good)
  flaxseeds—1 tbs at dinner (a good appetite suppressant)
  garlic, fresh—(ups metabolism and aids digestion)
  alfalfa tablets—550-mg tablets, 5 each at lunch and dinner (aids digestion and elimination)

Moderation Foods
- —monounsaturated fats (olives, olive oil, canola oil, avocados, almonds)—up to 2 tbs per day
- —spices (other than salt)—add to taste
- —honey, blackstrap molasses, maple syrup—up to 4 tbs per week
- —fruit and/or veggie juice—10 oz a day, if you're already lean
- —exotic meats (such as ostrich or buffalo)—6 oz, 2–3 times a month
- —caffeine—total of 200 mg per day or less (1 cup of coffee has approximately 100 mg)

Seldom Foods
- —high-saturated fats—egg yolks, meats (lamb, pork, beef, deli meats, organ meats, cold cuts), shellfish, all high-fat dairy, creams, cheeses, dips, sauces, spreads, butter
- —salts—meats; dairy foods; all canned, bottled, and packaged foods
- —alcohol—all types
- —refined grains or flours—cookies, cakes, bagels, breads, muffins, pretzels, pasta, crackers, cereals, biscuits, pancakes, waffles, noodles, croissants, popcorn, pastries
- —hydrogenated fats—any foods that are hermetically sealed or wrapped in plastic

Supplements
- —vitamins and minerals
    multiple (without iron, unless anemic)—1 x day
    vitamin C—2,000 mg, 2 x day
    vitamin E—400 IU at lunch
    selenium—200 mg at lunch
    women: calcium citrate—500–1,250 mg per day, split
        between morning and dinner; after menopause
        increase to 1,250–1,500 mg

To put your new way of eating into practice, use the following guidelines to plan your day's intake of fuel. A more detailed menu plan follows.

Ideal sample day's intake:

SMALL BREAKFAST: whole-grain cereal with fruit and skim or soy milk

SMALL A.M. SNACK: fruit, melon, or berries with nonfat yogurt or string cheese

MEDIUM-SIZED LUNCH: cooked and raw veggies, grains, and nonfat dairy

SMALL P.M. SNACK: fruit, melon, or berries with nonfat yogurt or string cheese

HEARTY DINNER: cooked and raw veggies, whole grains, nonfat dairy, white flesh

WARRIOR MENUS FOR ONE WEEK

(Recipes for starred items are in appendix A, pages 203–226)

Day 1

BREAKFAST—½ cup whole-grain hot cereal with Cherry Sauce* and skim milk

SNACK—½ cup nonfat dairy, veggie sticks, or ½ cup melon or berries

LUNCH—DeLayne's Tomatoes and Rice,* green salad with nonfat dressing

SNACK—½ cup nonfat dairy, veggie sticks, or ½ cup melon or berries

DINNER—Chicken Parmesan,* 2 oz whole-grain pasta with Red Sauce,* large green salad

Day 2

BREAKFAST—2 Crepe Shells* with nonfat yogurt and small piece fruit

SNACK—½ cup nonfat dairy, veggie sticks, or ½ cup melon or berries

LUNCH—veggie burger (such as Garden Burger) on multi-grain bun with Baked French Fries*

SNACK—½ cup nonfat dairy, veggie sticks, or ½ cup melon or berries

DINNER—Cajun Trout,* basmati rice (½ cup), steamed veggies, Mushroom Soup*

Day 3

BREAKFAST—¾ cup raisin bran, 1 banana, 1 cup skim milk

SNACK— ½ cup nonfat dairy, veggie sticks, or ½ cup melon or berries

LUNCH—whole-grain Pita Pizza,* Spinach Fruit Salad*

SNACK—½ cup nonfat dairy, veggie sticks, or ½ cup melon or berries

DINNER—roast turkey breast, steamed veggies, potatoes and Gravy,* ½ cup watermelon

Day 4

BREAKFAST—1 piece multigrain bread with jelly, ½ cup cantaloupe, 1 cup skim milk

SNACK—½ cup nonfat dairy, veggie sticks, or ½ cup melon or berries

LUNCH—whole-wheat Tortilla Roll-Up* with Basil Cream Cheese Spread,* 1 cup nonfat dairy

SNACK—½ cup nonfat dairy, veggie sticks, or ½ cup melon or berries

DINNER—grilled chicken with Mango Chutney,* Quinoa Pilaf,* steamed asparagus

Day 5

BREAKFAST—½ cup oatmeal with ½ cup berries and ½ cup skim milk

SNACK—½ cup nonfat dairy, veggie sticks, or ½ cup melon or berries

LUNCH—garden salad, grilled nonfat-cheese sandwich, ½ cup nonfat dairy

SNACK—½ cup nonfat dairy, veggie sticks, or ½ cup melon or berries

DINNER—4 oz baked sea bass, roasted winter squash, string beans, and broccoli stems

Day 6

BREAKFAST—Fruit and Oats* with nonfat yogurt

SNACK—½ cup nonfat dairy, veggie sticks, or ½ cup melon or berries

LUNCH—Warrior Vegetable Soup* and multigrain bread stick, 1 cup skim milk

SNACK—½ cup nonfat dairy, veggie sticks, or ½ cup melon or berries

DINNER—Jicama Orange Salad,* 4 oz white fish, steamed cabbage, 2 red potatoes

Day 7

BREAKFAST—Grape-Nuts cereal, small banana, ½ cup skim milk

SNACK—½ cup nonfat dairy, veggie sticks, or ½ cup melon or berries

LUNCH—vegetarian Taco Salad* with whole-grain tortilla and nonfat cheese

SNACK—½ cup nonfat dairy, veggie sticks, or ½ cup melon or berries

DINNER—Gazpacho Soup,* 4 oz baked salmon, grilled vegetables with olive oil

WARRIOR KEY #5:
Staying Focused

Even though the foods recommended in this plan are the ones you are genetically programmed to eat, and the exercise is the kind your body needs, it may not be easy switching all at once. Your cravings for unhealthful foods may persist for a while. You may find it difficult to make exercise a part of your life. The following tips will help you to maintain your focus and motivation, even when the going gets tough.

Craving Controls

As you remove the foods that give you feelings of power and energy at the cost of your health, you must replace those food-generated feelings with zone-time-generated feelings to stay balanced. If you try to eat this way without performing zone-time body motion, you will not feel well.

—Use pitta-dosha-type seasonings (Order from Ayurvedic Institute; see page 234). These will make your food taste better and help eliminate the cravings for adrenal-stimulating foods.

—Use sesame-oil gum massage (see page 81) before meals. This will aid your digestion and help you feel full before you are tempted to overeat.

—Drink water or herb tea.

—Substitute. Old habits die hard. If your body is used to eating a Big Mac every day at noon, try giving it a veggie burger instead. You can still have most of the fixings, and after a while you develop a preference for the leaner foods.

—Walk it off. If you do get a sudden "Mac attack," the best thing you can do is engage in some body motion—go for a bike ride, swim laps, or just take a walk around the block.

—Distract your consciousness. To prevent or minimize cravings, get your mind busy with projects, activities, or other people. Visit neighbors, call relatives, make music, or research your family genealogy.

Herbal Helps

The following herbal remedies will help control food cravings and balance your glandular secretions, helping you to get that "feeling" and stay on track:

Ginger, dandelion, and parsley-leaf teas as recommended on page 100.

Alfafa tablets as recommended on page 100.

Flaxseeds—1 tbs at dinner (sprinkled on a salad or soup).

Panax quinquefolius ginseng—follow label recommendations.

Garlic capsules—550 mg, 2 x day. Gradually add more until you're consuming 1,500–2,500 mg of garlic, but no more than 3,000 mg per day. Try also to include fresh minced garlic in your foods.

Aroma therapy (see page 187).

Let It Sink In

For many Warriors, the hardest part of switching to a largely vegetarian diet is learning new ways of shopping and cooking. Lisa, a forty-two-year-old homemaker and mother of five, solved her problem in two ways. First, she bought an audiocassette on the benefits of a vegetarian diet. "I listened to it over and over until what it said completely sank in and I realized that I did need to be more of a vegetarian," she told me. "I finally realized that I wasn't being deprived, but was actually improving my life. At the same time, I got a vegetarian cookbook. I learned how to use a Crock-Pot, to let foods simmer slowly through the day. I tend to cook big meals and freeze what's left over for menus later on."

Make It Easy on Yourself (Convenience Is the Key!)

If you keep quantities of your plenty foods easily available, they'll be there when you want to snack, and you won't be so tempted by your seldom foods. Among the proven tips Lisa and other Warriors use:

—Keep ready-to-eat fruits and vegetables handy in the refrigerator for snacks.
—Prepare baked french-fried potatoes as snack foods for the kids (see recipe, page 212).
—Cook large portions of brown or basmati rice and keep some in the fridge at all times for quick snacks or easy meals.

For more tips on ways to stick with your new eating plan, see chapter fourteen.

Working Body Motion into Your Busy Lifestyle

Because the Warrior needs so much body motion, it may seem impossible that you'll have time for all of it in a typical week. But the more than 60 million Americans who regularly exercise are living proof that it can be done, and that your overall lifestyle will be better as a result.

—Start slowly. In my own case, I started out just walking a few blocks to and from school, and right away I noticed that the body motion exhilarated me. I felt refreshed, and my mind was clear and ready for studies when I got home.

Physically, it was a little tougher. When I started, even moseying along slowly got me up in my target zone. In fact, I couldn't walk a block without stopping to huff and puff. Gradually, though, I began pace walking in order to keep the euphoric feeling I'd grown fond of. Before long, I was using the pace walking as a tool to keep my mind clear, my appetite down, and my spirits up.

—Get up early. My findings concur with fitness-industry research showing that those who exercise in the first four hours after waking up are most apt to continue. After I graduated from college, I continued to use body motion in the evening as a destressor from my workday. As my career responsibilities grew and I opened my own business, my personal time shrank, but I knew I still needed that body motion. I began getting up earlier in the morning to get the necessary zone-time. For a few weeks I didn't like it at all. Then I focused on the benefits of morning zone-time and have been a morning boy ever since.

One of my Warrior clients has a similar strategy. Marilyn, who owns a successful retail business in Ft. Lauderdale, had been slightly overweight her whole life, but had never felt she had the time to make body motion a big part of her world. After coming through the spa, she realized it was time to make a commitment to her own health. "I suddenly realized that I didn't have to go into work so early," Marilyn told me. "I realized that *I* was at least as important to me as my business was. I kept thinking about something you told us at the spa, that 'you can't give to others something you don't have.' So if I wanted to give good, positive vibes to my family and customers, I had to feel that way myself."

I know that exercising early in the morning may not be the answer for everyone, but I find that it's especially useful for overcommitted Warriors. It's a time of day when it's hard to find excuses. There really isn't much going on in the early hours of the morning, so give it a whirl. Of those who do it twenty-one days in a row, 40 percent never stop! Make it a ritual part of your day. Before long you'll find you're waking up, ready to go, whether the alarm clock is set or not.

When You Have Trouble Making Yourself Exercise

—Combine exercise with work. Study, read, listen to tapes, or watch educational TV while you do your zone-time body motion. This works especially well for busy, pragmatic Warriors who love using their time productively.

—Set goals. This tip too works well for task-oriented Warriors. Lisa, the local woman I mentioned earlier, found a way to ensure that she wouldn't get out of shape again. She joined the local running club and committed herself to participating in fun run/walks. She started with shorter distances and eventually worked up to the marathon.

"It's not that I'm even competitive," she says. "But I need a reason to stay at it. And to do longer runs, I simply have to put in the miles. Knowing a big race is coming up gives me the motivation to get out there and train."

For more tips on motivating yourself to work out, see chapter fourteen.

Dealing with Plateaus

Everyone who's ever tried to lose weight has experienced plateaus, those annoying times when your fat thermostat seems to get stuck, and no matter what you do you can't lose another ounce. These periods are caused by the body's having decided that you are at the correct weight for your current activity level and fuel blend, and it will do everything in its power to keep you there.

If you continue to follow the correct eating and body-motion plan for your type, the plateau will eventually give way to more weight loss. But to kick it into high gear and quickly break through the plateau, add the following strategies to your current foundation:

—Do more intervals. Instead of doing six intervals during one of your body-motion sessions, try doing them two or even three days for a few weeks. In my experience, there is no quicker method to rev your body up and lower the fat thermostat.

—Carry your lost weight. For every pound you lose, add a pound of weight to a backpack you carry during one or two of the six total zone-time body motion sessions per week. This fools your hypothalamus into thinking that you haven't lost any weight at all and helps to stimulate your metabolic rate to compensate. When you have lost twenty-five pounds, stop carrying the extra weight for six weeks, then, if you still need to lose more, begin the process again. Pace walking is best to avoid jarring the joints.

For more tips on beating plateaus, see chapter sixteen.

WARRIOR KEY #6:
Energy-Balancing Principles

Get Sunlight

Four or five times per week, get outdoors in the sunlight, without sunglasses (to allow the sunlight to stimulate your pineal gland), for at least thirty minutes. If possible, do so early in the day or late in the afternoon. If you can only go outside in midday in the summer, you should wear sunscreen; and bear in mind that *extended* exposure to sunlight can eventually cause cataracts.

Yogic Breathing

Warriors, especially those with controller personalities, can be highstrung and stressed. Yogic breathing not only helps calm you, it can invigorate, helping you to feel more alert by increasing oxygen delivery to your brain. Many Warriors find that the breathing routine also dissolves anxiety.

Two times per day, once in the morning and once in the evening, perform the following routine (or the use the power-stretch routine described on page 80):

Hold the tip of your tongue at the forward part of the roof of your mouth, just behind your top teeth. Inhale slowly through your nose, hold your breath, then exhale through pursed lips. Try to maintain a rhythm-count ratio of five to ten to three: inhale for a count of five; hold for a count of ten; and exhale for a count of three. Repeat for six full breaths.

This routine is especially helpful before dinner, as the calming effect will help you feel more easily satiated.

11

THE NURTURER'S WAY

Overview

The Nurturer is one of the two **strong** genetic types. If you're a Nurturer, you're a compassionate, caring person who is generally people-oriented. You enjoy taking care of things for those around you. You tend toward occupations that are service-oriented and can often be found in the healing, counseling, and teaching professions. You are intuitive and generally extroverted, but you can overdo it, either "smothering" other people or caring too much for others while ignoring your own needs.

Your anatomical type is mixed: you are larger from the waist down and smaller from the waist up. Your basic foundation is endomorphic or mesomorphic, especially in the lower half of your body, and mesomorphic or even ectomorphic from the waist up. The endomorphic (or mesomorphic) component, which derives from the embryonic endoderm (or mesoderm), gives rise to your generally larger or more solid lower body, and your "pear-shaped" figure. This component also determines your need for exercise, which is somewhat greater than for the sleek genetic types (see Key #1).

When you were young, you may have appeared to be a pure mesomorph or even an ectomorph, but with puberty your body began to thicken below the waist, becoming noticeably more muscular if you were athletic, and noticeably heavier if you were not.

When in balance, you have strong, muscular legs and buttocks and are quite curvy overall, with a small, well-defined waist. Your head is medium- or small-sized and generally heart-shaped, your shoulders are narrower than your hips, and you generally have a prominent rib cage and a well-defined, rounded tush. When out of balance, you gain weight first in the lower part of your body, starting with your buttocks, saddlebags, and thighs. You can often appear quite slender above the waist while carrying excess body fat below the waist.

Your glandular type is ovarian. The ovarian hormones estrogen and progesterone both stimulate the human nurturing drive, giving you your giving, generous qualities. You often crave foods that stimulate your dominant glands, especially creamy and spicy foods. These foods cause your ovaries to overproduce estrogen, which can throw all your sex hormones out of balance, leading to moodiness and menstrual and menopausal difficulties. You will be healthiest and most in balance on a diet that includes food with a high water content (fruits and vegetables) and is low in saturated fats. (For details, see Key #4.)

Your Ayurvedic energy type is predominantly kapha dosha, which gives you an easygoing, forgiving, and loving nature. It also gives you the potential to be somewhat sluggish, lethargic, and prone to weight gain, which can be avoided by plenty of body motion and a low-estrogenic diet (for details, see Keys #3 and #4).

Genetically, you have an abundance of estrogen receptors throughout your body; these may eventually leave you more vulnerable to cancers of the breast, cervix, ovaries, and uterus. You can help overcome this tendency by eating plenty of foods (such as soy and flaxseeds) that contain phytoestrogens (plant estrogens), which plug into the estrogen receptors in place of estrogen. You also need to minimize your intake of flesh foods, which contain growth hormones and other additives that have been implicated in female cancers. Getting plenty of aerobic body motion, which helps to clear excess estrogen from your bloodstream, will also reduce your susceptibility.

NURTURER KEY #1:
Body Motion—Cardiovascular Conditioning (Finding the Flow)

As a Nurturer, you need to be very physical, more so than the two sleek genetic types. The most important exercise principle for you is to get *lots* of cardiovascular (aerobic) body motion, preferably mixed with plenty of social interaction.

Why do you need so much aerobic body motion? You are one of the "strong" anatomical types, like the Warrior, and have a body that is made for physical exertion. You have a relatively strong biomechanical build, with thicker bones and stronger, shorter musculoskeletal connective tissues. Your constitutional essence is made for moving.

Nurturer types originated in Africa and South America. Until recent times, Nurturers engaged in a great deal of body motion during a typical day, since body motion went hand in hand with serving others.

Biochemically, your dominant ovarian function is overly efficient at pumping estrogen into your system, which, as research shows, can lead to major health problems. Exercise is one proven way to help remove excess estrogen from your bloodstream.

Recall that the flow is the level of intensity in the target zone that generates the release of beta endorphin and enkephalins, creating that euphoric, morphinelike high that makes zone-time feel so great. This elevated state stays with you for hours afterward. Exercising in the aerobic zone, but out of the flow zone, is helpful, but will not promote the euphoria necessary for long-term continuation. To become physically and psychologically addicted to exercise, you *must* find the flow.

Nurturers generally find the flow at an intensity level of 70–85 percent of aerobic capacity. If you combine your body motion with social activity, you also get that feeling of belonging that your type so intensely seeks.

In addition to keeping you balanced physically and emotionally, higher levels of exertion will also improve the overall health of your heart and circulatory system and are essential to keeping your weight down.

The best zone-time body motion activities for you are any that you can enjoy for extended time, and that include a social component. I'd especially recommend aerobic classes of any sort, spinning, jazz dance, step bench, and swim exercises. Pace walking/jogging, in-line skating, or cycling with a partner are also good.

Making regular body motion a part of your life is vital to your long-term success. I realize that you may face seemingly overwhelming obstacles in the form of family demands and a job. That's okay. Just do what you can for now, and as you become more fit, you can gradually increase the level of body motion until you are closer to the ideal for your genetic type.

Later on in this section I'll offer a number of practical, proven suggestions on how to fit body motion in as an enjoyable part of your lifestyle.

When to Do Body Motion

The best time for Nurturers to exercise is first thing in the morning. My research suggests that getting up early and working out is especially important for Nurturers, because you spend so much of your energy and time giving to other people. Once the day wears on and you're faced with conflicting demands, you simply won't choose to spend time on yourself.

Try to go to bed early enough to comfortably wake up early. As a kapha-dosha type, you feel best if you arise before kapha time, which begins at 6 A.M. Early zone-time body motion should also make child care less of a challenge.

If you absolutely can't manage morning zone-time body motion, evenings are another great time, because you get an energy burst then. Setting an 8 or 9 P.M. bedtime for children can do double duty if you also make it the designated time for your zone-time workout. See Key #5 for a number of tips and suggestions on how to easily work body motion into your life.

WARM-UPS AND COOLDOWNS.

Before your body motion sessions, always warm up by doing your scheduled activity at a slower pace for three to seven minutes. End your workout with a cooldown of about the same length of time.

Weight-Loss Tips

If you're trying to lose weight, or you want to reach the peak of leanness possible for you, you'll need to modify the basic program just a bit.

The best, most efficient way to achieve your ideal of leanness is to go for the flow. Sustain your exercising heart rate at 70–85 percent of your maximum capacity to find the flow. Try adding one more longer-distance zone-time workout to your basic foundation. Or add more intervals of maximum-activity bursts to your basic body motion workout, as detailed in the program below. By pushing your heart rate beyond the aerobic zone, you increase the release of ACTH by the pituitary gland. This adrenal-stimulating growth hormone lowers your body-fat thermostat.

Another way to speed weight loss is to fool your body into thinking it weighs more than it does. You do this by carrying nine pounds of weight while you pace walk. Your limbic system feels the weight and thinks, "Hey, we're feeling heavier than I remember. This just doesn't feel like us." Sooner rather than later, it resets the fat thermostat, and you lose more quickly.

Note: Don't wear ankle weights, which can injure your legs. Instead, carry a five-pound sack of grain in a backpack, and carry two-pound weights in each hand.

Still another strategy for the strong genetic types is to include at least three sessions per week of striding (pace walking, jogging, power walking). If your core zone-time exercise is one of these bipedal activities, you will quicken the balance of circadian rhythms in your brain, again lowering the fat thermostat.

Following is a stepped-level program that will allow you to gradually work up to the amount of body motion that your body needs.

Start at a level that is appropriate for you, and stay at each level as long as you need to. For some, that might mean staying at level one for several weeks or even months. If you have previously been sedentary and/or are recovering from any illness or injury, this is a good start and will get your body on the road to balance. It will also give you time to make the needed lifestyle changes that will enable you to work even more body motion into your life.

Level One

Amount of Body Motion

One to two sessions of cardiovascular activity, of ten to twenty minutes each, in your target heart zone (see page 55).

I suggest pace walking with a partner if possible, at least to start with, because it is effective, easy, and requires no equipment other than a good pair of shoes. Whatever zone-time body motion activities you choose, emphasize those in which you are standing (pace walk/jog, NordicTrack, aerobic class, etc.), in order to keep your bones strong. Do not emphasize the less weight-bearing activities such as lap swimming, pool exercise classes, and the recumbent-type cycle. If you cycle, use toe clips and sit straight up. The most important thing is to do something you like, something that you'll continue to do regularly that takes you to the flow zone.

When you can comfortably do two sessions per week of twenty minutes at your target heart rate, you are ready to move on to level two.

Level Two

Amount of Body Motion

Two to three sessions of zone-time body motion of fifteen to twenty-five minutes each, at your target heart rate.

Again, I recommend walking or some other activity with a social component if possible.

Speed Bursts

After you have been at this level for a week or two, it's time to add speed bursts to hasten weight loss and increase your fitness level. During one of your regular two to three zone-time body motion sessions, throw in one thirty-second burst of maximum-intensity effort. These sessions, combined with endurance sessions, which you will begin at level three, will get you lean sooner than any other training principle.

When you can do the maximum amount of body motion suggested for this level—three sessions of twenty-five minutes each, with one thirty-second interval of maximum-intensity effort during one of the sessions—move on to level three.

Level Three

Amount of Body Motion

Twenty-five to thirty-three minutes of zone-time activity, three to four times a week.

If you've reached level three, congratulations! You've done well, and you're much closer to your ultimate goal.

Speed Bursts

Add two more thirty-second bursts of maximum-intensity effort to one of your regular workouts, for a total of three bursts. Space the bursts five minutes apart, allowing your heart rate to decrease back down to your target heart zone before beginning the next burst.

Endurance Training

After you have been at this level for two or three weeks, it's time to extend one of your basic body-motion sessions for endurance and stamina. Gradually extend the time you spend on one of the weekly sessions to forty-three minutes of total zone-time.

When you can do the maximum amount of body motion suggested for this level—four sessions of thirty-three minutes each at your target heart rate, including three speed bursts of thirty seconds each, and one longer zone session of forty-three minutes—it's time to move on to level four.

Level Four

Amount of Body Motion

Thirty-three to thirty-eight minutes of zone-time activity, four or five times a week.

Speed Bursts

Add one more thirty-second burst of maximum-intensity effort to one of your workouts, for a total of four bursts. Space the bursts five minutes apart, allowing your heart rate to decrease back down to your target heart zone before beginning the next burst.

Endurance Training

Gradually extend the time you train during one of the weekly sessions to forty-eight minutes.

When you can do the maximum amount of body motion suggested for this level—five sessions of thirty-eight minutes each at your target heart rate, including four bursts of thirty seconds each during one of those sessions, and one longer session of forty-eight minutes—it's time to move on to level five.

Level Five

Amount of Body Motion

Thirty-eight to forty-three minutes of zone-time training, four to five times per week.

This is almost the top level. By now you're looking and feeling great. Look at you go!

Speed Bursts

Add one more thirty-second burst of maximum-intensity effort to one of your workouts, for a total of five bursts. Space the bursts five minutes apart, allowing your heart rate to decrease back down to your target heart zone before beginning the next burst.

Endurance Training

Gradually extend the time you train during one of the weekly sessions to fifty-eight minutes.

When you can do the maximum amount of body motion suggested for this level—five sessions of forty-three minutes each at your target heart rate, including five speed bursts of thirty seconds each during one of those sessions, and one longer session of fifty-eight minutes—you are ready for the max!

Level Six

Amount of Body Motion

Cardiovascular training five to six times per week, for forty-three to fifty-five minutes per session.

Great job! This is the top level—the one you thrive on and basically will be following for the rest of your healthy life. By now you feel and look better, you have more energy, and you feel more centered.

Speed Bursts

Add one more thirty-second burst of maximum-intensity effort to one of your workouts, for a total of six bursts. Space the bursts five minutes apart, allowing your heart rate to decrease back down to your target heart zone before beginning the next burst.

Endurance Training

Gradually extend the time you spend on one weekly session to sixty-three to sixty-eight minutes, which is about 20 percent longer than an average session.

I realize that this basic program may seem like a huge amount of body motion, because it is—by modern standards. But it is also the amount that will balance your body chemistry and keep you feeling and looking your best. Right now you may be wondering if you can ever do this much exercise, but you not only can, your genes are programmed to thrive on this amount.

Below is a progression chart that shows your cardiovascular training progression at a glance.

NURTURER-TYPE CARDIOVASCULAR CONDITIONING

Level Number	Total Number of Zone-Time Sessions per Week (Including Endurance Session)	Total Number of Zone-Time Minutes per Session	Total Number of Speed-Burst Sessions per Week and Number of Bursts per Session	Endurance Session
One	1 or 2	10–20	None	None
Two	2 or 3	15–25	1 session 1 burst	None
Three	3 or 4	25–33	1 session 3 bursts	1 session 43 minutes
Four	4 or 5	33–38	1 session 4 bursts	1 session 48 minutes
Five	4 or 5	38–43	1 session 5 bursts	1 session 58 minutes
Six	5 or 6	43–55	1 session 6 bursts	1 session 68 minutes

<u>NURTURER KEY #2:</u>
Strength Training

Because you have a naturally muscular lower body, you need to emphasize strength training for the upper part of your body only.

See the guidelines in chapter six on how best to perform strength exercises.

Two times per week *only,* perform two sets using free weights, selectorized machines, or stretch bands for each major muscle group in the upper body. Do twelve to fifteen repetitions per set. Perform three to five sets on the lats and deltoids (upper back and shoulders) to help the upper body become more balanced with the lower body. Always include abdominal crunches and back hyperextensions for the lumbar muscles when you do your regular strength workout. Don't lift weights with your legs or buttocks—save your legs for the cardio training. I know that this may sound strange if you have been listening to current approaches that emphasize weight training. But the best amount of lower-body heavy weight training for your type is . . . none . . . ever!

(Best for Nurturers are the exercises for Muscle Groups 2–7, and 9, pages 61–65.)

All varieties of toning, firming, sculpting, and calisthenics-type activities are fine. Just do not use heavy enough weights or high enough repetitions to reach muscle failure. When doing any strength-building activities, emphasize the full range of motion to increase your flexibility.

NURTURER KEY #3:
Flexibility

You are generally very flexible up until about age thirty, and then moderately flexible through menopause. Flexibility training will help prevent injuries to your muscles, tendons, and ligaments.

Refer to my guidelines on stretching in chapter six. The best way to limber up is to do static stretches—meaning that you hold the stretch, without bouncing, for about fifteen to thirty counts for each major muscle group. Do a flexibility routine at least three times a week, and increase to four to five times per week after menopause.

Remember that, just as the other genetic types can never hope to achieve the sculpted, curvy appearance you have naturally when you are in balance, you will never resemble a waiflike model, with a delicate look from head to toe. You can, however, optimize your genetic potential by following these principles.

EXAMPLE OF AN IDEAL EXERCISE WEEK
FOR THE NURTURER

Monday: A.M.—pace walk 30 minutes. P.M.—cycle 30 minutes; stretch.

Tuesday: A.M. or P.M.—aerobic dance; cardio weights, 45 minutes.

Wednesday: endurance walk/hike 68 minutes. P.M.—stretch.

Thursday: in-line skating or spin 45 minutes; cardio-weights
    routine.

Friday: pace walk/jog 50 minutes. P.M.—stretch.

Saturday: endurance walk/hike 68 minutes.

Sunday: Rest, relax.

NURTURER KEY #4:
Nutrition

Your basic theme as a Nurturer focuses on plant-based, high-water-content foods. Every day you should emphasize lots of plant foods, especially fruits and vegetables.

To remember the foods you need to avoid or minimize, think about "policing" your diet. Use the acronym COPS: C = Creamy, O = Oily, P = Processed, and S = Spicy. These are the foods that trigger your cravings and hunger.

Your main dietary challenge is your cravings for these COPS foods, all of which pull you out of metabolic balance. Unfortunately, the more unbalanced you become, the more your cravings intensify! Your appetite is strongest in the evening from 5 to 10 P.M., so you should eat a substantial evening meal. Your type should not have a hearty breakfast. You usually experience a letdown of energy and consequent cravings in the midmorning, so be sure you have some healthy, fruit- or vegetable-based snacks on hand.

The table below gives you three groups of foods. These are your **plenty** foods—you can basically eat as many of these as you like, within reason (unless otherwise noted); your **moderation** foods, those that you may have from time to time, or as a special treat; and your **seldom** foods, those foods that you should eat very rarely. Most of the foods in the seldom list are those that overstimulate your dominant glands, your ovaries, and cause you to become physically and mentally out of balance.

A list of recommended supplements is at the end of the foods list. These are micronutrients that are necessary for your body's basic processes. Including them as recommended will help ease cravings.

NURTURER FOOD CHOICES

Plenty Foods
—all fruits, especially melons and berries
—all vegetables, especially soy and broccoli
—all low-fat proteins
    nonfat dairy
    white flesh (skinless)
    pink fish (salmon or tuna)
—monofats (see list on page 73)
—extras
    alfalfa tablets—550-mg capsules, 5 at lunch, 5 at dinner
      (to aid digestion and elimination)
    flaxseeds—1 tbs with evening meal (a good appetite
      suppressant)

Moderation Foods
—all whole grains on list on page 73—1½ cups per day
—natural sweets (honey, molasses, etc.)—1 tbs per day
—caffeine—200 mg per day (green tea is best)
—exotic and extra-lean meats—4 oz per week
—juices—8 oz daily, *only* if you are at your ideal weight
—low-fat dairy products—1 cup, 3 times per week

Seldom Foods
—saturated fats—all higher-fat meats and dairy not listed in
  the column on pages 120 and 121. Especially avoid
  creams, dips, butter, cheese, dressings, sauces, spreads,
  gravies, puddings, and chocolate.
—hydrogenated fats—all processed foods that are hermetically sealed
—all spices (flavor enhancers)—salt, pepper, curry, hot sauces,
  salsas, chili powders, lemon juice and vinegar, MSG, savory
  foods made with spices (Cajun, Mexican, Thai, oriental,
  Indian)
—all refined grains and flours—breads, muffins, bagels, cookies, cakes, pretzels, pasta, pastries, crackers, cereals, biscuits, pancakes, waffles, croissants, noodles, popcorn

Supplements

　　—vitamins and minerals

　　　　multiple vitamin/mineral formula—1 × day

　　　　vitamin C—2,000 mg, 3 × day

　　　　vitamin E—400 IU, 2 × day, at noon and with evening

　　　　　　meal

　　　　selenium—200 mg at noon

　　　　calcium citrate—500–1,250 mg per day, split between

　　　　　　morning and dinner; after menopause increase to

　　　　　　1,250–1,500 mg

　　　　iron—20 mg, 1 × day*

　　*Note: Do not take iron once you have completed menopause.

To put your new way of eating into practice, use the following guidelines to plan your day's intake of fuel. More specific menu plans and
recipes follow.

Ideal sample day's intake:

SMALL BREAKFAST: 1 cup fruit with ½ cup nonfat dairy and 2 tbs
　　whole grain

SMALL A.M. SNACK: 1 cup fruit with ½ cup nonfat dairy

MEDIUM-SIZED LUNCH: veggies, fruits, nonfat dairy or white flesh,
　　1 cup whole grain

SMALL P.M. SNACK: fruit with nonfat dairy

HEARTY DINNER: veggies, flaxseeds, white flesh, fruit, 1 cup grains

NURTURER MENUS FOR ONE WEEK
(Recipes for starred items are in appendix A, pages 203–226)

Day 1

　　BREAKFAST—Fruit and Oats*

　　SNACK—1 cup berries, 1 oz string cheese

　　LUNCH—DeLayne's Tomatoes and Rice,* ½ cup cottage
　　　　cheese with ½ cup pineapple

　　SNACK—Nurturer Vegetable Soup*

　　DINNER—Chicken Parmesan* with whole-grain pasta and

tomatoes, green salad with flaxseed oil, 1 cup nonfat
yogurt

Day 2

BREAKFAST—1 cup nonfat fruit yogurt
SNACK—½ cup melon, 1 oz string cheese
LUNCH—Turkey Burger* with ½ whole-wheat bun and
   green salad
SNACK—Nurturer Vegetable Soup,* ½ cup nonfat yogurt
DINNER—Mushroom Soup,* Lemon Dill Trout,* rice and
   steamed veggies, 6 oz skim milk

Day 3

BREAKFAST—1 cup nonfat cottage cheese with 1 cup
   peaches
SNACK—½ cup watermelon, 1 oz string cheese
LUNCH—whole-grain Pita Pizza,* Spinach Fruit Salad*
SNACK—Strong Types Soup,* 1 oz string cheese
DINNER—roast turkey breast, steamed veggies, potatoes,
   ½ cup cantaloupe, 6 oz skim milk

Day 4

BREAKFAST—1 cup nonfat yogurt with raspberries
SNACK—½ cup mango, ½ cup nonfat cottage cheese
LUNCH—whole-wheat Tortilla Roll-Up* with Basil Cream
   Cheese Spread,* 1 cup fruit salad
SNACK—Nurturer Vegetable Soup,* 1 oz string cheese
DINNER—grilled chicken with Mango Chutney,* Quinoa
   Pilaf,* steamed asparagus, 6 oz skim milk

Day 5

BREAKFAST—1 cup nonfat yogurt with bananas and ½ slice
   whole-grain toast
SNACK—½ cup cantaloupe, ½ cup nonfat cottage cheese
LUNCH—garden salad, ½ grilled nonfat-cheese sandwich
SNACK—Strong Types Soup*
DINNER—4 oz Janice's Sea Bass,* roasted winter squash,
   string beans and broccoli stems, green salad

Day 6

　　BREAKFAST—1 cup Fruit and Oats*

　　SNACK—1 cup grapes, ½ cup nonfat yogurt

　　LUNCH—Nurturer Vegetable Soup,* ½ cup nonfat cottage
　　　　cheese, ½ pear

　　SNACK—Strong Types Soup*

　　DINNER—Jicama Orange Salad,* 4 oz Janice's Baked hal-
　　　　ibut,* steamed cabbage, 2 red potatoes, 6 oz. nonfat milk

Day 7

　　BREAKFAST—1 cup nonfat cottage cheese and ½ cup can-
　　　　taloupe

　　SNACK—½ cup melon or berries, 1 oz string cheese

　　LUNCH—vegetarian Taco Salad* with whole-grain tortilla
　　　　and nonfat cheese

　　SNACK—Nurturer Vegetable Soup*

　　DINNER—Gazpacho Soup,* 4 oz Baked Salmon,* grilled
　　　　vegetables with olive oil, 6 oz nonfat milk

NURTURER KEY #5:
Staying Focused

Even though the foods recommended in this plan are the ones you are genetically programmed to eat, and the exercise is the kind your body truly needs, it may not be easy switching all at once. Your cravings for less healthful foods may persist for a while. You may find it difficult to make exercise a part of your life. The following tips will help you to maintain your focus and motivation, even when the going gets tough.

Craving Controls

Old habits die hard. If your body is used to eating fettuccine Alfredo twice a week, it won't give it up without protest.

　　—Find the flow. Your zone-time body motion is the key.

　　—Try the energy-booster stretch on page 80.

　　—Use kapha-dosha-type seasonings (Order from Ayurvedic Institute;

see page 234). These will make your food taste better and help eliminate the craving for ovary-stimulating foods and spices.

—Drink herbal teas.

—Use sesame oil gum massage (see page 81) before meals. This will aid your digestion and help you feel full before you are tempted to overeat.

—Walk it off. When you do get a strong craving for a creamy pasta dish, a chocolate bar, or other food that overstimulates your ovaries, the best thing you can do is drink eight ounces of cool water and then engage in some body motion—swim some laps, go for a bike ride, or just take a walk around the block.

—Avoid spices. Spices stimulate your ovaries, releasing a hormonal flow and pulling you out of metabolic balance. Simply avoiding spices will help to prevent this imbalance and tone down your hunger between 5 and 10 P.M., your craving time.

—Avoid ginseng, which overstimulates your ovaries.

—Don't skip your afternoon snack. You tend to get an energy dip in the afternoon. Eating a snack will help lift you out of the dip and keep your appetite for dinner under control.

—Whenever you feel a craving, grab some fruit, especially a high-water-content fruit such as melon, and munch until the craving passes.

Herbal Helps

The following herbal remedies will help control food cravings and balance your glandular secretions, helping you to get that "feeling" and stay on track:

Ginger tea—drink at noon and 6 P.M. (red-clover tea is also good)

Flaxseeds—see page 75 (a good source of essential fatty acids and helps raise brain levels of serotonin, promoting satiety)

Fennel seeds—two 550-mg capsules with dinner (decreases gassiness and promotes satiety)

Soy lecithin—1 tbs at every meal (attaches to estrogen receptors, decreasing sites available for estrogen-mimicking carcinogens)

Evening primrose oil—2 gel caps with evening meal (contains gamma-linoleic acid [GLA], which helps regulate hormonal and metabolic functions)

Dong quai—(This nontoxic Chinese herb, from a plant in the carrot family, has long been used as a blood-building tonic, to increase circulation, and as a general tonic for women, regulating ovarian function. If you have menstrual or menopausal difficulties, take two 550-mg capsules a day; wait six to eight weeks to evaluate effectiveness.)

Make It Easy on Yourself (Convenience Is the Key)

If you keep quantities of your plenty foods easily available for when you want to snack, you won't be so tempted by your "seldom" foods.

—Keep fresh, washed, ready-to-eat fruits and vegetables handy for snacks.

—Prepare Baked French-Fries* as snack foods for the kids (see recipe, page 212).

—Cook large portions of brown rice and keep some in the fridge at all times for quick snacks or easy meals.

Brown Bag It

Bring your own, healthful lunch to work. Or buy a Nurturer-friendly meal in a local store. A group of nurses that I know take a brisk walk to the grocery at lunchtime, where they buy veggies and fruit and nonfat yogurt. Then they walk back to the hospital before enjoying their lunch. "I like the idea that we're setting a community example," says Shana, a twenty-six-year-old RN. "It's great that people see us walking along in our uniforms with healthy food."

Make It a Group Effort

Although dieting or working out with a group is often a good idea for all genetic types, for Nurturers it can spell the difference between failure and success. A number of my clients have reported success with "clustering," which is essentially getting together with like-minded people and sharing the responsibilities and chores involved in maintaining your good health. Rather than having to shop, wash, and prepare fresh foods daily, members of a group take turns preparing for the entire group.

LaDeane, a retired, fifty-five-year-old Nurturer who lives in Los Angeles, formed a food-preparation group with two neighborhood friends. Each woman had two days in each week to be responsible for preparing the food for all three families.

Say your days are Monday and Thursday—the other days of the week you don't have to do all that. All you need to do is pick up your food that's been prepared elsewhere. You know whose day it is, so you pop over at the appointed time to pick up your fresh veggies. This sort of cluster seems to work best with a core group of three to five participants.

For more information on clustering and other tips for ways to stick with your new eating plan, see chapter fourteen.

Working Body Motion into Your Busy Lifestyle

Because the Nurturer needs so much body motion, it may seem difficult to fit all of it into your typical week. But 22 percent of Americans exercise regularly and so can you. Your overall lifestyle will be more gratifying as a result.

—Start slowly. The ultimate body-motion goal for Nurturers is to systematically find the flow. This zone-time emphasis is the key to your long-term success. Just decide that you'll begin to do a little bit of zone-time body motion and only increase the amount as you feel like it. After all, it's taken years to get out of balance, so take the natural flow back to balance slowly.

No matter how out of shape and/or busy you are, you can certainly begin level one, which requires only one ten-minute body motion session per week to start. Resolve to do level one until you're comfortable enough to want to add a little more. Continue this process, seeking the flow step by step, until body motion has become an essential part of your life.

—Get up early. Getting up an hour earlier in the day is without a doubt the most effective way to add body motion to your life. The idea is to get out of bed and get moving before others are up. It's my experience that about 60 percent of those Nurturers who stay with it exercise in the first three hours of the day.

I know that exercising in the morning may not be possible for everyone, but it's especially useful for Nurturers. For one thing, the kapha dosha is active in the early part of the morning. Training early keeps you from feeling sluggish. It's also a time of day when it's hard to find excuses. Make your zone-time workout a ritual part of the day. Before long you'll find you're waking up, ready to go, whether the alarm clock is set or not.

For more tips on ways to work exercise into your life, see chapter fourteen.

When You Have Trouble Making Yourself Work Out

—Keep it social. Work as much social interaction into your life as possible. Involve other people in your zone-time activity at least three times a week. Ideal for Nurturers is working out on the buddy system: develop a plan that involves a group of three or more people who are committed to keeping each other focused on maintaining their body motion plan.

Shana, the twenty-six-year-old nurse I've told you about, is about as busy and service-oriented as a person can be. Not only is she a full-time nurse, she also has four-year-old twins. But she knows how important physical activity is to her life, and she's found an effective way to make sure she gets her body motion in. Shana brought together a small group of fitness-minded women who made a no-excuses agreement to get together first thing in the morning for body motion several times a week. The members of the group take turns being the drill sergeant, the one to give the others a wake-up call for the 6 A.M. meeting. And then, rain or shine, they meet and, depending on the weather, either pace walk outdoors or inside a mall. Once a week they also meet at a local roller-skating rink that opens early for adults. "That's my favorite," Shana told me. "They have lap lanes for cardio skating. Skating's fun, and it also has a purpose."

—Avoid boredom. Nurturers can easily get bored. Learn new and interesting ways to do body motion. Experiment with cardio boxing, in-line skating, jazz dance, mountain biking, spinning, power yoga, Tai bo, backpacking, and rowing. Don't hesitate to use a TV or Walkman to decrease monotony.

LaDeane, who is fifty-five and retired, invested in a treadmill so she can get her zone-time body motion in a climate-controlled environment. She set her treadmill up in front of the TV and does her thing right there. "I record my favorite TV shows on the VCR," she told me. "For example, I love to watch *Oprah*, but I'm seldom home when she's on. So I get up early and watch a day late. I keep my remote in reach and fast-forward through the commercials. That way I'm not wasting time."

For variety, LaDeane also attends a midmorning swim class twice a week for fifty-five minutes of aerobic toning and firming. "Those two activities are the mainstay of my cardio program," she told me. "I might learn something else if I get bored with them, but so far they work for me."

For more tips on maintaining your focus, see chapter fourteen.

Dealing with Plateaus

Everyone who's ever tried to lose weight has experienced plateaus, those annoying times when your fat thermostat seems to get stuck, and no matter what you do you can't lose another ounce. These periods are caused by the body's having decided that you are at the correct weight for your current activity level and fuel blend, and it will do everything in its power to keep you there.

If you continue to follow the correct eating and body-motion plan for your type, the plateau will eventually give way to more weight loss. But to speed the natural process and quickly break through the plateau, try the following strategies:

—Carry your lost weight. As you begin to lose weight according to the scale, add that same amount of excess weight to the weight you are carrying during one or two of your body-motion sessions per week. When/if you reach a total of twenty-five extra pounds, stop carrying the extra weights for six weeks. Following the six-week rest period, start over again by carrying ten pounds, once a week. Repeat this process until you reach your ideal weight.

—Do more bursts. Add four to eight thirty-second maximum-intensity bursts to a second day of your regular cardio workout. These bursts are the fastest, most efficient way to get your body back on track.

For more tips on beating plateaus, see chapter sixteen.

NURTURER KEY #6:
Energy-Balancing Principles

Get Sunlight

Three or four times per week, get outside in the sunshine, without sunglasses, for twenty to thirty minutes. If possible, do so early in the day or late in the afternoon. If you can go outside only during midday in the summer, you should wear sunscreen.

Lymphatic Stimulation

The lymphatic system, which is involved in removing the debris caused by cellular metabolism, is often sluggish in Nurturers, especially in the lower part of the body. Any activities that can help stimulate this system are great for you. Perform a quickie lymphatic massage on yourself four to five times a week, emphasizing your legs and buttocks area. (For details, see page 79.)

Yogic Breathing

To reduce stress and help control food cravings, practice yogic breathing a few times a week or whenever you are feeling anxious. For details on yogic breathing routines, see page 109.

12

THE COMMUNICATOR'S WAY

The Communicator is one of the two **sleek** genetic types. If you are a Communicator, you are creative, verbal, unpredictable, and easily bored. You like to organize information and impart it to others. You excel in professions such as writing, teaching, and acting. On the downside, you tend to moodiness. You can be didactic and impatient, an obsessive overachiever, driving yourself and those around you crazy with your perfectionism.

Your anatomical type is ectomorph, giving you a relative preponderance of skin and nerves, which derive from the ectomorphic embryonic layer. Since you have a naturally high metabolism, you only need a moderate amount of aerobic body motion. But you have trouble gaining strength and need more strength training than the two stronger genetic types. You are naturally quite flexible and can excel at yoga and tai chi.

When in balance, you have a slender, hourglass-shaped body, equally wide at the shoulders and hips, with prominent collarbones and a well-defined waist. Your head tends to be oval-shaped and you may have a long neck. You tend to be long and lanky, with long, thin arms and legs, bony hands and feet, and a relatively short trunk. When out of balance, you gain weight in the middle of your body—through the spare-tire area and upper thighs, giving you an apple shape. Even when you're quite overweight, your arms and legs, especially from the elbows and knees down, remain slim.

Your glandular type is thyroidal, which governs energy balance and is responsible for your unsteady energy levels and consequent tendency to up-and-down mood swings. You often crave foods that stimulate your

131

dominant gland—sweets, caffeine, and highly refined carbohydrates such as flour. You will be healthiest and most in balance on a diet high in leafy vegetables, monounsaturated fats, and lean protein, including all white meats, nonfat dairy products, eggs, some nuts, and soy protein. (For details, see Key #4.)

Your Ayurvedic energy type is vata dosha, which gives you your tendency toward changeability. Vata dosha is creative and volatile, and you tend to walk and talk fast. You are uncomfortable in a cool environment and often have cold hands and feet. To maintain balance, seek warm surroundings and strive for regularity in all aspects of your life.

Genetically, your dominant thyroid gland makes you vulnerable to circulatory and blood-sugar problems, including hypoglycemia and diabetes. Because of your preponderance of skin and nervous tissue, you also have a tendency to autoimmune diseases and allergies. Your system is oversensitive to stimuli in general; for instance, a little sugar intake can result in a noticeable insulin response, followed by a serious crash, followed by a feeding frenzy, and so on. Maintaining moderate body motion, eating several small meals during the day, and restricting snacks to protein can help maintain blood sugar levels, avoiding energy fluctuations and forestalling more serious problems.

COMMUNICATOR KEY #1:
Body Motion—Cardiovascular Conditioning

Because of your erratic energy levels and mood swings, you need the calming and stabilizing influence of moderate, frequent aerobic body motion. When you work out, be sure you are exercising within your target heart zone—Communicators tend to overdo exercise, exhausting themselves. It is even a good idea for you to take a week off every three or four months.

You will recall that what I call "the flow" is the level of intensity in the target zone that generates the release of beta endorphin and enkephalins, creating that euphoric, morphinelike high that makes zone-time feel so great. This elevated state stays with you for hours afterward. Exercising in the aerobic zone, but out of the flow zone, is beneficial, but will not promote the euphoria necessary for long-term continuation. To become physically and psychologically addicted to exercise, you *must* find the flow.

Communicators generally find the flow at an intensity level of 70–85 percent of aerobic capacity.

Because you are easily bored, your best choice for aerobic body motion is to cross-train, switching among different activities. In general, you should avoid repetitive, tedious activities, such as stair-climbing machines or running on a track, which will quickly drive you up the wall. Some activities to learn include cardio boxing, in-line skating, jazz dance, Tai bo, mountain biking, spinning, power yoga, backpacking, rowing, and running. Use a Walkman if you work out indoors, or exercise in front of a TV or with a friend, to decrease monotony.

Although the Communicator's body-motion program is less time-consuming than those for the strong genetic types, the amount of body motion you need may still seem overwhelming, especially if you have been sedentary for a while. And I know from my own experience that making body motion a part of your life is more than a matter of simply getting your body out the door. You may face seemingly overwhelming obstacles in the form of family and/or work demands.

That's okay—I understand. Many of my clients have voiced the same concerns. The important thing is to simply get started. Do what you can for now, and as you become more fit and more in balance, you can gradually increase the level of body motion until you are closer to the ideal for your genetic type. Remember that eating correctly for your type helps you feel like exercising.

See Key #5 for practical, proven ways you can fit body motion into your life.

When to Do Body Motion

As a Communicator you can do body motion at any time of the day that fits into your schedule. However, Communicators do best when they allow their bodies to warm up a little before they become active, so be sure to allow some extra time before your workout, especially if you schedule your body motion for first thing in the morning.

WARM-UPS AND COOLDOWNS.

Before your body motion sessions, always warm up by doing your scheduled activity at a slower pace for two to five minutes. End your workout with a cooldown of up to five minutes.

Weight-Loss Tips

If you're trying to lose weight, or you want to reach the peak of lean-ness possible for you, you'll need to modify the basic recommended pro-gram a little bit.

The best, most efficient way to achieve your ideal of body fitness is to make sure you're achieving the flow by working out at 70–85 percent of your maximum heart rate. Then add bursts of maximum activity to your basic zone-time body motion workout, as detailed in the program below. Pushing your heart rate beyond the aerobic zone stimulates the release of ACTH by the pituitary. This adrenal-stimulating growth hormone lowers the fat thermostat.

You can also try increasing the number of longer, zone-time endurance sessions per week, or increase your workouts to twice a day up to two times per week. For more detailed suggestions, see the section on "plateau busters" in chapter sixteen.

Following is a stepped-level program that will allow you to gradually work up to the amount of body motion that your body needs.

Start at a level that is appropriate for you, and stay at each level as long as necessary. For some, that might mean staying at level one for sev-eral weeks or even months. If you have previously been sedentary and/or are recovering from any illness, this is a good start and will get your body on the road to balance. It will also give you time to make the needed lifestyle changes that will enable you to work even more body motion into your life.

Level One

Amount of Body Motion

One to two sessions of cardiovascular activities, of ten to fifteen min-utes each, in your target heart zone (see page 55).

I suggest pace walking as a good way to get started, because it is effec-tive, easy, and requires no equipment other than a good pair of shoes. Whatever zone-time body motion activities you choose, be sure they are activities you like and can enjoy regularly.

When you can comfortably do two sessions per week of fifteen min-utes at your target heart rate, you are ready to move on to level two.

Level Two

Amount of Body Motion

Two sessions per week of fifteen to twenty-three minutes in your target heart zone.

Speed Bursts

After you have been at this level for a week or two, it's time to add speed bursts to hasten weight loss. During one of your regular zone-time body motion sessions, include two thirty-second bursts of maximum intensity effort.

When you can do the maximum amount of body motion suggested for this level—two sessions of twenty-three minutes each, with two thirty-second bursts of maximum-intensity effort during one of the sessions—move on to level three.

Level Three

Amount of Body Motion

Two to three sessions per week at twenty-three to twenty-eight minutes per session in your target heart zone.

If you've reached level three, congratulations! You're much closer to your ultimate goal. If you've been doing all of one sort of activity, now might be the time to begin some cross-training, switching to another activity.

Speed Bursts

During one of your regularly scheduled zone-time sessions, add two more thirty-second bursts of maximum-intensity effort, for a total of four bursts. Space the bursts five minutes apart, allowing your heart rate to decrease back down to your target heart zone before beginning the next burst.

Endurance Training

After you have been at this level for two or three weeks, it's time to extend one of your basic body-motion sessions for stamina and endurance. Gradually extend one of the zone-time sessions until you can comfortably sustain your heart rate for thirty-three minutes.

When you can comfortably perform the maximum activity for this level—three sessions of twenty-eight minutes each, including four bursts in one session, plus one extended session—you're ready to move on to level four.

Level Four

Amount of Body Motion

Three sessions of twenty-eight to thirty-three minutes each, in your target training zone.

Speed Bursts

During one of your training sessions, add two more thirty-second bursts of maximum-intensity effort, for a total of six bursts. Space the bursts four minutes apart, allowing your heart rate to decrease back down into the target zone before the next burst.

Endurance Training

Once you are doing three sessions a week, lengthen one of the sessions to an extended period of forty-three minutes.

When you can perform the maximum amount of body motion recommended for level four—three sessions of thirty-three minutes each, including six speed bursts and one longer session of forty-three minutes—it's time to move on to level five.

Level Five

Amount of Body Motion

Four sessions of thirty-three to thirty-eight minutes each.

This is almost the top level. By now you're looking and feeling great. Way to go!

Speed Bursts

During two of the workouts, do five thirty-second bursts of maximum-intensity effort. Space the bursts four minutes apart, allowing your heart rate to return to the target zone before beginning the next burst.

Endurance Training

Add five minutes to your extended session, increasing it to forty-eight minutes.

When you can perform the maximum activity recommended for this level—four sessions of thirty-eight minutes each, including five bursts in two of the sessions and one forty-eight-minute session—you are ready to move on to level six.

Level Six

Amount of Body Motion

Four or five sessions per week of training in your target heart rate zone. Each zone-time session length should be thirty-eight to forty-eight minutes.

Speed Bursts

During two of the workouts, insert one more thirty-second burst of maximum-intensity effort, for a total of six bursts. Space the bursts four minutes apart, allowing your heart rate to return to the target zone before beginning the next burst.

Endurance Training

Add five minutes to your extended session, increasing it to fifty-three minutes in your target zone.

Congratulations! You've reached the top level of exercise recommended for Communicators. Once you can perform the recommended levels of body motion, you'll be feeling and looking better. Your energy levels are steadier, you feel calmer and more centered.

I realize that this basic program may seem like a lot of body motion, because it is—by modern standards. But it is also the amount that will balance your body chemistry and keep you feeling and looking your best. Right now you may be wondering if you can ever do this much exercise. But believe me—you not only can, your genes are programmed for it.

Below is a progression chart that shows your cardiovascular training progression at a glance.

COMMUNICATOR-TYPE CARDIOVASCULAR CONDITIONING

Level Number	Total Number of Zone-Time Session per Week (Including Endurance Session)	Total Number of Zone-Time Minutes per Session	Total Number of Speed-Burst Sessions per Week and Number of Bursts per Session	Length of Endurance Session
One	1 or 2	10–15	None	None
Two	2	15–23	1 session 2 bursts	None
Three	2 or 3	23–28	1 session 4 bursts	1 session 33 minutes
Four	3	28–33	1 session 6 bursts	1 session 43 minutes
Five	4	33–38	2 sessions 5 bursts	1 session 48 minutes
Six	4 or 5	38–48	2 sessions 6 bursts	1 session 53 minutes

COMMUNICATOR KEY #2:
Strength Training

As a sleek Communicator, you tend to have a harder time than the strong types gaining muscle mass and strength, so you'll have to work a little harder in this area. To maintain good posture, lean body mass, and bone density, Communicator types *must* strength train.

Two or three times per week, perform two or three sets of strength-training exercises for each major muscle group, using enough resistance to "feel the burn" at twelve to fifteen repetitions. In addition to free weights, weight machines, or stretch bands, you may also use all varieties of toning, firming, sculpting, and calisthenics-type activities. You should also perform abdominal crunches and back hyperextensions at least three times a week (for instructions, see page 65).

Communicator types should perform exercises for all the muscle groups on pages 61–65.

COMMUNICATOR KEY #3:

Flexibility

Although Communicators tend to be naturally flexible, their joints can stiffen through lack of use and aging.

Please see my guidelines on stretching in chapter six. The best way for all types to limber up is to do static stretches (stretches where you hold but don't bounce) on each major muscle group for fifteen to thirty counts for each group. Perform stretches at least three times a week. Also excellent is yoga once or twice a week.

(For a suggested stretch routine, see pages 66 and 67.)

Remember that, just as the stronger genetic types will never be able to achieve the sleek, lanky look you have naturally when you are in balance, so you're unlikely to achieve the pumped-up, buff look of a muscle type. You can, however, greatly improve your posture, strength, and muscle tone, which will help your body to be the best Communicator type it can be.

EXAMPLE OF AN IDEAL EXERCISE WEEK FOR A COMMUNICATOR

Monday: step-bench aerobics 50-minute class (with hand weights).
Tuesday: stair-climber and weight train—45 minutes total.
Wednesday: rest or recreational sports activity such as tennis.
Thursday: walk/jog 40 minutes—weight train.
Friday: jazz dance or spin class 40–45 minutes.
Saturday: in-line skating, mountain bike, or hike 60 minutes.
Sunday: rest, relax.

COMMUNICATOR KEY #4

Nutrition

Your basic nutrition theme is MVP—monounsaturates, veggies, and protein. To remember this MVP acronym, think of yourself as your own Most Valuable Player. The closer you adhere to the basic theme required by your genetic programming, the more balanced and healthy you will be.

Monounsaturated oils—which include olives, olive oil, canola oil, avocados, peanuts, cashews, macadamia nuts, almonds, and peanut and almond oils—help balance your body chemistry, satisfy your appetite, and nourish your nervous system. You need lots of veggies for their phytochemicals and for the relatively small amount of carbohydrate you require. And most of all you need lots of good-quality protein. Unlike the other types, you can eat a lot of protein—basically as much as you want—including red meat, as long as you are careful to limit saturated fat. Especially good for you are white-meat poultry (with skin removed), fish, nuts, nonfat dairy, and soy foods.

Your main dietary challenge is your craving for sweets, refined carbos, and/or caffeine. Overindulgence in any of these thyroid-stimulating foods raises your insulin levels, causing a blood sugar drop later that results in even more cravings. To stop this vicious cycle, limit your intake of these foods and instead eat frequent small meals that always include the MVP combination.

When to Eat

Timing of food intake is more important for Communicators than the other genetic types, because of your volatile blood sugar levels. When you first begin your new way of eating, especially if you need to lose weight, minimize all carbohydrates before noon. This will keep insulin levels low, which helps to promote fat metabolism. Systematically eat protein every four hours to keep your blood sugar levels steady. Minimize your intake of all carbohydrates, and strictly avoid refined carbos (flour and sugar) and caffeine.

The table below lists three groups of foods. These are your **plenty** foods—you can basically eat as many of these as you like, within reason (unless otherwise noted); your **moderation** foods, those that you may have from time to time; and your **seldom** foods, those foods that you should eat rarely, if at all. Most of the foods in the seldom category are those that overstimulate your dominant thyroid gland and cause you to become physically and mentally out of balance.

Included under the plenty foods are "extras," herbs, condiments, and teas that are beneficial to Communicators and should be added to your daily regimen. These foods will help control your appetite and balance your biochemistry.

See also the list of supplements at the end of the foods list. These are micronutrients that are necessary for your body's basic processes. Including them as recommended will help ease cravings.

COMMUNICATOR FOOD CHOICES

Plenty Foods
—all leafy vegetables and vegetables grown above the
  ground, especially cruciferous vegetables such as broccoli
  and cauliflower
—all seaweeds—kelp, nori, kombu, bladder wrack, etc.
—all low-fat proteins
  white flesh (skinless poultry)
  exotic meats—ostrich, buffalo, elk, venison, emu
  all fish (except shellfish—see note on page 73)
  eggs/egg whites
  all nonfat and low fat dairy
—monofats
  olive oil and olives
  canola oil
  avocados
  almonds, peanuts, macadamia nuts, and cashews (note:
    nuts should be limited if you need to lose weight)
—extras
  spices, seasonings
  ginseng tea midday (to stimulate adrenals and give
    energy boost)
  flaxseeds (a good source of essential fatty acids)
  kelp tablets—100 mg, 1 at noon, 1 with evening meal
    (to improve digestion and regulate the thyroid)

Moderation Foods
—all fruits
  tropical and citrus—1 cup/day (note: whole fruits only,
    not juice)
  melon and berries—1 cup/day
—all whole grains—1½ cup/day
—all higher-fat proteins not on list (steak, etc.)—4 oz/week
—root vegetables and other starchy plants such as corn,
  beans, legumes, and squash

Seldom Foods
—all refined carbohydrates—sugars, juices, sodas, chocolate,

honey, jelly, syrup, flour, breads, muffins, bagels, pasta,
cereal, biscuits, cakes, cookies, crackers, pretzels, waffles,
pancakes, croissants, pastries, noodles, popcorn, white rice
—all alcohol, especially sweet wines
—organ meats, lamb, high-fat beef, deli meats, pork, cold cuts
—hydrogenated and saturated fats (see list on page 74)
    anything deep fried
    anything hermetically sealed or wrapped in plastic
    anything high in saturated fat, such as ice cream
—caffeine—including coffee, tea, gurana, kola nut, caffeinat-
ed sodas, and chocolate

Supplements
—vitamins and minerals
    multiple vitamin/mineral formula—1 × day in A.M.
    (note: mineral supplementation is especially important
        for Communicators, as it will help to stabilize blood
        sugar levels)
    extra B complex with iron,* magnesium, manganese
    selenium—200–400 mcg at lunch
    chromium piccolinate—200 mg, 2–3 × day
    E—800 IU at lunch
    C—1,000 mg, 2 × day
    women: calcium citrate—500–1,250 mg per day, split
        between morning and dinner; after menopause
        increase to 1,250–1,500 mg
—L-phenylalanine—500 mg 2 hours after lunch
    L-tyrosine—500 mg 2 hours after lunch

*Note: Do not take iron once you have completed menopause.

To put your new way of eating into practice, use the following guidelines to plan your day's intake of fuel. More specific menu plans and
recipes follow.

Ideal sample day's intake:
(*Note:* This sample is for those who have followed the Communicator
eating plan for several weeks. If you are just beginning the diet or have a
great deal of weight to lose, eliminate all carbos before noon.)

SMALL BREAKFAST: eggs, salsa, and 1 slice multigrain toast

SMALL A.M. SNACK: string cheese, small piece fruit (e.g., ½ peach, 1 small apple), 3 almonds

MEDIUM-SIZED LUNCH: veggies with olive oil and vinegar, any white flesh, ½ cup starch

SMALL P.M. SNACK: nonfat or low fat yogurt, small piece of fruit, 3 cashews

MEDIUM-SIZED DINNER: veggies, clean protein, any monounsaturated fat, ½ cup starch

COMMUNICATOR MENUS FOR ONE WEEK

(Recipes for starred items are in appendix A, pages 203–226)

Day 1

BREAKFAST—2 scrambled eggs with cooked veggies and salsa, 1 slice multigrain toast

SNACK—1 piece string cheese, 3 cashews

LUNCH—DeLayne's Tomatoes and Rice,* ½ cup skim milk

SNACK—Communicator Vegetable Soup,* piece of string cheese or turkey jerky

DINNER—Chicken Parmesan,* grated zucchini with Red Sauce,* salad with lemon and flaxseed oil, skim milk

Day 2

BREAKFAST—1 Crepe Shell* with 2 scrambled eggs wrapped inside

SNACK—½ cup sprouts, 3 almonds

LUNCH—Turkey Burger* on ½ bun, salad with oil and vinegar, skim milk

SNACK—small orange and 3 almonds

DINNER—Mushroom Soup,* Cajun Trout,* ½ cup basmati rice with green beans, ½ cup skim milk

Day 3

BREAKFAST—veggie omelet and 1 slice multigrain toast

SNACK—½ cup berries, 3 cashews

LUNCH—multigrain Pita Pizza* with chicken, with green salad, skim milk

SNACK—Sleek Types Soup,* piece of string cheese or turkey jerky

DINNER—roast turkey breast with steamed veggies, potatoes and Gravy,* spinach salad

Day 4

BREAKFAST—Spanish Egg Fritata,* ½ cup skim milk

SNACK—1 cup melon, 3 macadamia nuts

LUNCH—Tortilla Roll-Up,* Basil Cream Cheese Spread* dressing, green salad with almonds, skim milk

SNACK—Communicator Vegetable Soup,* piece of string cheese or turkey jerky

DINNER—grilled chicken with Mango Chutney,* Quinoa Pilaf,* steamed asparagus

Day 5

BREAKFAST—2 poached eggs, 1 slice multigrain toast

SNACK—1 cup berries, 3 cashews

LUNCH—garden salad with flaxseed oil, ½ tuna-salad sandwich, skim milk

SNACK—Sleek Types Soup,* piece of string cheese or turkey jerky

DINNER—green-leaf salad, 4 oz Janice's Sea Bass,* roast winter squash, string beans and broccoli stems

Day 6

BREAKFAST—scrambled eggs with vegetables, salsa, 1 slice multigrain toast

SNACK—½ cup nonfat yogurt, 3 macadamia nuts

LUNCH—green salad, 3-oz Turkey Burger*

SNACK—Communicator Vegetable Soup,* piece of string cheese or turkey jerky

DINNER—Spinach Fruit Salad,* 4 oz pork tenderloin, steamed cabbage, and 2 red potatoes

Day 7

BREAKFAST—cheese omelet and 1 slice multigrain toast

SNACK—½ cup berries, 3 cashews

LUNCH—Taco Salad* with lean hamburger and nonfat cheese, skim milk

SNACK—Sleek Types Vegetable Soup,* piece of string cheese or turkey jerky

DINNER—Gazpacho Soup,* 4 oz baked salmon, grilled vegetables with olive oil, skim milk

COMMUNICATOR KEY #5:
Staying Focused

Even though the foods recommended in this plan are the ones you are genetically programmed to eat, and the body motion is the kind your body truly needs, I realize it may not be easy switching your habits all at once. Your cravings for unhealthful foods may persist for a while. Some people find it difficult to make body motion a part of their lives. The following tips will help you to maintain your focus and motivation, even when the going gets tough.

Craving Controls

Old habits die hard. If your body is used to eating a Hershey's bar washed down with coffee every afternoon, it won't give them up without protest. The following tips will make it far easier to stick with your new eating plan.

—First and foremost, make sure you're getting enough zone-time cardio body motion to maintain the flow.

—Avoid all carbos in the morning. This is not as hard as it sounds, because you can eat the extra protein you need to keep your appetite under control.

—Eat protein every four hours to keep your blood sugar level in balance.

—Combine MVP at meals and snacks. That is, always have a bit of protein, a bit of veggie, and a bit of monounsaturated fat (such as a few nuts).

—Don't skip meals! This is important for keeping your sugar/insulin levels in balance.

—Don't eat large meals, which will flood your body with insulin, lead-ing to a rebound low-blood-sugar response a few hours later. A bet-ter strategy for you is to "graze," eating many smaller meals throughout the day, keeping your blood sugar levels steady.

—Avoid all caffeine, which stimulates your central nervous system, ultimately increasing your appetite.

Herbal Helps

The following herbal remedies will help control food cravings and bal-ance your glandular secretions, keeping you on track:

Kelp tablets—1 at lunch and 1 at dinner.
Flaxseeds—1 tbs at dinner.
Chamomile tea and/or valerian root—1 to 2 cups after dinner.

These herbs, along with kava kava, exert a relaxing and calming influ-ence on Communicators. They can take the edge off when you're feeling wound up and bouncing off the walls.

Keep It Pure

Because Communicators have the most limited food choices, you also face the greatest temptations of all the body types. Unfortunately, most popular convenience foods are your trigger foods.

Many Communicators have found the best way to deal with tempta-tion is to minimize it. Brenda, a forty-four-year-old homemaker with six children, simply doesn't keep tempting and unhealthful foods in the house. "I fill the fridge with Ziploc bags full of healthy snacks like sliced fruit, berries, veggies, string cheese, and peeled hard-boiled eggs," she explained to me. "I simply don't buy the other stuff, the packaged goods and sugary snacks. When I go to the grocery store, I don't even go down the aisles where they keep the Elmer's glue [our name for flour mixed with water]."

Working Body Motion into Your Busy Lifestyle

—Keep it interesting. More than any other type, you get bored easi-ly. Choose as many activities as you can for your body motion, and switch among them frequently. Or, if you really prefer one activity for your basic cardio workout, then vary the way you do it. For example, if you like to jog or pace walk, change your route. If you like to swim, use different strokes every few laps.

Brenda, the homemaker I mentioned earlier, likes to exercise first thing in the morning, before her kids and family get up. But she doesn't like doing the same old workouts. "I belong to a health club where I rotate between different classes," she told me. "Sometimes I do a jazz-dance cardio class, sometimes step aerobics, pretty much something different each time. That way I don't get bored with one instructor or one activity."

Brenda also keeps herself motivated by doing sports practice with her kids. "They're always into something active," she said. "So whether it's dancing or soccer, baseball or football, I get out there and practice with them. I also plan a lot of family activities—hikes, walks, and bike rides for the weekends."

—Have fun. Like Brenda, you can make your regular body-motion sessions enjoyable activities. Whether or not you have kids, schedule dancing, tennis, skating, mountain biking, or hiking for weekend fun.

When You Have Trouble Making Yourself Exercise

—Avoid boredom. Boredom is the number one reason for Communicators to give up on their body motion program. Follow the suggestions above for ways to keep your activities varied. Other tricks that work for Communicators are to listen to recorded books or music on headphones, and to work out with a buddy.

For more tips on maintaining your interest, see chapter fourteen.

Dealing with Plateaus

Everyone who's ever tried to lose weight has experienced plateaus, those annoying times when your fat thermostat seems to get stuck, and no matter what you do you can't lose another ounce. These periods are caused by the body's having decided that you are at the correct weight for your current amount of exercise and mix of fuel, and it will do everything in its power to keep you there.

If you continue to follow the correct eating and body-motion plan for your type, the plateau will eventually give way to more weight loss. But to speed up the process and quickly break through the plateau, try the following strategies:

—Do more speed bursts. Add four to eight thirty-second maximum-intensity bursts to a third day of your regular cardio workout. These bursts are the fastest, most efficient way to lower your fat thermostat.

—Give carbos the boot. For two or three days, try cutting out all carbohydrates, which can give your metabolism the boost it needs to start losing again.

For more tips on beating plateaus, see chapter sixteen.

Be Consistent

As a vata-dosha type, you tend to be erratic in your behaviors, which can severely drain your energy. More than the other genetic types, you need structure and consistency in your life. Try to schedule specific times for the important activities in your daily life, including arising, meals, work, zone-time body motion, and sleep.

By establishing regular habits, you accustom your body to expected pathways, for getting up and getting going, taking in nourishment, being active, and unwinding. Thus, if your body knows, say, to expect body motion at noon, it will be revved up and ready to go.

COMMUNICATOR KEY #6:
Energy-Balancing Principles

Get Sunlight

Two or three times a week, get outside in the sunshine, without sunglasses, for twenty to thirty minutes. If possible, do so early in the day or late in the afternoon. If you can only go outside during midday in the summer, wear sunscreen.

Take Classes

Your mind is quick and seeks novelty, so systematically expose yourself to fresh ideas, through classes, lectures, joining clubs, or the Internet.

See appendix C for an audiocassette catalogue from Nightengale/ Conant Corp.

Hot Baths

Take hot baths or a dip in a Jacuzzi four or five times per week, staying submerged long enough to sweat. As a vata-dosha type, you need to increase your circulation, especially to your extremities. A hot bath or hot tub can be especially relaxing for you toward the end of the day.

Filtered Water and Air

Drink only bottled or filtered water and keep an air purifier in the room where you sleep.

Aroma Therapy

See details in chapter fifteen.

Fresh Foliage

Communicators enjoy contact with the natural world. Keep fresh-cut flowers and living plants in your home.

Do Yogic Breathing

Daily, in the evening, lie on your back, your arms at your sides, your eyes closed, and inhale slowly through your nose, then exhale slowly through your mouth. Focus on the full breath cycle with the exhale as the start of the cycle. Maintain concentration on natural breathing for five to twenty minutes.

Meditate

Meditation is especially good for Communicators, as it helps to calm your quick, restless mind. Communicators in general are more high-strung than the other types, and more susceptible to life's vagaries. Try to meditate at least two to three times a week, at the same time of day. For instructions on how to meditate, see page 78.

13

THE VISIONARY'S WAY

The Visionary is one of the two **sleek** genetic types. As a Visionary, you're a cerebral, abstract, dreamy person who often "lives in your head." You are generally more of an idea person than a people person and may be introverted. Working with ideas, concepts, or principles is more natural for you than having to work with people. Visionaries are often scientists, entrepreneurs, poets, artists, and musicians. You have a tendency to become too analytical and detached, or reclusive, ignoring those around you and sometimes even ignoring your own needs.

Your anatomical type can be either ectomorph or endomorph, from the ectodermal or endodermal embryonic layers. If your type is ectomorph, the main focus of your body tissue is in the skin and nervous system. Since you are naturally lean, you don't need as much cardio-oriented body motion as the other types. On the other hand, if you are the endomorphic type of Visionary, you have a preponderance of body tissue related to assimilation and digestion. Of all the genetic types you have the hardest time building muscles and maintaining muscle tone, so you must concentrate on strength exercises.

When you're in balance, you have a naturally thin, straight body usually without a lot of curves. (Many top female models are Visionaries.) You generally have small hands and feet for your body size and a youthful appearance. Your head is noticeably large, your trunk is long, and your shoulders are narrow. Your chest area may even appear sunken. When out of balance, you gain weight all over your body—even your face, hands, and feet become pudgy. You first notice excess body fat right below the navel or between the knees.

Your glandular type is pituitary, which gives you your intellectual, analytical bent. You often crave foods that stimulate your pituitary gland, especially pungent or spicy foods, dairy, and/or sweets. These foods exacerbate your tendency to live in your head and ignore your body and its needs. You will be healthiest and most in balance on an Asian-type diet that includes lots of cooked vegetables, whole grains, and protein, especially soy foods (see Key #4).

Your Ayurvedic energy type is either kapha dosha, which gives you a slow, deliberate manner and a steadiness that some of the other types lack, or vata dosha, which lends volatility and a tendency to unsteady energy levels. You are uncomfortable in cold, damp weather, and although ectodermic Visionaries don't need as much body motion as the other genetic types, it is important for you to do body motion regularly to stay in balance and combat your tendency toward sluggishness (see Keys #1 and #2).

Genetically, you are vulnerable to lactose intolerance and diseases of the upper respiratory tract, including allergies, colds, asthma, and sinusitis. You can forestall these problems by minimizing dairy foods and flour, by practicing lymph stimulation/cleansing (see Key #6), and by getting enough body motion to keep your mind and body in balance.

VISIONARY KEY #1:
Cardiovascular Conditioning (Finding the Flow)

As one of the sleek anatomical types, you have difficulty gaining and maintaining muscle strength and tone. On the other hand, because you are naturally thin and lack the pent-up nervous energy found in some of the other types, you need less cardiovascular training than the other three genetic types.

Nevertheless, cardiovascular (aerobic) training is important for the health of your heart and lungs and overall balance. You also particularly benefit from the euphoria conferred by extended zone-time flow workouts. When you work out, be sure to exercise within your target heart zone (see page 55) for maximum results.

Remember that "the flow" is the level of intensity in the target zone that generates the release of beta endorphin and enkephalins, creating that euphoric, morphinelike high that makes zone-time feel so great. This elevated state stays with you for hours afterward. Exercising in the aerobic zone, but out of the flow zone, is great, but will not promote the euphoria necessary to become physically and psychologically addicted to exercise.

Visionaries generally find the flow in a heart range of 60–75 percent of maximum.

The best aerobic activities are those in which you are on your feet, carrying your own body weight—such as walking, jogging, in-line skating, and stair-stepping—because these will increase the strength and tone of your weight-bearing muscles and help reduce the risk of osteoporosis. Activities in which you do not carry your own weight, such as swimming, pool exercise routines, and recumbent cycling, should not form the foundation of your zone-time program. If you choose to cycle, use toe clips and sit straight up. (See the list of suggested activities on pages 48 and 49.)

Although the Visionary's body motion program is less time-consuming than those for the other three types, the amount of body motion you need may still seem like a lot if you have been sedentary for a while. I know from my own experience that making body motion a part of your life is not always easy. You may face serious obstacles in the form of family and/or work demands.

That's okay—I understand. Many of my clients have voiced the same concerns. The most important first step is to simply get started. Do what you can for now, and as you become more fit, you can gradually increase the level of body motion until you are closer to the ideal for your genetic type.

When to Do Body Motion

If at all possible, do all your scheduled zone-time body motion in the morning, within a few hours of getting up. Visionaries are basically morning persons, and usually super-early risers. The old saying "Early to bed, early to rise" feels right for your type. You generally feel most alive and mentally sharpest at the start of the day, and your energy tends to decrease as the day goes on. Unlike some of the other types, you don't usually experience increased energy after the evening meal.

Because you need to keep yourself regularly fueled, it's a good idea for you to have a little bite of something before you begin your morning body motion—a piece of fruit or a bite of brown rice—something to get your system going, but nothing heavy. Be sure to have a substantial breakfast after your body motion session.

WARM-UPS AND COOLDOWNS.

Always warm up by performing your chosen activity at a slower pace for five to ten minutes. End your workout with a similar cooldown of five minutes.

Weight-Loss Tips

If you're trying to lose weight, or you want to reach the peak of leanness possible, you'll need to do a little more than the basic recommended program. This is especially important if you reach a plateau. For a Visionary, there are several ways to reach your goal:

—Stay with the flow. Confirm that you are indeed working out in the target range that produces the flow (60–75 percent of maximum heart rate).

—Do speed bursts. The best, most efficient way to achieve your ideal body shape is to add speed bursts of maximum activity to your basic body motion workout, as detailed in the program below. Pushing your heart rate beyond the aerobic zone stimulates the release of ACTH by the pituitary gland. This adrenal-stimulating growth hormone helps you build muscle and also lowers the body-fat thermostat.

—Do more than the basics. Because the Visionary's cardio program is far less demanding than that for the other genetic types, you can easily add more sessions or make each session longer. For example, add an endurance session of up to sixty minutes of zone-time body motion once a week, as detailed in the body-motion program. Or add a second workout to your zone-time schedule (for detailed instructions, see chapter sixteen).

Following is a stepped-level program that will allow you to gradually work up to the amount of body motion that your body needs.

Start at a level that is appropriate for you, and stay at each level as long as necessary. For some, that might mean staying at level one for several weeks or even months. If you have previously been sedentary and/or are recovering from any illness, this is a good start and will get your body on the road to balance. It will also give you some time to make the needed lifestyle changes that will enable you to work even more body motion into your life.

Level One

Amount of Body Motion

One session of cardiovascular zone-time activity of ten to fifteen minutes, in your target heart zone (see page 55).

I suggest pace walking as a good way to get started, because it is effective, easy, and requires no equipment other than a good pair of shoes. Whatever zone-time body motion activities you choose, be sure they are activities you like and can enjoy regularly.

When you can comfortably do one session per week of fifteen minutes at your target heart rate, you are ready to move on to level two.

Level Two

Amount of Body Motion

Two sessions per week of fifteen to twenty minutes in your target heart zone.

Speed Bursts

After you have been at this level for a week or two, it's time to add speed bursts to hasten weight loss. During one of your two regular body motion sessions, include one thirty-second burst of maximum-intensity effort.

When you can do the maximum amount of body motion suggested for this level—two sessions per week at twenty minutes per session in your target heart zone, including one thirty-second speed burst in one of the sessions—, it's time to move on to level three.

Level Three

Amount of Body Motion

Two to three sessions per week of twenty to twenty-five minutes per session in your target heart zone.

If you've reached level three, congratulations! You're much closer to your ultimate goal. If you've been doing all of one sort of activity, now might be the time to begin cross-training, throwing in another activity.

Speed Bursts

During one of your three weekly sessions, add two more thirty-second bursts of maximum-intensity effort, for a total of three bursts. Space the bursts four minutes apart, allowing your heart rate to decrease back down into the target zone before the next burst.

When you can comfortably perform three sessions of twenty-five minutes each, including three thirty-second bursts, it's time to move on to level four.

Level Four

Amount of Body Motion

Three sessions per week of twenty-five to thirty minutes each in your target training zone (including one longer session, described below).

Speed Bursts

During one of your three training sessions, add two more thirty-second bursts of maximum-intensity effort, for a total of five bursts. Space the bursts four minutes apart, allowing your heart rate to decrease back down into the target zone before the next burst.

Endurance Training

Now is the time to extend one of your three sessions for musculoskeletal stamina and cardiovascular endurance. Gradually extend one of your workouts to thirty-eight minutes.

When you can perform the maximum amount of body motion recommended for level four—three training sessions of thirty minutes each, including one longer session of thirty-eight minutes, and five maximum-effort bursts of thirty seconds each—you are ready to move on to level five.

Level Five

Amount of Body Motion

Four sessions of thirty to thirty-five minutes each, including one longer session.

Speed Bursts

During two of the four total workouts, insert five thirty-second bursts of maximum-intensity effort. Space the bursts four minutes apart, allowing your heart rate to return to your target heart zone before beginning the next burst.

Endurance Training

Extend one of the regular sessions to forty-three minutes in your target heart zone.

When you can perform the maximum activity suggested for this level—four sessions in your training zone of thirty-five minutes each, including one longer session of forty-three minutes, and five thirty-second bursts during two of your regular sessions—it is time to move on to level six.

Level Six

Amount of Body Motion

Three to four training sessions per week in your target heart zone. Two or three of the zone-time session lengths should be thirty-three to thirty-eight minutes, and one should be forty-eight minutes.

Speed Bursts

During two of the three to four total cardiovascular workouts performed each week, add one more burst for a total of six thirty-second bursts of maximum-intensity effort twice a week. Space the bursts four minutes apart, allowing your heart rate to return to the target zone before beginning the next burst.

Endurance Training

One of the three to four zone-time sessions should last forty-eight minutes, which is about 20 percent longer than the average workout.

Congratulations! You have reached the top level of cardiovascular exercise recommended for Visionaries. Now that you can perform this level of body motion, you are feeling and looking better, have more steady energy, and feel calmer and more centered in your life.

I realize that this basic program may seem like a lot of body motion, because it is—by modern standards. But this is the amount that will balance your body and keep you feeling and looking at your best and healthiest. Right now you may be wondering if you can ever do this much exercise. But you can, and your genes are programmed to thrive on this amount.

Following is a summary chart so you can follow your zone-time cardio program step by step.

VISIONARY-TYPE CARDIOVASCULAR CONDITIONING

Level Number	Total Number of Zone-Time Sessions per Week (Including Endurance Session)	Total Number of Zone-Time Minutes per Session	Total Number of Speed-Burst Sessions per Week and Number of Bursts per Session	Endurance Session
One	1	10–15	None	None
Two	2	15–20	1 session 2 bursts	None
Three	2–3	20–25	1 session 3 bursts	None
Four	3	25–30	1 session 5 bursts	1 session 38 minutes
Five	4	30–35	2 sessions 5 bursts	1 session 43 minutes
Six	3–4	33–38	2 sessions 6 bursts	1 session 48 minutes

VISIONARY KEY #2:
Strength Training

As a sleek Visionary, you have a harder time than the strong types in gaining and maintaining muscle mass. To improve your posture, build lean body mass, and maintain bone density, you need strength training. This will probably be the most challenging part of your body motion regimen.

In addition to strengthening your musculoskeletal system, a complete strength-training regimen will also help to increase lymphatic system flow, which tends to be sluggish in Visionaries. The lymph system has no pumping mechanism as does the circulatory system, so it is largely dependent on major muscle contractions to move the lymph fluid along. (For more on the lymphatic system in Visionaries, see Key #6 and chapter eight.)

Please read through the section on progressive-resistance training in chapter six. Using free weights, stretch bands, or weight machines, perform two to three sets of fifteen repetitions for each major muscle group. Use a weight or resistance amount for each group that is heavy enough so that you feel a slight muscle burn at twelve to fifteen repetitions.

In addition to strength work on your major muscle groups, also work your hands, feet, wrists, ankles, and neck. (See exercises in chapter six.)

In place of one or two of your weight-training sessions, you might substitute whole-body exercises, such as calisthenics, toning, body sculpting, or Ashtanga-type yoga. These are also excellent for stimulating lymphatic flow.

VISIONARY KEY #3:
Flexibility

Although Visionaries tend to be more flexible than the strong body types, your joints can stiffen through lack of use and aging, so a flexibility program can help maintain the resilience of your joints.

The best way for all types to limber up is to do static stretches (stretches where you hold the stretch but don't bounce) on each major muscle group for fifteen to thirty counts. Perform these stretches three to four times a week in the evening, to increase energy and unwind. Yoga is excellent for your type, as is tai chi or any other slow stretching routine.

Remember that just as a Warrior is unlikely to achieve the sleek, lean look you have naturally when you are in balance, so you probably won't achieve the pumped-up, buff look of a weight lifter. You can, however, greatly increase your strength and muscle tone, which will help your body to be the best it can be, genetically.

EXAMPLE OF AN IDEAL EXERCISE WEEK FOR A VISIONARY

Monday: A.M.—cardio-style weight train, stretch/yoga. P.M.—
massage.
Tuesday: stretch/yoga.
Wednesday: A.M.—cardio-style weight train, stretch/yoga.
P.M.—massage.
Thursday: stretch/yoga.
Friday: A.M.—cardio-style weight train, stretch/yoga. P.M.—
massage.

Saturday: A.M.—cycle 45 minutes. P.M.—massage.
Sunday: A.M.—rest, relax. P.M.—massage.

VISIONARY KEY #4:
Nutrition

Your basic nutrition theme as a Visionary focuses on proteins, whole grains, and cooked vegetables. The closer you adhere to the basic theme required by your genetic programming, the more balanced and healthy you will be.

To remember the foods you need to minimize, use the acronym FAD: F = Flour, A = All sweets, D = Dairy.

Your best foods are soy proteins and vegetables. Unlike the stronger types, you can eat a lot of protein, but be careful to limit the saturated fats in your diet. Your digestive system will do best with warm foods and cooked vegetables. You do not do well with dairy products, which are likely to upset your stomach, and sweet foods, which disturb your energy balance.

Your main dietary challenge is your craving for dairy foods and sweets. Overindulgence in these foods throws your system out of balance, increasing cravings. To stop the vicious cycle, limit your intake of these foods.

When to Eat

Because your energy is highest in the midmorning, you are the type that needs a good, solid breakfast. You also need to eat regularly, throughout the day. Visionaries can sometimes become so absorbed in intellectual pursuits that they forget to eat. Avoid skipping meals, and eat your lightest meal in the evening.

The table on page 160 lists three groups of foods. These are your **plenty** foods, those you can basically eat as many of as you like, within reason (unless otherwise noted); your **moderation** foods, those that you may have from time to time; and your **seldom** foods, those foods that you should eat very rarely. Most of the foods in this latter category are those that overstimulate your dominant pituitary gland and cause you to become physically and mentally out of balance.

VISIONARY FOOD CHOICES

Plenty Foods
—veggies—all types including
>   leafy vegetables, squash, cruciferous vegetables such as
>   brussels sprouts and broccoli, all sea vegetables
>   starchy vegetables, including roots, potatoes, yams,
>   carrots, onions, turnips, parsnips, rutabagas, beets
>   legumes, including lentils, chickpeas, lima and butter
>   beans, peas, black-eyed peas, soybeans, hard and
>   soft tofu
>   other beans, including black, pinto, navy, kidney, white,
>   wax, and pole

—grains—whole only, including
>   oats, corn, rice, wheat, millet, barley, rye

—proteins
>   extra-lean proteins, including white and pink fish, eggs,
>   and skinless poultry
>   medium-fat proteins, including exotic meats such as
>   elk, emu, venison, and ostrich; and free-range
>   beef and pork

—all spices

Moderation Foods
—monounsaturated fats—2 tbs per day
>   olive oil and olives
>   canola oil
>   avocado
>   almonds, peanuts, and cashews (note: nuts should be
>   limited if you need to lose weight)

—all fruits
>   tropical and citrus—½ cup per day
>   melons and berries—½ cup per day

—higher-fat proteins—8 oz per week
>   lamb, pork, beef, organ meats, deli meats

Seldom Foods
—all refined carbohydrates—sugars, juices, sodas, chocolate,
  honey, jelly, syrup, flour, breads, muffins, bagels,
  pasta, cereal, pretzels, waffles, pancakes, croissants,
  pastries, noodles, popcorn, alcohol
—hydrogenated and saturated fats
  anything deep fried
  anything hermetically sealed or wrapped in plastic
—all dairy foods—milk, cheese, yogurt, goat's cheese,
  cream, cream cheese, butter, ice cream, milk chocolate

Supplements
—vitamins and minerals
  multiple vitamin/mineral formula—1 × day
  B complex with extra magnesium and manganese*
  selenium—200 mg with lunch
  E—400 IU at lunch
  C—1,000 mg, 2 × day
  women: calcium citrate—500–1,250 mg per day, split
    between morning and dinner; after menopause
    increase to 1,250–1,500 mg
—L-glutamine—300 mg 2 hours after lunch

*Note to women: Do not take iron after menopause.

To put your new way of eating into practice, use the following guidelines to plan your day's intake of fuel. More-specific menu plans and recipes follow.

Ideal sample day's intake:

HEARTY BREAKFAST (main meal of day): egg(s), grains, veggies, light
  protein
MEDIUM-SIZED LUNCH: veggies with oil and vinegar, any white flesh,
  brown rice
LIGHT DINNER: veggies, light protein, any monounsaturated fat,
  brown rice

VISIONARY MENUS FOR ONE WEEK**
(Recipes for starred items are in appendix A, pages 203–226)

Day 1

    BREAKFAST—soy milk and whole-grain cereal

    LUNCH—Chicken Stir-Fry*

    DINNER—spiced eggplant with Mango Chutney* and
       Quinoa Pilaf*

Day 2

    BREAKFAST—soy milk and rice porridge

    LUNCH—mixed green salad, Chicken Curry*

    DINNER—Janice's Sea Bass,* roasted winter squash, green
       beans and broccoli

Day 3

    BREAKFAST—scrambled eggs and veggies

    LUNCH—tuna-salad sandwich with Spinach Fruit Salad*

    DINNER—curried lentil soup with ginger

Day 4

    BREAKFAST—whole-grain cereal with soy milk and multi-
       grain toast

    LUNCH—grilled chicken with Visionary Vegetable Soup*

    DINNER—Baked Salmon,* red potatoes, mixed vegetables

Day 5

    BREAKFAST—Spanish Egg Fritata*

    LUNCH—Turkey Burger* with salad greens

    DINNER—Artichoke Veggie Loaf* with mixed salad greens

Day 6

    BREAKFAST—scrambled tofu and vegetables

    LUNCH—Tortilla Roll-Up*

    DINNER—teriyaki beef

**Note: Visionary types generally do not snack, but mixed nuts (almonds, cashews, macadamia, peanuts, soy nuts) are good when necessary.

Day 7

    BREAKFAST—omelette of greens and herbs
    LUNCH—Taco Salad*
    DINNER—Chicken Curry*

VISIONARY KEY #5:
Staying Focused

Even though the foods recommended in this plan are the ones that you are genetically programmed to eat, and the exercise is the kind your body truly needs, it may not be easy changing your habits all at once. Your cravings for less healthful foods may persist for a while. You may find it difficult to make zone-time body motion a part of your life. The following tips will help you to maintain your focus and motivation, even when the going gets tough.

Craving Controls

Old habits die hard. If your body is used to eating chocolate or ice cream occasionally, it won't give them up without protest. The following tips will make it far easier to stick with your new eating plan.

—Minimize carbos in the morning. This is not as difficult as it may sound, because you can eat extra protein to keep your appetite under control.

—Always have breakfast. This is especially important for Visionaries, who tend to skip meals.

—Minimize caffeine. If you need a pick-me-up, try green tea, which has much less potent caffeine and also contains a number of healthful phytochemicals.

—Eat as many of your veggies cooked as possible.

—Don't skip meals.

Herbal Helps

The following herbal remedies will help control food cravings and balance your glandular secretions, helping you to get that "feeling" and stay on track:

Kelp—150-mg tablets, 1 at each meal.

Ginger tea—1 cup in the evening, for relaxation and to aid digestion.

Flaxseeds—1 tbs in the evening with your dinner.

Panax ginseng or ginseng tea.

Gotu kola or Saint-John's-wort, as per instructions on the label.

Wild yam or DHEA, as per instructions on the label.

Conceptualize Your Progress

Visionaries love to intellectualize things, sometimes to their detriment. But you can also turn your cerebral bent into an ally in your quest for a healthier self. When Nichole, a twenty-nine-year-old studio musician from New York, came to the spa, she was seriously emaciated. By following the Visionary eating and body-motion program, she has regained a healthy amount of weight, but it hasn't always been easy.

"To stay on track I made a collage," she told me. "I found some pictures of myself looking gaunt and sickly. I put them on an image board that I take out and look at a few times a week to remind myself to eat. If I feel myself slipping back into my old habits, I close my eyes and visualize how I looked and felt before I started taking good care of myself." (For instructions on making a motivational collage, see chapter fourteen.)

Working Body Motion into Your Busy Lifestyle

As a Visionary, you have an easier program than the other genetic types when it comes to cardiovascular body motion, although the amount may seem like a lot to you right now if you have been sedentary for a while.

—Fit body motion into your world. When Nichole, whom I described above, came to the spa, she was underweight and low in energy. Just looking at her poor posture you could tell that she had little confidence in her physicality.

I convinced Nichole that adding body motion to her day would actually give her more energy rather than draining the little bit she had. After only a few weeks on the program, Nichole was vastly improved and is now hooked on the zone-time high.

"I feel so much better now!" she told me recently. "I do very intense work from six to eleven in the morning, and when I'm through, I'm usually exhausted. But when work's over, I have a snack and then take what I think of as a mind-refresher break. That's when I do my body motion. I'm so goal-oriented in my work that I try not to have goals when I work out. I just take my headset and listen to music or daydream as I walk/jog for half an hour or so."

Nichole prefers to do her strength-training and lymphatic stimulation right after the zone-time workout, when her heart rate is still up. She memorized an at-home weight-training routine using dumbbells, which she does twice a week. "Since I memorized it, all I have to do is come in and go through it without really thinking about it," she told me. "I also do yoga once a week, to stay centered. When I look back on it now, I can hardly believe I'm spending so much time exercising. But once I experienced the benefits, I realized it had to be a priority in my schedule."

—Make it convenient. Another Visionary client, Nancy, a sixty-one-year-old lawyer in Chicago, fought for years to lose ten pounds. Once she began regular zone-time body motion, she lost the extra weight. "I never exercised before because it seemed too inconvenient," she told me. "But I felt my health was slowly sliding downhill. I decided to give your program a try."

Nancy bought a stationary recumbent cycle with a reading rack and took it home. Now two or three times a week she gets her zone-time body motion in while doing professional paperwork or reading. "I also do power yoga," Nancy told me. "That's the only inconvenience—and I love it so much I don't mind going out a couple of times a week for class."

For more tips on working body motion into your life, see chapter fourteen.

When You Have Trouble Making Yourself Exercise

As a Visionary, you need plenty of time to yourself. Make your body-motion period a time to be alone. Enjoy the "loneliness of the long-distance runner," go for a solitary walk in the woods, or find a quiet, secluded mountain trail.

Dealing with Plateaus

Everyone who's ever tried to lose weight has experienced plateaus, those annoying times when your fat thermostat seems to get stuck, and no matter what you do you can't lose another ounce. These periods are caused by the body's having decided that you are at the correct weight for your current activity level and fuel mix, and it will do everything in its power to keep you there.

If you continue to follow the correct eating and body-motion plan for your type, the plateau will eventually give way to more weight loss. But to kick it into high gear and quickly break through, try doing more body motion than the basic program—either working out more days or adding more bursts. (For more plateau-busting ideas, see chapter sixteen.)

VISIONARY KEY #6:
Energy-Balancing Principles

Do Yogic Breathing

All types of yogic breathing can be beneficial for Visionaries, but I especially recommend the Energy-Boosting Power Stretch routine. For details, see pages 80 and 81.

Defend Your Solitude

Make sure that you take some time—every day, if possible—to be by yourself to ponder and think. More than the other types, Visionaries need time alone to think things through.

Lymph Self-Massage

One of the main functions of the lymphatic system is to cleanse the body of toxins by filtering them through the lymph glands. These toxins are largely the by-products of metabolism. Metabolism consists primarily of ingestion, digestion, absorption, and elimination. The latter part is somewhat analogous to cleaning up a dirty kitchen once the food has been cooked, served, and eaten.

In Visionaries, this elimination or cleanup phase is sometimes sluggish. The lymph fluid that surrounds our cells is supposed to pick up the debris of cellular metabolism and carry it to the filtration sites, but in Visionaries, this process can sometimes have trouble keeping up with the rest of the metabolism. So the next time you need to take in food, it's almost like going into a kitchen where the mess from the last meal is still being cleaned up. It makes metabolism less efficient.

To keep the body better cleansed, and also to help decrease puffiness and sluggishness, enhance the lymphatic system through any type of body motion. As the muscles move, lymph fluid is forced to flow.

In addition, Visionaries greatly benefit from a daily self-massage to get their normally sluggish lymph system flowing. (For instructions on lymphatic self-massage, see page 79).

PART FOUR

Helpful Hints from the Real World

14

BREAKING THE SETBACK CYCLE AND OTHER WAYS TO STAY ON TRACK

Why do some people begin a diet and exercise program and then, just when things are starting to work, stop doing it? Why do others manage to eat and exercise right for years? Nobody knows all the answers, but in this chapter I'll offer you some strategies that will maximize your chances of continuing the Body Code diet and body-motion plan that is optimal for your genetic type.

The Pain and Pleasure Principle; the Carrot and the Stick

It's common wisdom that people will do things for a positive benefit— that is, by focusing on all the pleasures and positive feelings something will give them. And, in fact, many people do adopt a set of strategies or follow a specific diet or exercise plan that will move them toward a favorable outcome. So offering a "carrot" can certainly be beneficial. But the *opposite* approach is more likely to work for some of us.

Eighteen years ago I asked the late, great Earl Nightengale, "Why do people pay money and take time to go to a wellness retreat to learn how to be well, and then either quit the program after a short time or not follow it at all?"

He looked at me seriously and said, "Jay, I'm going to tell you a secret. If you'll remember it, it will change your life. It applies to money or success or exercise or diet or any other human endeavor. The secret is that people are concerned with good health or money or whatever *to the extent that they don't have it.*"

I've thought about those words many times through the years, and I've come to believe that they are surprisingly true. Let me give you an example. The number one cause of death in America is heart disease. Some version of this disease will kill most of us between the ages of sixty and eighty. It is appropriately nicknamed the Silent Killer because in most cases you can't feel it coming, you don't have any noticeable symptoms, until suddenly there it is. You have a heart attack.

Most people don't think much about possible heart disease because, even though they may be genetically susceptible, they aren't feeling it. It isn't impacting their lives in any way. But take a man who's been having some pain in his chest and finally goes to the cardiologist. The doctor says, "You've got three years to live if you don't do something about your heart disease." Now, all of a sudden that man has big-time motivation! He *has to* do something about the way he's been living his life—or that life will be over prematurely. And for many of us, that type of pain-preventing motivation is what's needed to start on a healthier way of living.

This is not to say that you have to be diagnosed with a potentially fatal disease in order to stick with a diet and exercise program. But when you think about it, the reason that most people do what they do, especially when it comes to making life-altering changes, is because the cost of doing what they have been doing has become too great. The poor-health-related pain they are suffering, whether psychic or physical, has grown to the point that they're willing to take steps to move away from that pain. They get to the point where they say, "I must," or, "I have to make some changes."

In my own case, I remember when I was a sophomore in college and weighed 242 pounds. One day after school I walked past my twelve-year-old brother's bedroom. He had one of his friends in there, and I overheard the friend say, "What's the matter with your brother? Why is he so fat?" And I heard my brother answer, "We don't know what it is. He has something medical wrong with him that causes it."

I could hardly believe my ears. Here was my little brother making up a story about why I was so fat. The pain of that remark stabbed right through me. Not long after that, I was Christmas shopping for my girlfriend when I happened to glance into a store window on the other side of the street. I saw someone who looked like the Goodyear blimp, just a grotesquely obese man. Then it hit me just after the reflection disappeared: that was me. I had to back up and look again to make sure it was really me. I was flabbergasted!

Being across the street had changed my perspective so that I could see the "big" picture. I was a big, obese mess. I was so fat I was embarrassing my family. I hadn't realized till that point how far out of control I had become. It's like with a drug addict or alcoholic—you get to a place where you hit bottom, and the pain you experience is bad enough that you know you have to do something to move away from that pain. In my case it led to my seeing a doctor, who told me I had only ten years to live if I didn't shape up, and so I began my recovery.

Maybe you can identify with what caused me to change my behavior. Perhaps you've had some experience in life where you chose to change a behavior because of the mounting pain. But moving away from pain is only the beginning, and it can lead to a complete, permanent change in behavior. But often that change is only temporary. Sometimes the move in a positive direction becomes short-circuited, and the old, destructive, pain-causing behaviors are revived.

I call this sort of regression the setback cycle, where we slip back into those old familiar ways. To see how it works, examine the following diagram:

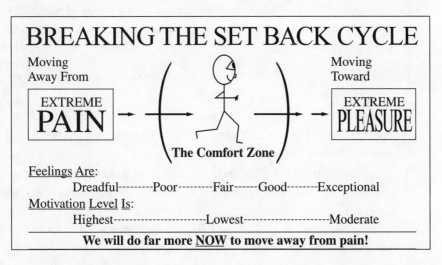

BREAKING THE SET BACK CYCLE

Moving Away From

EXTREME PAIN

The Comfort Zone

Moving Toward

EXTREME PLEASURE

Feelings <u>Are</u>:
Dreadful--------Poor---------Fair------Good-------Exceptional

Motivation <u>Level</u> <u>Is</u>:
Highest----------------------Lowest---------------------Moderate

We will do far more <u>NOW</u> to move away from pain!

As you can see by the diagram, your motivation for change is highest when you are in extreme pain. That is the time when you realize, "I have to do something about this." You have decided to change your habits. Deciding is half the battle.

But as you move from extreme pain toward the comfort zone, where you have not yet reached your goals but are feeling much better, your motivation diminishes. In fact, *your motivation to continue your new behavior is at its lowest level when your feelings are neutral.* At this time, many people falter or stop. They have forgotten the feelings of pain.

It seems that once we are in the comfort zone, we forget what it was like to be so miserable. Thus, the nicotine addict forgets what his lungs felt like; the alcoholic forgets that he lost his family and was lying in the gutter; the overweight person forgets the discomfort and embarrassment of being fat. This cycle can continue throughout life, from pain to the comfort zone and back to pain again, unless we do something to break the cycle. And to break it, what we need is not more knowledge, but an effective reminder of the things that we already know.

We need *effective* reminders of reasons to continue the beneficial behavior. These reminders can bring back the pain memories or they can be positive reminders of the way the future will be if we continue to fol-low our health-promoting lifestyle. Either way, the goal is to stay focused and keep our feelings *out* of the comfort zone.

Below are some suggestions on ways to continue to follow the Body Code wellness plan without slipping into the setback cycle.

- *Construct an effective collage that will bring back feelings of pain.* (To be *effective*, the reminders in this collage must generate strong feelings in you.)

  1. Think back through your life and recall three to six specific mem-ories that cause you to feel pain.

  2. Project into the future now, and picture how you will look, move, act, and feel if you don't change some of your habits now. See yourself in two years and in ten years.

  3. Visualize your family of origin. Are you built similarly to someone in your gene pool? Do you have a preview of coming attractions by observing your parents, grandparents, aunts, or uncles? Have they taken good care of themselves? From your gene pool, which dis-eases or susceptibilities are you likely to face?

  4. Cut out graphic pictures from magazines of people with these ail-ments.

  5. Find photos of yourself at your worst, and magazine pictures of how you will look if you don't change. Create an "Extreme Pain Collage" of these pictures that cause painful feelings in you. The pictures, symbols, and/or words on your collage must cause you to think or say, *"I must change now!"*

• *Construct an effective collage that causes feelings of pleasure.*

1. Project into the future again, and this time picture how you will look, move, feel, and act if you *do* change now. See yourself in two years, in ten years. Now you are quite a picture of health, aren't you?

2. Go through magazines and find six pictures of body types like yours in the fit, trim version. Cut the pictures out, decapitate them, and paste your own neck and head onto the bodies. Attach these pictures with any motivational symbols, sayings, goals, or events that you have upcoming onto your "Extreme Pleasure Collage" to create a moving and motivating concept of the future you. Remember that if the pictures and other visuals you use do not cause genuinely strong feelings in you, this exercise will not work.

• *Use both collages systematically to keep your feelings out of the comfort zone.*

Set aside some personal time every day or two to look at your collages long enough to rekindle the feelings they evoke in you. Force yourself to remember and reexperience the discomfort and pain you felt before you began the Body Code plan. Then look at the positive collage and picture yourself a few months from now, healthy, energetic, and at your physical and mental best.

One of my clients who lives alone brings out her collages at dinnertime. She tells me that looking at them not only keeps her on track in general, it is an effective way to avoid overeating . . . every day!

Once you understand the concept of the pain/pleasure setback cycle, you can do many creative things to keep your feelings out of the comfort zone. Another client, a sixty-one-year-old Visionary, made a monetary agreement with several other people who are committed to losing weight. Each month, each member of the group places $100 in a kitty. (The administrator, the person in charge of the kitty, changes each month.) At the end of the month, everyone in the group gets on a scale in front of the administrator. Those who have lost weight divvy up all the money in the kitty. Those who have gained weight lose their $100.

It's important in this sort of arrangement to keep the dues small enough to be fun—but high enough to be painfully motivational. The amount of money should be great enough that its loss hurts—anything from $20 a month to $100 a week, depending on your income level. Also, participants are allowed to quit only when they have lost weight in the most recent month.

Staying in the Flow

One of the most effective ways for anyone to stay motivated is to regularly get in the "flow," the state of euphoria caused by exercising in the aerobic zone long enough to cause the release of pleasure-giving brain chemicals. Once you have regularly experienced the euphoric, centered, and calm feelings of the flow, your body and mind will crave it. The feeling of flow will become something that you really do physically and psychologically feel that you need to have. It isn't something that only happens to a secret few—it will happen to you too.

In my experience, the major reason people give up on a body motion program, or fail to sustain one, is that either they fail to work out within their target heart range and thus never find the flow (this is most common with Communicators and Visionaries), or they don't stay in the flow long enough to become psychologically addicted (more common with Warriors and Nurturers).

Whatever your type, your primary fitness goal is to work out often enough and long enough to find the flow regularly. Once you do that, you will become "addicted" to body motion and find it easier to continue. Until you reach that level, however, remember the following principles, slightly different for each genetic type:

Communicators need to keep their minds occupied. This is why I recommend listening to headphones, working out with someone you can talk to, or doing zone-time body motion on machines in front of a television set or while reading a book.

Warriors, on the other hand, are task-oriented. They do best if they exercise with a purpose—whether training for an upcoming race or fun run, training to climb a mountain, or preparing to complete a weeklong bicycle excursion. Since Warriors hate to waste time, they can also benefit by working out on a treadmill or stationary cycle with a book rack, so they can do work-related things while getting zone-time body motion.

For **Visionaries,** the problem is just the opposite. Visionaries need to be in a place where they can let their minds go and wander, ponder, and sort through things. Cycling and running are especially good for Visionaries, because they allow detachment, letting the body operate on automatic pilot while the brain is elsewhere.

Nurturers need to get their body motion as much as possible in a social context. Most Nurturers do well exercising where other people are involved, such as exercise or dance classes, or simply working out with a group of friends. When forced to do solitary workouts, Nurturers have a harder time. It is much easier for a Nurturer to continue exercising when she has a sense of connectedness and belonging.

Avoiding Temptation

I'm sometimes asked by clients how to strengthen their willpower in food choices. I've come to believe through the years that the easiest answer is simply to minimize temptations. Don't keep snack foods in your home. If they're not there, you won't be visually reminded as often and will hence be less tempted to eat them. Research has proven this is true.

Marilyn, the businesswoman and young mother I mentioned in chapter ten, told me that she keeps her home "pure." "I only keep basic food," she said. "I simply won't buy or bring junk into my home. I'm raising my children with the idea that fruit and veggies are the power snacks to have."

Marilyn is extremely busy, so she buys plates of salads, veggies, and fruits prepared for her at the local grocery. A less expensive alternative is to buy prewashed and precut veggies and fruits at a salad bar. Most supermarkets now offer prewashed salads and bags of healthy treats.

Prioritize Your Time and Money

Many people have said to me, "I'd love to start exercising, but I just don't have the time."

After twenty years and thousands of clients, that excuse just cracks me up. As I like to tell my clients, all modern presidents of the United States from Jimmy Carter on have found time to exercise systematically. Who could possibly have a busier schedule than the U.S. president? So I think that when you claim you don't have time, it's more a matter that you aren't choosing to take the time to do what you need to stay well.

Learn to prioritize your time. The best strategy is to get up an hour early and do your zone-time body motion then. Simply get up and out the door before you have a chance to talk yourself out of it. If you absolutely, positively can't get your body motion in first thing in the morning, then *make* an extended lunchtime at work. Or stop off at the gym on the way home from work. The important thing is to set aside a definite, scheduled time, as a commitment to yourself, and keep that commitment no matter what.

If your excuse is bad weather, then join a health club or buy an exercise machine—a treadmill, a NordicTrack, or a rowing machine. Wait—I can just hear the excuse: "An exercise machine is too expensive!" This is simply another excuse. How much do you spend on your yearly vacation? How much did you spend on your home entertainment system, or your computer? How about the yearly cost of sodas and snack foods? It's really easy to spend $2,000 or $3,000 on any of these items, yet many of us regard the purchase of a $1500 treadmill as something we can't afford.

If you can choose to vacation, you can really afford to buy an exercise machine. The vacation will be over with in a week or two, but the benefits of the treadmill will last for the rest of your life.

Group Dynamics and the No-Excuses Contract

I've emphasized the importance of social interaction for Nurturers. Some aspects of involving others can work for all genetic types, including the solitary-inclined Visionary. Several of these strategies are detailed in chapter eleven (see pages 126 and 128). Other group-oriented approaches:

—Involve the workplace. One of my clients, a Communicator, approached the company owners of the large firm where she works and asked them if she could organize a contribution pool to which workers would donate money until they had enough to buy a treadmill, a Lifecycle, and a multiworkout station. The company owners were so impressed with the idea that they contributed a workout room, fans, a TV, and storage areas.

The plan was so successful that the company allows those who have good work attendance to take three hours a week of paid time to exercise.

—Hire a chef. This is not as extravagant as it sounds. The same Communicator, Susan, got together with some other women in her company to hire a person who three times a week brings in low-fat, healthy food choices for each genetic type. "We found her on the bulletin board at the local health-food store," Susan told me. "It's great for her, because she's been able to make this into a part-time job. And it's great for us, because it doesn't really cost more than going to a restaurant, but the food she provides is much tastier and healthier."

—Sign a "no-excuses contract." This is another variant on the buddy system, in which you and one or more friends agree to meet for zone-time body-motion sessions, *no matter what*. The only excuse allowed is a certifiable life-and-death emergency, or real illness—if you're running a fever, for example. (See appendix B.)

—Start a recipe exchange. A number of my clients have tried this. Put a note up on the bulletin board in your condo, fitness center, or YMCA that there will be a healthy-foods get-together. The guidelines are that each participant prepares and brings a low-fat recipe of his or her choice, so that everyone who attends the get-together has a sample. Each participant also brings copies of the recipe.

A fifty-five-year-old Nurturer client told me this idea was a great success at her fitness center. "We've had literally a hundred recipes at a time," she told me. "There were soups, entrées, snacks, desserts, baked goods, plenty of delicious things that aren't in cookbooks."

—Dine out wisely. For many of us, the greatest temptations come when dining out. Not only are restaurants likely to offer delicious-sounding foods that are wrong for your body type, restaurant meals are often gigantic, tempting you to overeat.

Dining out is much less of a problem if you plan. Know where you're going and what the food choices are. Once you understand the basic theme for your genetic-type diet, it is usually possible to find something to eat at most places. If you're a Warrior, order a vegetarian special or a plate of pasta. If you're a Nurturer, have a fruit salad and half a sandwich. Communicators and Visionaries can always find grilled meat or fish and vegetables. Never be afraid to ask for something that's not on the menu; most places will accommodate you.

"Never look at a menu." That advice comes from Shana, the Nurturer nurse I've already told you about. "The best way to deal with all those choices is to ignore them," she explained. "When I go to a restaurant, I order a fruit bowl for an appetizer. Then I have a house salad with dressing on the side, a baked potato, and stir-fried or steamed veggies. Almost every place can make those, they're on my diet, and they're delicious."

As for those huge portions, the best way to deal with them is to think of that heaping plate as a two-for-one deal and take half home for another meal. Or share a meal with a friend.

Airline meals, like meals in restaurants, are usually somewhat less than healthful for any of the genetic types. For the strong types, I recommend pre-ordering a vegetarian meal, which is likely to be better tasting and healthier than the standard fare. Communicators and Visionaries are usually better off bringing a "survival kit" of foods to eat while aloft, including, for Communicators, small cans of water-packed tuna, boiled eggs, and string cheese, and for both types packages of nuts.

Involve the Family

One of the main reasons people fail to follow through on a food and body-motion plan is that they let the demands of family life, with its pressures and temptations, sabotage them. You can avoid this trap by including your family in your new way of eating. They may not all have the same genetic type as you, but everyone in your family can benefit from eating more whole, pure foods.

When you look at the Western diet in general, we've given up real, whole, natural, unrefined foods in favor of packaged, processed, refined foods containing additives and preservatives. In your own family, the best thing you can do for those you love is to move back toward basic foods. Buy fruits, vegetables, whole grains, and nuts. When you eat flesh foods, buy them from health-food stores, where you can be assured that they are free of antibiotics and hormones. Most of us can benefit by cutting down on the amount of fat and animal protein in our diets, anyway.

Organize family meals around salads, soups, stir-fries, casseroles, and shish kebabs. Try grilling exotic vegetables. These fundamental foods are good for all genetic types. Keep plates of fresh-cut veggies, berries, and melons in the refrigerator for quick snacks. The hurry-up pace of modern life has conditioned all of us to look for convenience, so make eating right as convenient as eating fast foods or packaged foods.

Investigate the worlds of soy, beans, and the new whole grains, such as basmati rice, millet, and amaranth. A number of products out there can be substituted for more traditional ingredients in family recipes. Spend some time in the local health-food store. Take an hour or more to see what they have. Ask questions. Read brochures. Learn about the products that are available.

Take these good, pure foods as the foundation foods for your family meals. Then, depending on individual body types, you can decide how to refine your menus. For example, make a big veggie stir-fry with a side of lean, free-range meat. The Communicators and Visionaries in the family can eat more of the meat; the Warriors and Nurturers can have a small amount of meat slivered in the stir-fry.

In my family, we do a lot of veggie and bean dishes, as well as whole-grain-pasta concoctions. My elder daughter, McCall, and I are both strong types, so we're always looking for good vegetarian dishes. We discovered that the best way to get used to whole-grain pasta is to make the switch gradually. Start out with just a little whole-grain pasta in a big pot of refined white pasta. Gradually increase the percentage of whole-grain pasta. Eventually you'll come to prefer its rich, nutty taste and chewier texture over the gluey white-flour version.

The same process can work for nearly any healthier version of foods. Whole milk, for example, tastes cloyingly rich once you have become accustomed to skim milk.

I don't recommend putting children on the genetic-type diets until they reach puberty or older. But you can start them eating fresh, wholesome foods at a young age. Until the age of eighteen months or so, follow the recommendations of your pediatrician, and let them breast-feed or drink milk. At that age they have a great need for fatty and amino acids. But after eighteen months, be very aware of supplying them with a variety of healthy foods. Have wholesome snacks available all the time, to help establish good habits.

As for body motion, lead by example and by all means encourage your children to be active, but also don't overdo it. No marathons, for example, until after puberty—or even better, sometime in the twenties, because the stress of ultra-endurance activity can damage the still-growing musculoskeletal system.

Miscellaneous Ideas

Over the years, my clients have come up with some excellent tips for sticking with the Body Code wellness plan. Read through the following, and maybe one or more ideas will be just what you need to make your journey more enjoyable and/or productive.

—Get a dog. One of my Warrior-type clients realized that she needed a reason to get out of bed in the morning and do her body motion, so she adopted a greyhound from a local rescue association. "That dog *has to be* jogged every day," she told me. "You can't just walk a dog like that. He's my built-in motivation, no matter what the weather's like."

—Reach for a sugarless sweet. Some of my Communicator and Visionary clients keep bowls of sugar-free rock candy around, for whenever they want a little taste of something sweet. The candy lasts a long time in your mouth and can take the edge off a sugar craving.

—Make a little cheese go a long way. One of my male clients, a Visionary, is the family chef, and his favorite food was always cheese. He could rattle off the names of cheeses I'd never heard of. Unfortunately, his love for fatty cheese was challenging his health. "I started experimenting with the no-fat cheeses, like hoop and ricotta," he told me. "I found out I could mix them in the blender with just a little bit of supersharp specialty cheeses and then use them in recipes just like the real thing."

—Make bread. Buy one of the new bread-making machines and make your own delicious whole-grain breads. Add nuts, veggies, spices, and seeds for added nutrition.

—Keep your gym bag packed. This tip works well for professionals who are always too busy to get body motion. I recommend keeping your gym bag loaded with everything you need for a workout, so all you have to do is grab it and stop at a health club on the way home. Or hire a personal trainer who fires you after a few no-shows. If you have a definite appointment that you pay for even if you don't show up, it's harder to make an excuse not to do it.

—Keep a record. This works especially well for task-oriented Warriors, but can also be a motivational boost for anyone beginning a body motion program. Get a pocket notebook or diary, and every day record your progress in achieving your body motion goals. Write down what you did, how it felt, and the amount of time you worked out and/or the distance you went in pace walking or swimming. Having this record to look back on at the end of a week or a month can provide the motivational boost to help you reach your ultimate goals.

—Slow down and smell the tea. To help prevent overeating, turn on a pot of hot water for herbal tea at the start of your evening meal. Time it so that ten or fifteen minutes into the meal you'll be forced to stop eating, get up, and tend to the tea and the teabags. Sometimes that little interruption is all it takes to keep you from overeating.

—No news is good news. Dr. Andrew Weil, the alternative-medicine-oriented physician, recommends going on a news fast from time to time. During that period—whether it's a day or a week—resolve not to read a newspaper or listen to the news on radio or TV. When you stop the break, the world will still be there, but you may find yourself surprisingly upbeat, calmer, and more centered.

The Six Essential Things to Do Today

As a general way to stay on track physically and psychologically, make a copy of one of the two following lists and post it someplace where you will see and think about it every day. The lists are similar—they just say the same thing in different ways. Choose the list that most resonates with your psyche.

These lists are written, effective reminders of the most important things you can do for yourself today—every day—to keep your body and mind healthy and balanced. Even if you don't achieve another thing during the day, if you manage to complete the six items on your list, you'll be well on your way to a happier and healthier lifestyle.

The Six Essential Things for Me to Do Today
(Using the acronym HEALTH)

H = Healthy-foods plan
  Think about/arrange for

E = Exercise and energize
  Think about/arrange activity

A = Attitude affects life
  Choose to seek the positive

L = List tasks
  Write down today's essentials

T = Thankful expressions to Creator
  Pray/meditate

H = Help others (service)
  Give of your time and talents

The Six Most Important Things for Me to Do Today
(Using the acronym TARGET)

T = Thank Creator
Stay plugged in to your spiritual lifeline

A = Arrange nutrition
Plan today's food choices

R = Reconfirm attitude
Choose to find the positive

G = Give of yourself
Serve your spouse, family, friends, career, community

E = Exercise and energize
Body motion gives you more

T = Think about goals
Write down the essentials: "What gets measured gets done."

Celebrate Your Uniqueness

Finally, realize that there has never been, nor will there ever be, another human exactly like you. So be willing to experiment, to find *your way* of using effective reminders to help keep your food choices wholesome and your lifestyle regenerating.

15

FINE-TUNING

Back in the section on your own genetic type, I offered you a list of recommended supplements and herbs that will help your type stay in balance. In this chapter I'll go into a little more detail, in case you would like a more specific supplement regimen.

I'll also address some of the areas that weren't covered earlier, such as what to do if you have special dietary restrictions or other problems.

If fine-tuning for you means getting those last few pounds off, you'll find helpful information in chapters fourteen and sixteen, as well as in the section on your own body type. Many of us are tempted to jump past the basics to the supplements in hope of quickening the process. But the best way to reach your goals is *first* to follow the guidelines for your genetic type, including the zone-time body motion plan.

Help! I'm a Vegetarian Communicator!

Of all the four genetic types, Communicators, with their greater need for protein, are by far the least well suited to a vegetarian diet. Visionaries too should try to include a lot of protein in their diets. With some planning, even a vegan (pure vegetarian) Communicator or Visionary can thrive on the Body Code eating plan.

The most important thing a sleek-type vegetarian can do is to become aware of the kinds of alternative protein products that are available. I listed several in chapter seven (page 73). In addition to those, a plethora of new soy products are constantly coming on the market. Besides classic silken tofu, you can often buy Chinese-style tofu, deep-fried tofu cutlets, deep-fried tofu pouches, tofu pudding, tofu burgers, grilled tofu, freeze-dried tofu, pressed (chewy) tofu, even instant powdered tofu. You can drink soy milk, eat soy cheese, even luxuriate in soy-milk ice cream. Add soy powder or soy lecithin to juice for a protein drink. Many of these products are available in regular supermarkets; for others, check out the nearest health-food store.

A number of companies now make "meat analogues," or vegetable-protein meatlike foods, ranging from vegetable "chicken" to fake bacon. Garden Burgers and Boca Burgers are among the best known of the national brands; many excellent products are out there—try several and find which ones you like.

Beans, legumes, and nuts are relatively high in protein and, when combined with grains, can approximate the complete protein found in animal foods.

For those Communicators and Visionaries who eat some animal products, such as milk (lacto-vegetarians) and eggs (lacto-ovo-vegetarians), the problem of getting sufficient protein is more easily solved. All skim dairy products are good for Communicators (but not for Visionaries), and both types can eat eggs (preferably free-range). If you're watching your weight, limit yourself to egg whites, which can be scrambled like whole eggs, or hard-boiled, cut up in a salad.

Kosher Eating on the Body Code Plan

If you eat kosher, you should have no problem following the Body Code eating plan; simply substitute soy products for either meat or dairy in menu plans that include both meat and dairy.

Food Allergies

Food sensitivities and allergies should not be a problem in the Body Code eating plan. If you are sensitive to dairy, for example, either use

Lactaid, which helps digest the milk sugars in dairy products, or substitute soy milk, rice milk, or soy cheese in recipes. If you're one of the many people with wheat intolerance, substitute other grains in sandwiches and tortillas.

In both cases, you may find it helpful to chew gingerroot as a digestive aid, or try fennel seeds or dandelion root.

With allergies in general, including seasonal hay fever, the best thing you can do to boost your immune functions is to take antioxidant supplements, including 1,000–3,000 mg of vitamin C a day, 400–800 IU of Vitamin E, 200 mcg of selenium, up to 100 mg a day of coenzyme Q-10, and up to 150,000 IU of beta-carotene. Also, increase the garlic and ginger in your diet.

Fine-Tuning Vitamin Intake

Vitamins are a sometimes controversial topic. Some say that we have no need for extra vitamins provided we eat a balanced diet. My own belief is that if you're on a calorie-restricted eating plan or reside in a metropolitan environment, you need nutritional insurance in the form of multivitamins. With all the contaminants in the environment, taking antioxidants can be greatly beneficial. Furthermore, many of the products available today offer definite benefits in curbing cravings.

My basic supplement recommendation is as follows:

1. A multiple vitamin and mineral supplement with breakfast, and 1,000–2,000 mg of additional vitamin C.

2. 400 IU of vitamin E and 200 mcg of selenium at lunch.

3. 1,000–2,000 mg of vitamin C again at the evening meal.

4. Specialty nutrients according to the label directions.

I elaborated on the above vitamin and mineral plan for each genetic type in the section for that type. For those who wish to further fine-tune their supplement intake, the following chart gives you a better idea of what to look for in choosing multiple vitamin/mineral supplements.

MULTIPLE-VITAMIN/MINERAL CHART

Nutrient	N	W	C	V
Vit A (IU)	5,000	5,000	5,000	5,000
Vit C (mg)	1,000	4,000	2,000	3,000
Vit D (IU)	400	400	400	600–800
E (IU)	400	800	400	400
K (mcg)	100	1,000	100	100
B_1 (mg)	25	25	25	25
B_2 (mg)	25	25	25	25
B_3 (mg)	50	100	50	50
B_6 (mg)	100	100	50	50
Folic acid (mcg)	400	600	400	400
B_{12} (mcg)	50	50	150	100
Pantothenic acid B_5 (mg)	20	20	20	20
Calcium citrate* (mg)	1,000	750	1,000	1,500
Chromium (mcg)	400	400	800	600
Copper (mg)	2	2	2	2
Magnesium (mg)	100	100	500	500
Manganese (mg)	2	2	10	10
Phosphorus (mg)	500	500	500	500
Selenium (mcg)	200	200	100	100
Zinc (mg)	25	25	50	50

*Note: Women need more calcium than men, and should increase intake after menopause. See individual genetic-type sections for more-exact guidelines.

Fine-Tuning Herbal Supplements

One of the best ways to promote optimum well-being is to judiciously use herbs. Most of these plants have been time-tested for generations in conventional folk medicine. The following chart offers you a list of basic herbs and some other helpful substances for specific functions. Experiment with these products and see how you feel after three months. For correct dosage, follow the label recommendations.

Purpose	Nurturer	Warrior	Communicator	Visionary
1. General tonic	Ashwaganda	Astralagus	Ginseng	Ginseng
2. Digestive adaptogen	Garlic Alfalfa	Alfalfa Garlic	Kelp Ginger	Ginger Kelp
3. Appetite control*	Garcinia cambodia Flaxseeds	Garcinia cambodia Flaxseeds	Flaxseeds Gymnemia sylvestre	Spirulina St.-John's-wort
4. Mental enhancement	Kola nut	Guarana	Gingko biloba	Ma huang
5. Specific needs	Evening-primrose oil	Milk thistle	Valerian root	St.-John's-wort DHEA
6. Best teas	Dong quai Red clover	Dandelion Parsley leaf	Skullcaps Chamomile	Mullein Licorice
7. Aroma oil**	Clove	Rose	Lavender	Eucalyptus

Note: Echinacea/goldenseal and maitake combinations make great cold remedies for all types.

*Choose only one from category 3.

**A note on scents: The highly evolved human schnoz understands a vast vocabulary of smells, about ten thousand total. The odors first dissolve in the moisture of the nasal tissues and are thereafter passed straight to the hypothalamus by a special group of olfactory cells. These olfactory cells are nerves, the only ones in the entire body directly exposed to air, though they are protected by a thin layer of mucus. These special cells replace themselves about every three weeks. That smells go straight to the hypothalamus is significant, because this tiny organ regulates several vital functions, including thirst, hunger, blood sugar levels, sleep cycles, growth, sex drive, and the basic emotions. Smells thus send immediate messages from the hypothalamus to the limbic system, which processes emotions, and on to the hippocampus, the brain area responsible for memories. This helps explain why certain smells bring back past memories so vividly, sometimes triggering déjà vu.

Essential oils—scents such as those recommended in the above chart—can have a profound positive effect on our sense of well-being. Try the scents recommended for your genetic type, and see how they make you feel.

A Glossary of Recommended Herbs

Alfalfa—see discussion in chapter seven, page 108.

Astralagus—this Chinese herb is used as an immune-system booster. It is also helpful against infections and as a general "pep-up" tonic.

Ashwaganda—sometimes called Indian ginseng, this herb is considered a restorative and general tonic.

Chamomile tea—long used in folk medicine, chamomile tea promotes relaxation before bedtime and can soothe an upset stomach.

Coenzyme Q-10—this nutrient, which is not an herb, is helpful in increasing blood flow to the heart. It is also used to fight gum infections.

Dandelion tea—this common plant is used as a natural diuretic and digestive aid. It has also tested as helpful in reducing high blood pressure.

DHEA—this substance is not an herb, but a hormone. Some researchers believe that it can help prevent many of the ailments associated with aging.

Dong quai—this Chinese herb has long been used to treat "female disorders," including cramps, PMS, and menopausal symptoms.

Evening-primrose oil—this is an excellent source of essential fatty acids and can help relieve menstrual-related problems.

Fennel seeds—fennel is used both as a cooking spice and as a digestive calmative.

Garcinia cambodia—this Ayurvedic remedy is a fruit from Southeast Asia that contains HCA (hydroxycitric acid), which helps block the conversion of glucose to fat in the liver. It is used as a weight-loss aid.

Garlic—see the discussion in chapter seven, page 75.

Ginger—see the discussion in chapter seven, page 75.

Gingko biloba—another ancient Chinese remedy, gingko helps protect cells from damage by free radicals and increases blood flow to the brain, aiding memory.

Ginseng—this ancient herb was once believed to have magical properties. It has been considered a sexual aid and an all-around general tonic. Of the two forms, *Panax* ginseng is more of a stimulant, while *Panax quinquefolius* ginseng is more of an adaptogen.

Gotu kola—the Chinese use this herb to increase longevity. Science has proven it to have anti-inflammatory and antibacterial activity. It is also believed to increase blood flow, improving concentration and memory.

Guarana—this Amazonian vine is used as a stimulant. Use it with caution, as it is higher in caffeine than coffee.

Guggul (Indian bedillium)—an herb from the Ayurvedic tradition that helps promote fat metabolism.

Gymnemia sylvestre—see discussion in chapter seven, page 75.

Hawthorn—the small, reddish fruit of this thorny tree has long been used to enhance the health of the heart. Research has shown that it does have beneficial effects on the cardiovascular system.

Kava kava—a calming herb used widely in the South Pacific.

Kelp—this seaweed, high in iodine and chlorophyll, is good for thyroid-support.

Kola nut—this tropical nut used to flavor cola drinks has long been used as a stimulant because of its caffeine. You can find kola powder and tea in many health-food stores for a quick pick-me-up.

Licorice tea—licorice root is a powerful herb that has been used for centuries for various ailments. As a tea, it calms the digestive tract.

L-phenylalanine—not an herb, but rather an amino acid, this preparation can be quite helpful in dampening appetite.

Ma huang (Chinese ephedra)—this powerful herb has long been used both as a stimulant and in the treatment of allergies, including asthma and sinus problems. Because it increases metabolism, ma huang is sometimes used in weight-loss programs. This herb should not be taken by anyone with insomnia or by pregnant women, as it can cause uterine contractions.

Milk thistle—this herb has long been used to protect against liver damage by alcohol or environmental toxins. Its active ingredient, sylimarin, is also a natural antioxidant.

Mullein—this soothing tea is not only calming when taken in the evening, it is also a tried-and-true folk remedy for respiratory congestion and coughs.

Parsley-leaf tea—a natural diuretic and breath-freshener, this herb is also used for its calming effects.

Red-clover tea—the blossoms of this common plant have long been used to treat skin and respiratory disorders, and as a general cleansing agent for the body.

Saint-John's-wort—this medicinal herb has been in the news lately as an antidepressant. It is also commonly used to soothe stomach problems and decrease appetite.

Skullcaps tea—a proven nervine (substance that produces a calmative effect) from the dried herb of this North American plant.

Spirulina—an edible alga, often taken as an immune-system booster and general tonic.

Valerian root—this herb, a nervous-system relaxant and soother, has been used for centuries to ease insomnia.

Yerba mate—a South American drink that is used both for its relaxing and energizing effects.

16

MOST COMMONLY ASKED QUESTIONS

I agree that your program sounds great. But I'm so out of shape and sluggish, I barely have enough energy to get through the day. How can I possibly start such a difficult program?

I've often had clients who considered the idea of changing to a healthier lifestyle hopeless. But I promise you it's not. I'd suggest first of all that you don't look at the ultimate goal, but just take the program for your genetic type one step at a time. Start out with ten minutes of body motion once or twice a week. Ease into your new way of eating gradually, cutting down on your old favorites bit by bit while you add the new foods in. Mixing your pastas and cereals to include some whole grain is a great way to start.

Even those small steps will effect a positive change in the way you feel, making it easier for you to gradually do more.

Is food cooked in microwave ovens safe to eat?

There is some controversy about the safety of food that's been cooked in a microwave oven. I can't say that I know all the answers. Probably, in a perfect world, it would be better to cook food in a more conventional way. But the reality is that most cooks are far too busy to spend hours in the kitchen preparing meals. I feel that the food itself is more important than the way it is prepared. As long as you are eating basically pure, wholesome, unadulterated foods, go ahead and use the microwave, especially if it makes it easier for you to use those foods.

Likewise, frozen vegetables and fruits lose some of their natural nutrients, but not all, so use them for convenience.

191

How can I get rid of cellulite?

Cellulite is a conglomeration of white fat cells. When these cells aren't completely full of fat, they are compacted into a smaller area. However, once they are full, they form pockets between strands of connective tissue, resulting in a dimpling in the surface of the skin.

To make things worse, these deposits of fat are part of a survival mechanism left over from the days when famine was a common part of life. They are intended for long-term storage. They have a relatively poor supply of blood and are the last part of your body-fat stores to be used.

The good news is that if you eat right and get the correct amount and intensity of body motion for your type, eventually these fat stores will be used, and the cellulite will noticeably diminish.

I've reached a weight-loss plateau that I just can't seem to break. I tried all the recommendations in my genetic-type section, but nothing helped. How can I get to losing again?

A weight-loss plateau is a kind of biological and metabolic accounting period. Your body is evaluating where you are and deciding whether you need to keep going in order to be as trim as you're genetically programmed to be.

Before you decide that you're really stuck, you need to check a couple of things. The first, and most important, is to make sure that you're training in your target zone for the amount of time recommended for your genetic type. I am continually surprised at the many experienced exercisers who assume they are in the flow zone but really are not. If you haven't done so already, now would be a good time to buy a Polar pulse monitor to help you keep track of your true zone-time. (For ordering information, see appendix C.)

After you've confirmed you're in the target zone for the specific amount of time for your type, then experiment within that target range. If you've been working out at 65–75 percent of your maximum heart rate, go to the 75–85 percent range two or three times a week. Or if you've been doing your zone workouts at the high end, try dropping back to the low end for a few sessions.

Another strategy that often works is to increase total training time by 10 percent.

A more difficult but often effective way to break away from a plateau is to go into "boot camp" mode. For two or three days during the week, work out a second time for twenty-five to thirty-five minutes.

Then continue with the double workout days three times a week until you begin losing weight again.

Another approach that is often successful is either to add another endurance session or to increase your regular sessions by 10–20 percent. Don't add more than two extra-long sessions, and be sure to drink plenty of water, especially if you work out more than sixty to sixty-five minutes at a time.

If all else fails, you can try what I call controlled shock therapy, the purpose of which is to keep your body from getting too comfortable where your fat thermostat is currently set. This isn't realistic for everyone and is only practical if you plan for the time. To do it, plan a long, tough body-motion excursion. Go for a fifty-mile bike ride; hike down and back up the Grand Canyon. Backpack one hundred miles in a week. Go climb a mountain. This kind of challenging activity will definitely turn down your body's fat thermostat and get you back into the losing mode.

The bottom line is that plateaus are just a metabolic accounting. If you ride it out, as long as you're doing the right amount of body motion for your type (including speed bursts), then within two to six weeks you will get through the plateau.

The three charts below summarize the steps I take when helping clients break through plateaus. One approach uses body motion, one uses foods and herbs, and one uses eclectic methods. Choose whichever approach most appeals to you and follow the steps in order. Each of the steps is explained in detail elsewhere in the book.

CHART 1 (USING BODY MOTION): PLATEAU BUSTERS/WEIGHT LOSS

1. Make sure you're getting enough zone-time exercise at the correct intensity level.
2. Increase speed-burst sessions.
3. Increase time of endurance sessions.
4. Make sure your zone-time body motion is based on "striding" (works only with Warriors and Nurturers).
5. Carry your lost weight (works only with Warriors and Nurturers).
6. Try twice-a-day workouts two or three times a week.
7. Change intensity level (up or down within the target zone).

CHART 1 (CONTINUED)

8. Add a quick stroll at noontime.
9. Add a stroll before bedtime.
10. Change your routines—shake things up.

CHART 2 (USING FOOD AND HERBS):
PLATEAU BUSTERS/WEIGHT LOSS

1. Make sure you're following the correct nutrition plan for your genetic type.
2. Make sure you're getting enough fluids.
3. Make sure you're not eating too many calories.
4. Add herbal digestive aids.
5. Add herbal adaptogens and/or thermogenics.
6. Fast once a week.

CHART 3 (USING ECLECTIC METHODS):
PLATEAU BUSTERS/WEIGHT LOSS

1. Add breath routine.
2. Add stretch/breath routine.
3. Add meditation.
4. Add aroma therapy.
5. Add touch therapy/massage.

I hate doing speed bursts. Since I'm not overweight, can I skip that part of my body motion regimen?

If you're in the right range—both in body weight and fat percentage, you don't really have to do the speed bursts. But take care that you don't become too complacent in a comfort zone. For optimal toning and conditioning, your body requires moving out of that comfort zone from time to time. If you can't bring yourself to do speed bursts, then challenge yourself regularly in other ways, by carrying a heavy pack up a steep trail, doing a long hike, or an equivalent activity.

Why do I want to eat when I'm not hungry?

This is a common problem, one that many of my clients have reported. Hunger and cravings are often caused by the body's signaling that it needs an increase in some kind of nutritional building block or micronu-trient. In other words, even though your stomach may be full, your body is still missing something that it needs.

Many of us modern Americans represent a paradox: we are overfed, yet undernourished. We fill ourselves up with dead foods and empty calo-ries that don't contain the basic nutrients that we need for cell regenera-tion. Until we give our bodies what they need, in the form of whole, nutritious foods, they will continue to send us signals of hunger and crav-ing.

Also, overstimulation of your dominant gland can cause cravings. Stop overstimulating your dominant gland with the wrong foods!

There's so much information out there on nutrition, exercise, healthy lifestyle. A lot of it is contradictory. How can I sort out the good information from the bad?

I think many of us feel confused in this information age, where we are constantly bombarded with advertisements and news stories that tell us to do this or don't do that—then turn around and say the opposite. I think the soundest way to sort through all this information is to use good old common sense.

First, think about how life used to be for your grandparents, and their grandparents. If you didn't know your grandparents, take a look at a movie set in the time when they were young, or read a book about it. Become aware of the amount of body motion that was necessary for them each day. Think about the food choices that were available to them. And then compare those body motion and food choices to the way we live today.

It's true that we have many medical miracles that weren't available to our grandparents. But it's also true that we need them more, because of the diseases, such as heart disease and many cancers, that are caused at least in part by our lifestyle. What I'm saying is that, deep inside, you already know these answers. You know what is the best thing for your body and mind. It's just a matter of repositioning your beliefs in a way that causes you to choose to make good health a priority in your life right now.

I've read that one day soon there will be a pill people can take to safely lose weight. So why should I bother to diet and exercise?

A number of drugs throughout the years have promised safe, painless weight loss, but have then turned out to have horrendous—even fatal—

side effects. Although scientists have learned a great deal in recent years about the causes of obesity and may one day find a cure, I still believe that it all boils down to a basic law of the universe, which is that each and every one of us needs a certain amount of consistent body motion in combination with pure, natural, whole foods in a balanced lifestyle to enable our bodies to heal themselves.

You may read about leptin, the hormone that stops obese mice from overeating, or Venacol, the protein that blocks the abosrption of fat, or other miracle molecules and drugs. But these discoveries are by no means the whole story. Obesity researchers now have overwhelming evidence that there are a number of types of obesity. A number of genes are involved in weight regulation. It would take an arsenal of pills to treat every different pathway to obesity, even if we were able to develop effective treatments.

I'm afraid that the bottom line is that there's no quick fix for obesity, and there's no miracle drug without a downside.

How can I tell if I'm the right size for my genetic type?

The insurance industry publishes suggested height-weight charts that supposedly tell people what they should weigh for a given height. These charts should be taken only as guidelines, however. Depending on your body type, you may need to weigh more or less than the "ideal" according to the chart. A fit, muscular Warrior will always weigh noticeably more than a more delicate but still fit Visionary of the same height.

One way to get an idea of your ideal weight is to look at pictures of people with your body type who look good to you and compare. Take an honest look at your body. If you don't have obvious excess amounts of body fat, if you feel good and have enough energy to do the things you want to do, you are probably about where you're biologically programmed to be. Don't keep trying to lose weight in an effort to starve yourself into someone you're not.

Is it all right to eat the new fake fats and no-fat snacks?

I fundamentally believe that any time we try to reach for a quick-fix solution, we're treading on dangerous ground. In the case of the "fake fats," such as Olestra, there are three main problems. In the first place, these are chemically manipulated fats that can no longer be absorbed through the intestinal wall. Unfortunately, this also makes it impossible to absorb some of the fat-soluble vitamins and minerals that are bound up with the fat. In the second place, these fake fats are usually found in "foods" that are high in refined carbohydrates, and therefore unfit for human consumption. In the third place, some people suffer flatulence, diarrhea, and other disturbances of the digestive tract when they eat these fats, though this is less of a problem for Warriors and Nurturers than for the sleek types. If you really want to try these snacks, a little bit certainly won't kill you—at least not quickly. But they are not wholesome, real foods, and you shouldn't make them a part of your fundamental diet. Partake of them sparingly, and don't stock them in your home or work environment.

The fat-free snacks currently crowding the supermarket shelves suffer from the same problem of being basically unhealthful foods. They are usually made of refined flour with sugar and/or salt and therefore provide mostly empty calories. Communicators and Visionaries should stay completely away from these foods because of their high glycemic index. Warriors and Nurturers can eat them occasionally as a hurry-up snack, but again, these are not foods that you should make part of your foundation.

Is it all right to do my body motion when I'm sick?

My own experience and that of thousands of clients has taught me that, most of the time when you're not feeling well, going ahead and doing your body motion session will usually make you feel better. If you have a cold, PMS, or you're generally out of sorts, go on and push yourself out the door for at least a token workout. Just don't overdo—make it one of your lighter days, but at least go through the motions. The one exception is if you're actually running a fever—in that case, forgo all body motion in favor of rest and give your body the necessary time and energy to heal.

Do vitamins and herbs really work?

Many research scientists agree that they do. And many of these products have been used for literally thousands of years with good results.

The newest studies say that 70 percent of Americans are turning to alternative-health-care measures. But be leery of any claims made by those trying to sell you these products. And be aware that the claims for some products are far better substantiated than for others. Be an informed consumer: read health magazines and be alert for the latest news about products you are interested in. (See the following question for more details.)

How can I stay up on what's happening in the health and fitness world?

You can't! That is, you can't stay up on all of it—there's too much going on these days. The important information that survives the scrutiny of experts is available through a number of reliable sources. If you want the basics, check out any of the many reputable magazines such as: *Shape, Women's Health, Fitness, Natural Health, Men's Health, Prevention.* Your library and the Internet are loaded with information. I especially recommend the great newsletter put out by Dr. Andrew Weil. For subscription information, call 1-800-523-3296. Finally, my own newsletter will be available in June 1999. Visit my Website at: www.JayCooper.com.

How can I get my family to eat healthy food?

Don't try to switch your diet all at once. Do it gradually, starting perhaps with leaner cuts of meat and adding a small amount of whole grains to your family's starch choices.

Numerous research studies have demonstrated that we like what we're accustomed to eating. I remember when all we had was whole milk. Then 2 percent milk was introduced, and we all hated it. We said, "No way will this stuff survive." But it did, and we got used to it. Then came 1 percent and skim milk. Now try going back to drinking whole milk again. For most of us it is too rich. We now actually prefer the lesser-fat versions.

The strange thing is that if we had tried to switch straight from whole milk to skim, most of us would not have made it. But we did it gradually, in steps. This process works for other things too. Switching gradually from white pasta to whole-wheat pasta is only one of a number of examples. As your taste buds slowly change, you'll come to prefer the leaner, cleaner types of food.

Do I have to go to a gym or fitness center to learn how to exercise?

No; many resources are available to you. Consult the resources section of this book for details. Your local library has many great books and videos available. Personal trainers will also come to your house. If cost is a factor, buddy-up to minimize the expense. Many fitness-equipment companies also offer training videos, products, and materials designed for those desiring to exercise at home.

Do I have to visit a spa to learn how to eat right and exercise?

I would be delighted to meet you if you do choose to come to Green Valley Spa, but you don't have to. Everything you need to succeed is in this book. But as you well know, the hardest part of many of the things we do is just getting started. The next hardest part is sticking with it when the going gets tough. Research shows that many of us do better if we remove ourselves from life's daily distractions by taking a jump-start approach in a retreat-style atmosphere. This not only gets us off to a great start physically, but also provides us with nutritional cleansing benefits. Experiencing a program in person also creates powerful memories of real-world people just like you who have found ways to succeed.

The spa industry has really changed. No longer are spas just pampering palaces for wealthy ladies to come to luxuriate. Today's top-destination spas offer an invigorating variety of mind/body wellness experiences. For instance, at Green Valley Spa, we offer a great range of life-changing services and experiences, from the luxuriating traditions to cutting-edge adventures. We even have a new program that teaches golf to businesswomen so they'll be able to crack the "old boys" club on the golf course. All these programs and services are offered in one of the most beautiful settings you can imagine—the heart of southern Utah's famous red-rock canyon country.

17

THE SEASONS OF OUR LIVES

In Ecclesiastes, we learn that "to every thing there is a season." I believe that our lives go through seasons also, no matter what our genetic type. Just as the seasons of the year signal predictable changes in the natural world, the seasons of our lives reflect profound changes in each of us too. Our metabolism, body shape, psychology, and spiritual focus are all influenced by biochemical changes programmed into the DNA helix.

Although the foundation of our body's genetic code remains the same from cradle to grave, many of the ways it is manifested can change.

In the first season of our lives, the spring, we are new and fresh. As children, our metabolism is revved way up to facilitate growth. We have more brown fat, a calorie-burning mechanism governed by the hypothalamus. We also burn calories just in growing. As long as we're fairly active, we can eat quite a bit and never become fat. Psychologically, we're trying to find out who we are, why we're here, and where we're going. Our energies are focused on growth and learning.

Sometime after we hit puberty, and for several decades afterward, our focus shifts. During this summer season we're more focused on the most basic drive of all—perpetuating the species. At this time we have a great deal of carnal energy and ambition.

These instinctive drives became obvious to me when I was an adult and for the first time got a dog. If you've ever raised a puppy or kitten, then seen it get pregnant and raise a litter, you'll know what I mean. Watch the maternal instincts your pet was blessed with. She didn't learn anywhere how to take care of her babies, she just instinctively knows these things.

200

Sometimes we fail to give enough recognition to how many of our human behaviors are instinctive, coded into the genes. Yet many of the specific things we do in the different seasons of our lives, we do because of those genetically coded instinctive promptings.

In addition to behavioral changes, we undergo physiological changes from season to season. By the twenties, most of our anatomical growth has stopped. We begin more easily to store excess calories as body fat. By the thirties or forties, most of us can gain weight quite easily, especially if we don't keep our activity level up. Our metabolisms are no longer as crisp and functional as they once were. Every little overindulgence, every holiday, every vacation, every illness and injury, sets us back a little bit more.

I've had clients come to me and say, "But why do I need to eat this certain way? When I was a kid, I ate anything I wanted and never gained an ounce."

The answer is that when we were kids, our bodies were more forgiving because our metabolisms were fast and growth spurts would burn up the excess energy. We could get away with eating concentrated foods. But as we age, we need to pay more attention to both the intake and the output parts of the equation. We need to establish and maintain an active lifestyle and a calculated food intake. Our food choices, in fact, become more important as we age, because our digestive systems aren't as efficient and our recuperative powers aren't as effective. We simply can't overload our systems with excesses and expect to stay well.

The optimum nutrition and body-motion program that I recommend for each genetic type is aimed primarily at men and women in the prime of life. As we get older, these lifestyle choices are just as important, but the intensity with which we pursue them may decrease as our priorities shift.

Once we reach female or male menopause, the fall season of life, there is a predictable decrease in basic biological functions. Our metabolic functions decline by about 1 percent per year in the forties and fifties. Our lung capacity goes down, and so does our capacity to perform aerobic activity.

Our food and exercise choices may need to be modified at this time too. We may develop new cravings—a woman I know who never cared for sweets suddenly developed a sweet tooth after menopause. Another woman, somewhat older, began to find meat distasteful and became a vegetarian. Both were balanced and in tune with their biological promptings.

At about this time, most of us begin to enter what I think of as the age of enlightenment. It's the time when we tend to open up spiritually, look more at the true meaning of life, come to appreciate the things that money can't buy, develop a greater appreciation for all the Lord's creations. As our physical bodies are declining, our spirits are expanding.

In the winter season, our genetic coding causes us to change again and look at things from an even more spiritual perspective. Our spiritual focus becomes clearer and we discover the pure joy and pleasure in the things money can't buy. We gravitate back to the essence of who we really are. I visualize it this way: we come into the world as huge spirits with small, wrinkled bodies curled up in a fetal position; then our bodies grow and sometimes take over the spiritual influence in us as we go through our lives doing our earthly thing; then, if we've lived to a ripe old age, we transform back to being huge spirits with small, wrinkled bodies again curled up in a fetal position.

Some of us may get lost or sidetracked in one season or another of life, but as the seasons change and our body chemistry changes, most of us are nudged toward our true spirituality.

Although we never completely lose our need for body motion, once we have reached the age of enlightenment, it is not necessary to do the same amount and intensity of activity as before. Our focus in activity will shift from trying to look trim and to feel energetic toward feeling joy from the simpler pleasures in life. Grandparents, kids, and pets all seem to have time for the small, important things.

APPENDIX A

RECIPES FROM THE GREEN VALLEY KITCHEN

by
Chef Janice Coon
Chef DeLayne Whiting
Chef Tadd M. Gunther

Items Used in Recipes

Bragg Liquid Aminos—a low-sodium, liquid soy product that can be purchased in health-food stores. Lite soy sauce may be an alternative.

Jensens Protein Seasoning—a low-sodium, dry soy seasoning developed by Bernard Jensens. It is used to make broth and add flavor. Available in health-food stores.

Cajun Dust—a dry Cajun seasoning made from all-natural herbs and spices. Available in some grocery stores around the meat department.

Jan-De's Seasoning—a seasoning created by the chefs at Green Valley Spa. The recipe is as follows:

> 2 parts Jensens protein seasoning
> 2 parts onion powder
> 1 part garlic powder
> ½ part thyme

All of the above seasonings are available from Jan-De's Cupboard, Green Valley Spa Chefs. 1-877-688-0782.

Breakfast Entrées

Cherry Sauce
(WARRIOR)

½ cup dried cherries
1 cup water
½ cup cherry juice concentrate
2 tsp cornstarch
¼ cup water

In a small sauce pan combine cherries, water, and juice. Bring to a boil and turn down to low. Simmer until cherries are reconstituted and plump. Stir cornstarch into ¼ cup of water. Pour slowly into cherry mixture, stirring constantly. Mixture will become thick and clear. Simmer an additional 5 minutes. Serve over hot cereal.

Makes 4 ¼-cup servings.

Spanish Egg Fritata
(COMMUNICATOR, VISIONARY)

½ red bell pepper
½ green bell pepper
10 medium mushrooms
¼ medium onion
4 ½ cups egg whites
½ cup Egg Beaters
¼ cup Parmesan cheese (optional)

Chop bell peppers, mushrooms, and onion into small pieces. Pour eggs in a large bowl and add chopped vegetables and cheese, then mix together. Spray a 10-inch glass pie dish with vegetable spray and pour the egg mixture in. Bake for 45 to 50 minutes at 400 degrees.

Note: Visionaries should substitute soy cheese for Parmesan.

Makes 8 servings.

Fruit and Oats
(NURTURER, WARRIOR)

1 cup of fruit mixture
½ cup uncooked oats
¾ cup nonfat plain yogurt
2 tbs frozen white-grape-juice concentrate
½ tsp vanilla

To make fruit mixture, use any three or more of the following fruits: cantaloupe, honeydew melon, blueberries, strawberries, raspberries, raisins, bananas, pears, or peaches. Cut into small pieces to equal 1 cup. Add oats and mix together. Mix yogurt with juice concentrate in a small bowl, add vanilla, and mix. Fold into fruit-and-oat mixture.

Makes 2 servings.

Crepe Shells
(COMMUNICATOR, WARRIOR)

1½ cup whole-wheat flour
½ tsp baking powder
1 tbs frozen apple-juice concentrate
2¾ cups skim milk
4 large egg whites
½ tsp vanilla

In a medium bowl, mix whole-wheat flour and baking powder. Add apple juice (may be used frozen), skim milk, egg whites, and vanilla. Mix with a whisk until smooth. Batter should be the consistency of heavy cream. Spray a 6- or 7-inch nonstick frying pan with vegetable spray and put on medium-low heat. When pan is hot, pour ¼ cup of batter in pan and quickly tilt pan around until batter fills the bottom and up the sides about ½ inch. Place pan back on burner and cook until golden brown. Use a spatula to raise one side of crepe, and with your fingers quickly turn the crepe over to cook the other side. For Communicators, fill crepe with scrambled eggs. For Warriors, fill crepes with Fruit Yogurt filling. Crepe shells keep well in the fridge for up to 4 days and make good snacks.

Makes about 16 crepe shells.

Fruit Yogurt
(NURTURER, WARRIOR)

1½ cup nonfat yogurt
1 cup fruit*
¼ cup white-grape-juice and peach-juice concentrate

Put a coffee filter or a cheesecloth into a colander and pour yogurt in. Place a bowl under the colander to catch the liquid that will drain out. Let stand overnight in the refrigerator. Pour off the liquid and put yogurt cheese in a bowl, and with a wire whisk stir in juice concentrate until smooth. Cut fruit into small pieces and add to yogurt mixture.

*Berries, bananas, pineapple, peaches, and pears are all good. You may use cherry-juice concentrate with berries. For a variety, use almonds or sunflower seeds.

Makes 2 servings.

Salads and Soups

Spinach Fruit Salad
(COMMUNICATOR, VISIONARY)

5 cups spinach
1 cup strawberries
3 kiwi fruit
1 tbs honey
6 oz pineapple juice
½ tsp ground ginger

Wash and towel dry spinach leaves. Slice strawberries, and peel and slice kiwi into circles. Mix honey with pineapple juice and ginger and pour over spinach leaves.

Garnish spinach with kiwi and strawberries. Should be used right away.

Makes 5 servings.

Jicama Orange Salad
(NURTURER, WARRIOR)

1 clove garlic
½ cup rice vinegar
½ cup water
2 large oranges
⅛ tsp orange-rind zest
⅓ cup apple-juice concentrate
1 tsp lime juice
1 pinch red-pepper flakes (omit for Nurturer body types)
2 medium jicamas
6 green leaf-lettuce leaves

Mince garlic clove and put in a shaker jar along with rice vinegar, water, the juice from one orange, orange zest, apple-juice concentrate, lime juice, and red-pepper flakes. Place in fridge for at least 4 hours or overnight. Peel and grate jicamas. Peel and cut the other orange into small pieces. Toss grated jicama and orange pieces with dressing. Serve on a lettuce leaf.

Makes 6 servings.

The Strong Types Soup
(WARRIOR, NURTURER)

1 rounded cup carrots cut into bite-sized pieces
⅔ rounded cup chopped yellow onion
3 cups water
2 tbs and 2 tsp Bragg liquid aminos
⅔ rounded cup small mushrooms, cut into quarters
1 rounded cup yellow squash, cut into bite-sized pieces

Place carrots, onion, water, and Bragg liquid aminos into a small stock pan and turn on high, bring to a boil, then reduce heat to medium. Cook for 15 minutes. Add mushrooms and yellow squash, cover, and turn off. Let stand for 5 minutes. Refrigerate unused soup for up to 4 days.

Makes 4 one-cup servings.

The Sleek Types Soup
(COMMUNICATOR, VISIONARY)

⅔ rounded cup or 1 leek, sliced
⅔ rounded cup celery, diced
3 cups water
1 tbs Jensens protein seasoning
1 rounded cup or 1 zucchini, cut into bite-sized pieces
1 rounded cup string beans, cut into 1-inch pieces

(If using fresh string beans, add them to the water with leeks and celery. If using frozen, add them with zucchini.) Bring leeks, celery, water, and protein seasoning to a boil. Reduce heat to medium and cook 15 minutes. Add zucchini and string beans and cover with a lid, turn off heat, and let stand for 5 minutes. Refrigerate unused soup for up to 4 days.

Makes 4 one-cup servings.

Mushroom Soup
(NURTURER, COMMUNICATOR, WARRIOR)

6 cups water
2½ cups sliced white mushrooms
2½ cups sliced portabella mushrooms
2 tbs Jensens protein seasoning
1 12-oz can evaporated skim milk
¼ cup cornstarch

In a 6-quart pot, add water, sliced mushrooms, and protein seasoning. Over high heat bring soup to a boil and then turn down to low and cover. Let cook for at least 45 minutes to 1 hour. Pour evaporated skim milk in a small bowl and mix in cornstarch with a wire whisk. Add cornstarch mixture and stir until soup becomes thickened.

Makes 6 servings.

Gazpacho Soup
(NURTURER, WARRIOR, COMMUNICATOR)

5 medium-sized garlic cloves
¼ cup water
1 small red onion
24 oz low-sodium tomato juice
24 oz low-sodium V-8 juice
½ cup red wine vinegar
¼ cup lime juice
1 medium cucumber
1 medium yellow or green bell pepper
1 7-inch zucchini
1 celery stalk
1 15-oz can kidney beans
¼ cup minced cilantro
   red pepper sauce to taste—omit for Nurturer

Mince garlic and put in a small saucepan along with water and red onion. Cook for 2 minutes or until slightly softened. In a large bowl pour tomato juice, V-8 juice, vinegar, and lime juice. Dice cucumber, bell pepper, zucchini, and celery, and add to juice mixture. Stir in cooked garlic mixture, beans, and cilantro. Serve cold. This will last up to 4 days in the fridge. Makes a good snack food.

Makes 8 servings.

Vegetable Soup
(COMMUNICATOR, VISIONARY)

3 lbs fresh tomatoes or 1 36-oz can diced tomatoes
3 cups water
4 bay leaves
½ cup sun-dried tomatoes
1 cup diced baby carrots
2 tbs Jensens protein seasoning
2 cups broccoli
2 lbs ground turkey breast
4 garlic cloves
4 tbs fresh, minced basil leaves
½ tsp black pepper
1 15-oz can drained kidney beans
Parmesan cheese

Peel and dice tomatoes (if using fresh) and put them along with water and bay leaves into a 6-quart pot. Bring to a boil, reduce heat, and cook for an hour. Cut sun-dried tomatoes into small bits and put in pot, or put in 1 cup of water to rehydrate, let set for 20 minutes, and then swirl in the blender until they begin to be cut into small pieces (not smooth). Add them to soup pot, along with baby carrots and protein seasoning. Bring to a boil and cook for 15 minutes. Add broccoli, bring to a boil, and cook for 15 more minutes. While soup is cooking, spray a frying pan with vegetable spray and crumble ground turkey into the pan. Cook until all signs of pink have disappeared. Put garlic cloves and basil in the blender with ¼ cup of water and swirl just enough to mince garlic and basil. Add basil-and-garlic mixture and pepper to soup pot. Mix together and let cook about 5 to 10 minutes. Add cooked ground turkey and kidney beans. Garnish each bowl with ½ teaspoon grated Parmesan cheese. This soup will store in the fridge for up to 4 days and may be used for snacks.

Makes 12 servings.

Vegetable Soup

(NURTURER, WARRIOR)

3 lbs fresh tomatoes or 1 36-oz can diced tomatoes
3 cups water
4 bay leaves
½ cup sun-dried tomatoes
1 cup diced baby carrots
2 tbs Jensens protein seasoning
2 cups broccoli
1 cup shell pasta
4 garlic cloves
4 tbs fresh, minced basil leaves
½ tsp black pepper
1 15-oz can drained kidney beans
  Parmesan cheese

Peel and dice tomatoes (if using fresh) and put them along with water and bay leaves into a 6-quart pot. Bring to a boil, reduce heat, and cook for an hour. Cut sun-dried tomatoes into small bits and put in pot, or put in 1 cup of water to rehydrate, let set for 20 minutes, and then swirl in the blender until they begin to be cut into small pieces (not smooth). Add them to soup pot, along with baby carrots and protein seasoning. Bring to a boil and cook for 15 minutes. Add broccoli, bring to a boil, and cook for 15 more minutes. While soup is cooking, cook pasta shells. Put garlic cloves and basil in the blender with ¼ cup of water and mix just enough to mince garlic and basil. Add basil-garlic mixture and pepper to soup pot. Mix together and let cook about 5 to 10 minutes. Add cooked pasta and kidney beans. Garnish each bowl with ½ teaspoon Parmesan cheese. This soup will store in the fridge for up to 4 days and may be used for snacks.

Makes 12 servings.

Main Dishes

Baked French Fries

2 baking potatoes
1 tsp Jensens protein seasoning
lemon pepper

Wash and slice potatoes into ¼-inch rounds. Place in a bowl with enough cold water to cover. Let sit for two to three hours. Spray a baking sheet with vegetable spray and sprinkle potato rounds with 1 tsp protein seasoning and lemon pepper to taste. Bake at 375 degrees for 40 to 45 minutes.

Serves 4.

Tortilla Roll-Up
(COMMUNICATOR, WARRIOR, NURTURER, VISIONARY)

½ lb ground turkey breast
¼ cup zucchini (small)
¼ cup yellow crookneck squash
¼ cup carrot
¼ cup red bell pepper
2 banana peppers (cut into slices)
¼ cup beets (cooked)
2 12-inch whole-wheat tortillas
¼ cup Basil Cream Cheese Spread (page 214)
Dijon mustard

In an 8-inch nonstick frying pan, crumble turkey breast and cook over medium heat until slightly browned or all pink disappears. Shred each vegetable separately. Lay tortilla on a plate and spread ⅛ cup Basil Cream Cheese Spread, leaving an inch from the edge. Sprinkle half of the turkey on each tortilla one inch from the edge. Layer each vegetable on top. Roll up the tortilla and trim ½ inch off each end. Slice roll-up in half.

For Visionary and Communicator, use Dijon mustard instead of basil spread.

For Warrior and Nurturer, omit the turkey.

Makes 4 roll-up halves.

Pita Pizza
(NURTURER, WARRIOR, COMMUNICATOR)

4 *pieces whole-wheat Greek-style pita bread*
1 green pepper, minced
½ small red onion, minced
6 medium button mushrooms, sliced
1 cup grated lowfat mozzarella cheese
2 garlic cloves, minced
10-ounce jar spaghetti sauce

Place pitas on a sprayed baking sheet and spread sauce on pitas. Layer green peppers, onions, garlic, and mushrooms. On top put mozzarella cheese, 2 ounces per pizza. Preheat oven at 350 degrees. Cook for 20–25 minutes.

For Communicator, add 1 cup cooked ground chicken or turkey to the spaghetti sauce.

Serves 4.

Gravy
(COMMUNICATOR, WARRIOR, NURTURER)

1½ cup water
½ cup chicken or turkey stock
½ teaspoon minced fresh rosemary
1 teaspoon minced fresh sage
1 teaspoon minced fresh parsley
1 tablespoon Jensens protein seasoning
⅓ cup cornstarch
½ cup warm water
  pepper to taste

In a medium sauce pan put 1½ cups water, chicken stock, rosemary, sage, parsley, protein seasoning, and pepper. Bring to a soft boil, then remove from heat. Add corn starch to ½ cup warm water and mix until smooth. Place gravy back over heat and pour cornstarch mixture in, stirring to a soft boil. Gravy should be slightly thick with a slight shine.

Makes 5 ½-cup servings.

Basil Cream Cheese Spread
(NURTURER, COMMUNICATOR, WARRIOR)

½ cup nonfat cream cheese
¼ cup chopped water chestnuts
¼ cup chopped pimentos
¼ tsp Dijon mustard
1 tsp minced basil
¼ tsp lite soy sauce
pepper to taste

In a medium-sized bowl stir cream cheese until smooth. Then add remaining ingredients and mix. Spread on tortilla or bagel.

Cajun Trout
(COMMUNICATOR, WARRIOR)

⅓ cup water
⅓ cup Bragg liquid aminos
4 4-oz trout fillets
2 tsp Cajun dust

Put water and Bragg liquid aminos in a low dish to be used for marinating. Add the fillets and place in the fridge for a few hours. Take fillets from marinade and place on a baking sheet. Sprinkle each fillet with Cajun dust. Use more if you like it hot, less if you like it mild. Cover with foil and bake in preheated oven at 450 degrees for 10 minutes. Remove skin and serve.

Serves 4.

Lemon Dill Trout
(NURTURER)

⅓ cup water
⅓ cup Bragg liquid aminos
4 4-oz trout fillets
1 lemon
6 large sprigs fresh dill

Put water and liquid aminos into a low bowl for marinating; place trout fillets in the bowl, and place in the refrigerator for a couple of hours. Take trout from marinade and place in a baking pan. Cut the lemon in half and squeeze the juice of the lemon over the trout. Mince dill and sprinkle over the trout. Cover with foil and bake in a preheated oven at 450 degrees for 10 minutes.

Serves 4.

Turkey Burgers
(NURTURER, COMMUNICATOR, VISIONARY)

½ cup zucchini
½ cup carrots
1 lb ground turkey breast
1 tbs dehydrated onions
½ cup Bragg liquid aminos
  whole-grain buns

Grate zucchini and carrots. Add them to ground turkey with onions and liquid aminos and mix well. Use a large scoop to shape burgers. Spray wax paper with vegetable spray and put the scooped burger on paper. Press down and form into a circle. Cook burgers on a grill or pan that has been heated on medium and sprayed with vegetable spray. Turn each patty when the edges start to look firm and cooked, about 5 minutes on each side. Serve on a whole-grain bun.

Serves 4.

Janice's Sea Bass
(NURTURER, COMMUNICATOR, WARRIOR, VISIONARY)

8 oz fresh Chilean sea bass
⅓ cup water
⅓ cup Bragg liquid aminos
4 sprigs fresh dill
4 large parsley florets
1 lemon

Cut sea bass into 2 4-ounce pieces. Put water and Bragg liquid aminos in a shallow dish suitable for marinating. Place the sea bass in marinade and set in fridge for a few hours, turning once or twice. Mince fresh dill and parsley. Take fish from marinade and place on a baking pan. Squeeze the juice from the lemon over the bass. Sprinkle with minced dill and parsley. Cover with foil and bake at 450 degrees for 15 minutes. (If fish is ½ inch or thinner, bake 10 minutes.)

Serves 2.

Baked Salmon and Caper Dill Sauce
(NURTURER, COMMUNICATOR, WARRIOR)

2 4-5-oz salmon fillets
1 lemon

SAUCE
1 medium carrot
1 celery stalk
½ medium onion
2 oz trimmings from salmon (the tail)
¼ cup chicken stock
1 tsp capers with juice
1 lemon
4 sprigs fresh dill
1 tbs cornstarch
4 oz evaporated skim milk

Chop carrot, celery, and onion and place in a stock pan. Add fish trimmings and chicken stock and enough water to cover the vegetables. Cover and bring to a boil, then turn down and let simmer for up to 45 minutes. Strain off the liquid into another pot; discard vegetable mixture. Put liquid back on the stove and turn on medium. Add capers, the juice and zest of a lemon, and dill. Mix cornstarch with evaporated milk, and when liquid comes to a boil, add milk mixture and stir until thick and creamy.

Cut salmon into 4- to-5-ounce pieces and place on a baking pan. Slice a lemon into circles and place on top of the salmon. Bake in a preheated oven at 450 degrees for 13 minutes. Serve sauce over salmon.

Serves 2.

DeLayne's Tomatoes and Rice
(NURTURER)

8 medium ripe tomatoes
1 cup tomato juice (low sodium)
2 tbs dehydrated onions
2 tsp cumin
1 tsp coriander
½ cup frozen apple-juice concentrate
8 corn tortillas
2 cups cooked basmati rice (or long-grain brown)
3 cups shredded lettuce
¾ cup mozzarella cheese
2 green onions
¾ cup nonfat plain yogurt

Blanch tomatoes (put in boiling water) for 2 minutes. Peel and chop tomatoes and place in a large saucepan. Add tomato juice, onions, cumin, coriander, and apple juice. Cook and stir over medium heat. Bring to a boil, then reduce heat and simmer for at least 20 minutes. Spray grill (or pan) with vegetable spray, turn on medium heat. Warm tortillas on both sides and roll up, then wrap each tortilla in foil. Lay ½ cup of rice on plate and spoon 1 cup of tomato mixture over rice. Place lettuce on one side of the plate and 2 wrapped tortillas on the other. Top with mozzarella cheese and chopped green onions. Add a dollop of nonfat yogurt on top.

Makes 4 servings.

DeLayne's Tomatoes and Rice
(COMMUNICATOR)

8 medium ripe tomatoes
½ cup green chilies
1 cup tomato juice (low sodium)
2 tbs dehydrated onions
2 tsp cumin
1 tsp coriander
½ tsp red pepper flakes
¼ cup frozen apple-juice concentrate
1 lb ground turkey breast
8 corn tortillas
1 cup cooked basmati rice (or long-grain brown)
3 cups shredded lettuce
¾ cup mozzarella cheese
2 green onions
¾ cup nonfat plain yogurt

Blanch tomatoes (put in boiling water) for 2 minutes. Peel and chop tomatoes and place in a large saucepan. Add green chilies, tomato juice, onions, cumin, coriander, red pepper flakes, and apple juice. Cook and stir over medium heat. Bring to a boil, then reduce heat and simmer for at least 20 minutes. In a nonstick frying pan, brown ground turkey. Spray grill (or pan) with vegetable spray and turn on medium. Warm tortillas on both sides and roll up, then wrap each tortilla in foil. Lay ¼ cup of rice on the plate and spoon ½ cup browned ground turkey and 1 cup of tomato mixture over rice. Place lettuce on one side of the plate and 2 wrapped tortillas on the other. Top with mozzarella cheese and chopped green onions. Add a dollop of nonfat yogurt on top.

Serves 4.

DeLayne's Tomatoes and Rice
(WARRIOR)

8 *medium ripe tomatoes*
½ *cup green chilies*
1 *cup tomato juice (low sodium)*
2 *tbs dehydrated onions*
2 *tsp cumin*
1 *tsp coriander*
½ *tsp red pepper flakes*
½ *cup frozen apple-juice concentrate*
8 *corn tortillas*
2 *cups cooked basmati rice (or long-grain brown)*
3 *cups shredded lettuce*
¾ *cup mozzarella cheese*
2 *green onions*
¾ *cup nonfat plain yogurt*

Blanch tomatoes (put in boiling water) for 2 minutes. Peel and chop tomatoes and place in a large saucepan. Add green chilies, tomato juice, onion, cumin, coriander, red pepper flakes, and apple juice. Cook and stir over medium heat. Bring to a boil, then reduce heat and simmer for at least 20 minutes. Spray grill (or pan) with vegetable spray and turn on medium. Warm tortillas on both sides and roll up, then wrap each tortilla in foil. Lay ½ cup of rice on the plate and spoon 1 cup of tomato mixture over rice. Place lettuce on one side of the plate and 2 wrapped tortillas on the other. Top with mozzarella cheese and chopped green onions. Add a dollop of nonfat yogurt on top.

Serves 4.

Taco Salad

(NURTURER, COMMUNICATOR, WARRIOR, VISIONARY)

½ cup water
2 limes (juice from)
2 tsp lite soy sauce
½ cup cauliflower florets
½ cup cubed zucchini
½ cup broccoli florets
½ red bell pepper, chopped
½ cup kidney or black beans, cooked
¼ cup green chilies, chopped
¼ tsp chili powder
½ tsp coriander
1 tsp cumin
½ tsp minced cilantro
1 garlic clove, minced
1 cup cooked quinoa
4 cups cut green leaf lettuce
1 medium tomato, cubed

In a frying pan place water, ½ lime juice, soy sauce, cauliflower, zucchini, broccoli, red bell pepper, and beans. Cook on medium high for 4 minutes, stirring often. Then add green chilies, chili powder, coriander, cumin, cilantro, and garlic. Cook for another 2 minutes, then add quinoa and mix. Put filling in medium-sized bowl, add lettuce, then top it off with tomatoes. Squeeze remaining ½ lime juice on lettuce. Goes great topped with some fresh salsa and yogurt or lite ranch dressing.

For Visionary and Communicator types, add cooked lean ground beef to mixture.

For Visionary types, omit yogurt.

Serves 4.

Quinoa Pilaf
(NURTURER, COMMUNICATOR, WARRIOR, VISIONARY)

2 cups cooked quinoa
½ cup bell peppers (use red and green)
½ cup carrots
½ cup onion
1 tbs garlic
1 tsp grated ginger
1 tsp Bragg liquid aminos
1 tsp low-sodium soy sauce
1 tsp Jensens protein seasoning

Put 2 cups of cooked quinoa in a medium-sized bowl. Finely mince bell peppers, carrots, onion, and garlic; add to quinoa. Mix together and add ginger, liquid aminos, soy sauce, and protein seasoning. Stir again. Spray a loaf pan with vegetable spray and pour mixture in and cover with foil. This may be made ahead. Bake at 350 degrees for 45 minutes to 1 hour.

Serves 4.

Mango Chutney
(NURTURER, COMMUNICATOR, WARRIOR, VISIONARY)

¼ cup bell pepper (red and green)
⅛ cup onion
1 tsp garlic
½ medium mango
1 tsp minced cilantro
½ tsp rice vinegar
1 tsp honey
1 lime

Chop bell pepper, onion, garlic, and mango into small pieces. Put into a small bowl and add cilantro, rice vinegar, honey, and the juice and some zest of the lime and stir. This may be made ahead. Keep refrigerated.

Baked Salmon

(VISIONARY)

8–10 oz salmon fillet
1 lemon

Preheat oven to 450 degrees. Cut salmon into 4- to-5-ounce pieces and place on a baking pan. Slice a lemon into circles and place on top of the salmon. Bake for 13 minutes.

Serves 2.

Red Sauce

(COMMUNICATOR, WARRIOR)

8 lbs ripe roma tomatoes
½ large onion
1 carrot
3 celery stalks
¼ cup dehydrated onion flakes
1 tbs dried Italian seasoning
2 tbs Jensens protein seasoning
1 pinch red pepper flakes
¼ cup apple-juice concentrate
¼ cup extra-virgin olive oil
1 garlic bulb
½ cup minced fresh oregano
⅔ cup minced fresh basil

Peel and dice tomatoes. Peel and dice onion, carrot, and celery. In a heavy, large pot put tomatoes, onion, carrot, celery, onion flakes, Italian seasoning, protein seasoning, red pepper flakes, and apple juice and turn on medium high. In a small frying pan put olive oil and garlic that has been peeled and separated into cloves. Sauté over low heat until garlic is translucent. Pour garlic and oil into pot with tomato mixture and continue to cook for about 2 hours, stirring occasionally to prevent sticking. Sauce will be done when carrots become very tender (overcooked). Add oregano and basil. Let cool and then blend until smooth. Reheat and use over pasta or any other Italian dish. Red Sauce will freeze well or last in the fridge for up to a week.

Chicken Parmesan
(NURTURER, COMMUNICATOR, WARRIOR)

4 boneless, skinless chicken breasts
⅓ cup Bragg liquid aminos
⅓ cup water
4 tsp fresh shredded Parmesan cheese
4 tsp fat-free, grated Parmesan cheese
1 tsp dried basil leaves
½ tsp Jan-De's seasoning

Cut all visible fat from chicken with kitchen shears. Mix liquid aminos together with water and pour in a shallow dish suitable for marinating. Place chicken in marinade and let sit in the fridge for at least 2 hours. Combine the two cheeses with basil and Jan-De's seasoning. Take chicken from marinade and coat with the cheese mixture. Place in a baking pan that has been sprayed with vegetable spray. Lay each breast side by side without touching. Cover with foil. Bake in a preheated oven at 450 degrees for 13 minutes or until juices run clear.

Serves 4.

Chicken Curry
(VISIONARY)

4 chicken breasts
2 cups cooked rice
2 medium Granny Smith apples
2 stalks celery
2 medium carrots
½ small pineapple
1 cup silken tofu
1 tbs honey
½ tsp lite soy sauce
¼ cup rice vinegar
½ tsp curry
⅛ cup walnuts
⅛ cup raisins
4 lettuce leaves

Preheat oven to 450 degrees. Place chicken breasts on a baking sheet and bake for 13 minutes. Cook rice as directed on the package. Cut apples, celery, carrots, and pineapple into small pieces, about ¼-inch square. Cube chicken into ¼-inch cubes. In a large bowl, add chicken, rice, apples, celery, carrots, and pineapple. In the blender, combine tofu, honey, soy sauce, vinegar, and curry. Blend until smooth and pour over chicken-rice mixture. Fold together until all ingredients are incorporated. Finely chop walnuts. Sprinkle with walnuts and raisins. Serve on a lettuce leaf.

Serves 4.

Artichoke Veggie Loaf
(VISIONARY)

½ cup minced artichoke hearts
¼ cup sliced mushrooms
¼ cup minced cauliflower
¼ cup minced carrots
¼ cup minced Swiss chard
1 cup cooked white or brown rice
3 tbs minced onion

2 tsp minced fresh garlic
3 tsp minced sun-dried tomatoes
1 cup tofu
3 cups egg whites
2 tsp lite soy sauce
3 tsp Jensens protein seasoning
2 tsp onion powder
¼ cup sliced almonds

Preheat oven to 400 degrees. Cook rice according to the package. Mix artichoke, mushrooms, cauliflower, carrots, Swiss chard, minced onion, garlic, and tomatoes together. Crumble tofu into mixture and add egg whites. Stir in soy sauce, protein seasoning, and onion powder. Add rice and mix everything together. Put into a loaf pan that has been sprayed with vegetable spray. Fill ¾ full. Bake 1 hour. Place almonds in a baking dish and bake for 2 to 3 minutes in the oven while heating loaf. Roasted, sliced almonds may be sprinkled on top.

Chicken Stir-Fry
(COMMUNICATOR, VISIONARY)

4 4-ounce chicken breasts
½ cup red onions, sliced
½ cup green bell peppers, sliced
½ cup broccoli florets
½ cup cauliflower florets
¼ cup snow peas
¼ cup bean sprouts
¾ cup chicken stock
½ teaspoon fresh ginger, minced
1 teaspoon garlic, minced
1 tablespoon soy sauce
1 tablespoon Worcestershire
1½ teaspoon cornstarch
pepper to taste

In a small bowl combine chicken stock, soy sauce, and Worcestershire. Slice chicken into strips. Heat wok. Add ginger, garlic, pepper, and half of the liquid mixture. Add cornstarch to the other half and whisk, then set aside. Put chicken in wok, cook 1 minute, and add the onions, peppers, broccoli, and cauliflower. Toss over medium-high heat until broccoli becomes bright green. Add peas and sprouts. Pour in cornstarch mixture and stir until a glossy texture, about 3 minutes.

Serves 4.

Janice's Halibut
(NURTURER)

4 halibut filets
4 tbs Bragg liquid aminos
4 tbs water
4 tbs nonfat yogurt
1 tbs lemon pepper
1 tbs grated Parmesan cheese
1 tsp Jan-De's seasoning

Whisk together Bragg liquid aminos and water. Place filets in a baking dish and space evenly. Spoon Bragg liquid aminos and water mixture over filets and marinate in refrigerator for three hours. Drain off excess. In a bowl, combine yogurt, lemon pepper, and Jan-De's seasoning. Stir until smooth. Spoon over filets and spread evenly. Cover with foil and bake at 450 degrees for 13 minutes.

Serves 4.

APPENDIX B

BIBLIOGRAPHY

Abravanel, Elliot, and E. King. *Body Type Diet*. Bantam, 1983.

Adams, G., and H. Devries. "Effects of Exercise on Women." *Journal of Gerontology* 28 (1973).

A.H.A. Exercise Commission. *Exercise Testing of Apparently Healthy Individuals: A Handbook for Physicians*. A.H.A., 1972.

Atkins, Robert C. *Dr. Atkins' New Diet Revolution*. Avon Books, Inc., 1992.

Bailey, Covert. *The New Fit or Fat*. Houghton-Mifflin, 1977.

Balderer, G., and A. Borberly. "Effect of Valerian on Human Sleep." *Psychopharmacology* 87 (1985): 406–9.

Bannister, Roger. "Human Beings Are Not the Same." *Physician and Sportsmedicine*, September 1974.

Baschetti, R. "Chronic Fatigue Syndrome with neurally mediated hypotension." *Journal of the American Medical Association*, June 1996: p. 49.

Beach, Frank A. *Hormones and Behavior*. Paul B. Hoeber, Inc., 1948.

Benson, Herbert. *The Relaxation Response*. William Morrow, 1975.

Berkowitz, Gerald. *The Berkowitz Diet Switch*. Arlington House, 1981.

Bertoli, A. "Gender Differences in Insulin Receptors." *Journal of Clinical Endocrinology* 50 (1980): 246–50.

Bicchieri, M. G. *Hunters and Gatherers Today*. Holt, Reinhart and Winston, 1972.

Bieler, Henry. *Food Is Your Best Medicine*. Random House, 1966.

Bland, Jeffrey. "Back to Basics." *Let's Live*, April 1995.

Bolton, S., and G. Null. "Caffeine, its effects, uses and abuses." *Journal of Applied Nutrition* 33, no. 1 (1981): 35–53.

Bonner, Michael. "Sit Down and Relax." *Runners World*, June 1976.

Bowen, D. J., and N. E. Grunberg. "Variations in appetite across the menstrual cycle." *Physiology and Behavior* 47 (1990): 287–91.

Boyd, William C. *Genetics and the Races of Man.* Boston University Press, 1950.

Brody, Jane. "Drug Researchers Working to Design Customized Estrogen." *New York Times,* March 1997.

———. *Guide to Personal Health.* Time Books, 1976.

———. "Jogging Is Like a Drug." *New York Times,* November 1976.

Brown, P. J. "An Anthropological Perspective on Obesity." *Annals of the New York Academy of Science* 499 (1987): 29–47.

Brown, R. *An Introduction to Neuroendocrinology.* Cambridge University Press, 1994.

Brunani, A., ed. "Influence of Insulin on beta-endorphin levels in normal weight and obese subjects." *International Journal of Obesity and Related Metabolic Disorders* 20, (1996): 710–14.

Cabot, Sandra. *The Body Shaping Diet.* Warner, 1995.

Carter, J. *Food—Your Miracle Medicine.* HarperCollins, 1997.

Cassidy, A. "Biological Effects of Diet of Soy Protein in Iso-Flavones on the Menstrual Cycle of Post Menopausal Women." *American Journal of Clinical Nutrition* 60 (1994): 333–80.

Chopra, Deepak. *Perfect Health.* Harmony, 1991.

———. *Quantum Healing.* Bantam, 1990.

Clementz, G. L., and J. N. Dailey. "Psychotropic effects of caffeine." *Journal of American Medical Anesthesia* 37, no 4. (1995): 167–72.

Colbin, Annemarie. *Food and Healing.* Ballantine, 1995.

Colgan, Michael. *Optimum Sports Nutrition.* Keats, 1996.

Consolazio, Johnson, and R. A. Nelson. "Protein Metabolism During Intensive Physical Training in the Young Adult." *American Journal of Clinical Nutrition* 14 (1975): 103.

Cooper, Kenneth H. *The Aerobics Way.* Bantam, 1968.

Cooper, Mildred. *Aerobics for Women.* Bantam, 1972.

Costill, David. "Muscular Exhaustion During Distance Running." *Physician and Sportsmedicine,* October 1974.

D'Adamo, James. *One Man's Food.* Richard Marek Publishers, 1980.

D'Adamo, Peter. *Eat Right 4 Your Type.* Putnam, 1996.

Daoust, Gene, and Joyce Daoust. *40-30-30: Fat-Burning Nutrition.* Wharton, 1996.

Darwin, C. R. *On the Origin of Species by Means of Natural Selection.* Murray, 1859.

DeMaisons, Kathleen. *Potatoes Not Prozac.* Simon & Schuster, 1998.

Demitrack, M. A. "Evidence for impaired activation of the hypothalamic-pituitary-adrenal axis in patients with chronic fatigue syndrome." *Journal of Clinical Endocrinology and Metabolism,* 1991.

DeVries, Herbert. "Exercise Intensity Threshold for Improvement of Cardiovascular-Respiratory Function in Older Men." *Geriatrics,* April 1971.

Doll, R., and R. Peto. "The Causes of Cancer: Quantitative Estimates of Avoidable Risks of Cancer in the United States Today." *Journal of the National Cancer Institute,* 1981.

Drewnowksi, A. "Changes in mood after carbohydrate consumption." *American Journal of Clinical Nutrition* 46 (1987): 703.

Duke, James. *The Green Pharmacy.* Rodale, 1997.

Eaton, S., and M. Konner. "Paleolithic Nutrition: A Consideration of Its Nature and Current Implications." *New England Journal of Medicine* 5 (1985): 283–84.

Fernstorm, J. D., and R. J. Wurtman. "Brain Serotonin." *Science,* December 1971.

Fonda, Jane. *Jane Fonda's Workout Book.* Simon & Schuster, 1981.

Friedl, E. *Women and Men: An Anthropologist's View.* Holt, Rinehart & Winston, 1975.

Frye, C., and G. Demolar. "Menstrual cycle and sex differences influence salt preference." *Psychology and Behavior* 55, no. 1 (1971): 193–97.

Geliebter, A. "Effects of strength or aerobic training on body composition." *American Journal of Clinical Nutrition* 66 (1997): 357–63.

Genassani, A. R. "Deficiency of beta-endorphins in alcohol addicts." *Journal of Clinical Endocrinology and Metabolism* 55, no. 3 (1982): 583–86.

Gianoulakis, C. "Different pituitary beta-endorphin and adrenal cortisol responses to ethanol." *Life Sciences* 45, no. 12 (1989): 1097–1109.

Gilmore, C. P. "Taking Exercise to Heart." *New York Times,* March 1977.

Gittleman, Ann Louise. *Beyond Pritikin.* Bantam, 1988.

———. *Your Body Knows Best.* Pocket, 1996.

Glasser, William. *Positive Addiction.* Harper & Row, 1976.

Green, M., and K. Keville. *Aromatherapy: A Complete Guide to the Healing Art.* Crossing Press, 1995.

Guyton, Arthur. *Physiology of the Human Body.* Sanders Co., 1979.

Gwinup, Grant. "Effect of Exercise Alone on the Weight of Obese Women." *Archives of Internal Medicine,* May 1975.

Haas, Robert. *Eat to Win.* Signet, 1983.

———. *Eat Smart Think Smart.* The Publishing Mills, Inc., 1994.

Halstead, B., and L. Hood. *Siberian Ginseng.* Oriental Healing Arts Institute, 1984.

Hartman, Taylor. *The Color Code.* Taylor Don Hartman Publications, 1987.

Hendricks, Gay. *Conscious Breathing*. Bantam, 1995.

Higdon, Hal. *Fitness After Forty*. World Publications, 1977.

Hirschi, James L. *The Healing Power of Herbs*. Prima, 1995.

Hooton, Ernest A. *Up from the Ape*. McMillan, 1946.

Hoskins, R. J. *Endocrinology*. W. W. Norton & Co., 1941.

Howell, Edward. *Enzyme Nutrition—the Food Enzyme Concept*. Avery, 1985.

Jackowski, Edward. *Hold It, You're Exercising Wrong*. Simon & Schuster, 1995.

Kanarek, R. B. "Differential effects of sucrose, fructose, and glucose on obese rats." *Journal of Nutrition* 112 (1982): 1546–54.

Keim, N. L. "Effects of exercise and diet on obese women." *Appetite* 26, no. 1 (1996).

Kelly Foundation. *The Metabolic Types*. Kelly Foundation, 1976.

Kleijnen, J. "Gingko biloba for cerebral insufficiency." *British Journal of Clinical Pharmacology* 34, no. 4 (1992): 32–358.

Krizmanic, Judy. "The Best of Both Worlds," *Vegetarian Times*, March 1995.

Kuppurajan, K. "Effect of Ashwaganda." *Journal of Research in Ayurveda and Sidha* 1, no. 1 (1980): 247–58.

Lad, Vasant. *Ayurveda*. Lotus Press, 1985.

Lance, Kathryn. *Running for Health and Beauty*. Bobbs-Merrill, 1977.

Lappe, Frances M. *Diet for a Small Planet*. Ballantine, 1971.

Leaf, A. "Cardiovascular Effects of Omega-3 Fatty Acids." *New England Journal of Medicine* 318 (1988): 349–57.

Lee, R., and I. DeVore. *The Making of Mankind*. Aldine, 1968.

Lewin, R. *Human Evolution: An Illustrated Introduction*. W. H. Freeman, 1984.

Liberman, Jacob. *Light—the Medicine of the Future*. Avery, 1991.

MacDiarmid, J., and M. Hetherington. "Mood modulation by food." *British Journal of Clinical Psychology*, February 1995.

Manson, J., C. Stamapafer, H. Hennekens, and W. Willett. "Body Weight and Longevity: A Reassessment." *Journal of the American Medical Association* 257 (1987): 353–58.

Mazel, Judy. *The Beverly Hills Diet*. McMillan, 1982.

McDougald, John. *The McDougald Plan for Maximum Weight Loss*. New Win, 1994.

McMurray, W. C. *Essentials of Human Metabolism*. Harper & Row, 1977.

Morley, J. E. "The role of endogenous opiates as appetite regulators." *American Journal of Clinical Nutrition* 35 (1982): 757–61.

Morris, Barbara J. *My Life With the Eskimo*. McMillan, 1951.

Mowery, D. *Herbal Tonic Therapies*. Keats, 1993.

Murray, M., and J. Pizzorno. *Encyclopedia of Natural Medicine*. Prima, 1991.

Murray, Michael T. *Healing Power of Herbs*. Keats, 1992.

Myss, C., and N. Stanley. *The Creation of Health*. Beacon Press, 1993.

Nelson, Miriam E., with Sarah Wernick. *Strong Women Stay Young*. Bantam, 1997.

Newman, H. H. *Twins: A Study of Heredity and Environment*. University of Chicago Press, 1937.

Nightengale, Earl. *Earl Nightengale's Greatest Discovery*. Dodd-Mead, 1987.

Northrup, C. *Women's Bodies, Women's Wisdom*. Bantam-Doubleday, 1995.

Ornish, Dean. *Dr. Dean Ornish's Program for Reversing Heart Disease*. Ballantine, 1992.

———. *Eat More, Weigh Less*. HarperCollins, 1993.

Orr, Warren H. *Hormones, Health and Happiness*. Macmillan, 1954.

Oscai, L. B., and J. O. Haloszy. "Effects of weight changes produced by exercise, food restriction or overeating on body composition." *Journal of Clinical Investigation* 48 (1969): 2124–28.

Page, Melvin. *Body Chemistry in Health Disease*. Biochemical Research Findings, 1949.

Page, Melvin, and L. Abrahms. *Your Body Is Your Best Doctor*. Keats, 1972.

Pavlov, K. N., W. P. Steffee, R. H. Lerman, and B. A. Burrows. "Effects of dieting and exercise on lean body mass, oxygen uptake, and strength." *Medical Science, Sports, and Exercise* 17 (1985): 471–77.

Picton, Lionel. *Nutrition and the Soil: Thoughts on Feeding*. Devin-Adair, 1949.

Pierce, E. "Beta-endorphin responses to endurance exercise." *Perceptual Motor Skills* 77 (1993): 767–70.

Pilbeam, D. *The Origin of Homo Sapiens: The Fossil Evidence*. Harper & Row, 1986.

Pottenger, Francis. *Symptoms of Visceral Disease*. C. V. Mosby Co., 1919.

Prasad, A. *Trace Elements in Human Metabolism*. Plenum, 1978.

Price, Weston. "Nutrition and Physical Degeneration." *American Association of Applied Nutrition*, 1988.

Pritikin, Nathan. *Live Longer Now*. Keats, 1974.

Proctor, Dean. "Physically Fit Women Have Fewer Complaints." *Physicians and Sportsmedicine*, March 1974.

Puhn, Adele. *The 5-Day Miracle Diet*. Ballantine, 1996.

Rappoport, L. "Gender and age differences in food cognition." *Appetite* 20, no. 1 (1993): 33–55.

Remmington, D., G. Fisher, and E. Parent. *How to Lower Your Fat Thermostat*. Vitality House, 1981.

Robbins, John. *Diet for a New America*. Random House, 1987.

Rowe, John W., M.D., and Robert L. Kahn. *Successful Aging*. Pantheon, 1998.

Rubin, Herman H. *Glands, Sex, and Personality.* Funk, Inc., 1952.

———. *Your Life Is in Your Glands.* W. Funk, Inc., 1948.

Saltin, M. "Maximal oxygen uptake in athletes." *Journal of Applied Psychology* 23 (1967): 353–58.

Schwarts, Bob. *Diets Still Don't Work.* Breakthrough, 1990.

Sears, Barry. *The Zone.* Regan, 1995.

Sheehan, George. "Bloody Urine: Don't Panic, Collect a Specimen." *Physician and Sportsmedicine,* May 1975.

———. "Carbohydrate Loading Doesn't Work for Everyone." *Physician and Sportsmedicine,* June 1976.

Sheldon, William. *Atlas of Men.* Harper & Bros., 1954.

Shirley, John L. *Body Watchin Is Fun.* Taylor Publishing Co., 1973.

Simmons, Richard. *Never Say Diet.* Warner, 1980.

Smith, Cameron. "Gold Medal Herbs." *Natural Health,* May/June 1994.

Somer, E. *Food and Mood.* Holt, 1995.

Stein, Diane. *The Natural Remedy Book for Women.* North Point Press, 1995.

Stevens, T., and B. Tucker. *The Varieties of Human Physique.* Harper & Bros., 1940.

Thomas, Vaughan. *Science and Sport: How to Measure and Improve Athletic Performance.* Little, Brown, 1970.

Ucko, H. *Endocrine Diagnosis.* Staples Press, 1951.

Vihjalmur, Stefansson. *The Fat of the Land.* McMillan, 1957.

Waitley, Denis. *Seeds of Greatness.* Pocket, 1983.

Watson, George. *Nutrition and Your Mind.* Harper & Row, 1972.

Weil, Andrew. *Eight Weeks to Optimum Health.* Ballantine, 1997.

———. *Spontaneous Healing.* Ballantine, 1995.

Werbach, Melvyn. *Nutritional Influences on Illness—Sourcebook of Clinical Research.* September Bounty, 1998.

Wheeler, P. E. "Loss of functional body hair in man." *Journal of Human Evolution* 14 (1985): 23–28.

Wiley, R. *Biobalance.* Life Science Press, 1989.

Williams, Roger. *Biochemical Individuality.* Wiley and Sons, 1956.

Wilmore, Jack. "Exploring the Myth of Female Inferiority." *Physician and Sportsmedicine,* May 1974.

Wilt, Fred. "How They Train." *Track and Field News,* July 1959.

Wood, Curtis H. *Overfed but Undernourished.* Exposition Press, 1959.

Wood, P. "Effect of Physical Activity on Obese Women." *American Journal of Clinical Nutrition,* February 1996.

Wood, Peter. "Bos(huff)ton (puff) or (sigh) Bust." *New York Times,* April 1975.

Wurtman, J. "Mood changes and carbohydrates." *American Journal of Clinical Nutrition* 44 (1986): 772–78.

————. *The Serotonin Solution*. Fawcett Columbine, 1996.

Zorilla, DeRubeis, and Redei. "Pituitary-adrenal hormone levels' effect on self-esteem." *Psychoneuroendocrinology* 20, no. 6 (1995): 591–601.

Zuti, W. "Comparing diet and exercise as weight reduction tools." *Physician and Sportsmedicine*, January 1976.

APPENDIX C

PRODUCT AND RESOURCES INFORMATION

American College for Advancement in Medicine. 800-532-3688
American Council on Exercise. 800-529-8227
American Foundation for Alternative Health Care. 914-794-8181
Aqua-Jogger pool-exercise products. 800-922-9544
Ayurvedic Institute dosha-type products. 800-255-8332
Body Code–Metabolic Typing Programs. www.JayCooper.com
Complete guide to exercise videos. 800-433-6769
Cybex International. 800-677-6544
Eden's Acres, Inc., organic foods directory. 517-456-4288
Exercise videos catalog (free). 800-201-5444
Green Valley Spa, St. George, Utah. 435-628-8060
Herbal Research Foundation. 800-381-2700
National Women's Health Resource. 202-293-6045
Nature's Way Products. 435-962-8873
Nicotine Anonymous. 415-750-0328
Nightengale/Conant Corp. personal-development audiocassettes. 800-525-9000
NordicTrack fitness equipment. 800-892-2174
Polar Pulse Monitors. 800-227-1314
Power Eights exercise resistance bands. 435-674-5836
Powerbelt walking products. 800-797-2358
Precor Fitness Equipment. 206-486-9292
Trotter Treadmills. 800-677-6544
Twin Labs. 800-645-5626

SAMPLE GROUP AGREEMENTS

The Buddy System: Zone-Time Training Agreement

The group-support approach to exercise can be a great tool when used properly. The purpose of a written group agreement is to help clarify the serious intentions of all group members. This is accomplished by clearly stating the purpose of the group and outlining the basic responsibilities of each group member.

All this formality and structure do not mean that you can't have lots of fun. But it will help assure that your group attracts only serious members who understand the benefits of a structured approach. I have used the following basic ideas in maintaining successful long-term buddy-system groups.

1. Draft a simple, generic agreement that states the group's purpose and the members' responsibilities. For example, your group's purpose could be: *To provide a positive support group of like-minded individuals who are committed to maintaining a structured zone-time program.*

2. Maintain a group size of between three and six members.

3. Each month, alphabetically rotate the group leadership responsibilities.

4. Make sure that everyone understands the group leader's responsibilities, including giving daily wake-up calls to other members, and handling all relevant communications.

5. The minimum length of membership is three months.

6. The minimum frequency of meeting for zone-time body motion is three times per week.

7. The minimum duration of each zone-time session is thirty minutes (forty-five to sixty minutes is better).

8. All members commit to daily use of an alarm clock.

9. Unanimous agreement is required on admitting new members.

10. A small fine ($1 to $5) is levied for negative conversation (whining, gossiping, or whatever your group decides is counterproductive to its purpose).

11. A monthly cash fee ($20 to $100—enough to hurt if you lose it) is submitted to the group leader. At month's end, those who have attended as scheduled and lost weight split the contributions of those members who have not.

12. Schedule at least one non-body-motion get-together each month (healthy dinner or lunch).

13. Schedule a monthly special fitness activity (a Saturday-morning hike, a moonlight walk).

14. Members may drop out of the group only after a successful prior month.

15. A documented and serious medical injury or ailment negates all contractual obligations.

16. Acceptable excused absences include the eleven major holidays, out-of-town travel, fever, or an illness requiring a doctor visit. No other exceptions or excuses are acceptable.

17. Two unexcused absences per month are allowed for all members except for the member serving as the group leader.

The Food-Exchange Group Agreement

A food-exchange group can be a great tool when used properly. The purpose of the group approach is to feed your family effectively while dramatically decreasing the time and effort required. Here is how it works: a group of three to six people agree to provide the fresh veggies for all members' evening meals on a specific day or days each week. For example, in a three-person group, your days might be Monday and Thursday. On those days, you prepare enough for all three families in the group, including your own family. Not only does this plan reduce the time you spend shopping, washing, and chopping, it also increases veggie consumption and variety.

A written agreement is essential for several reasons: to express the serious intentions of all group members; to clearly state the standards to be followed; and to minimize any possible misunderstandings. All this formal structure will help assure that you attract only members who understand the benefits and responsibilities. I have found the following guidelines effective for maintaining successful long-term food-exchange groups.

1. Draft a simple agreement that states the group's purpose and the members' responsibilities. For example, your group's purpose might be: *To maintain a group of individuals who are committed to sharing the responsibility of providing fresh, wholesome, high-quality foods without having to prepare them individually each day.*

2. Maintain a group size of between three and six members.

3. Maintain assigned days of the week without switching.

4. Maintain members who live within five minutes of each other.

5. The minimum length of membership is three months.

6. Grocers, produce, and other quality standards should be mutually decided upon.

7. Use interchangeable plastic bowls and bins, such as Tupperware.

8. National holidays and weekends are excluded from the agreement.

9. No leftovers—no exceptions.

10. No substandard substitutions, including cooking by an incompetent spouse or child.

INDEX